D1288028

Economic Structures of the Ancient Near East

MORRIS SILVER
Professor of Economics
City College of the City University of New York

BARNES & NOBLE BOOKS
Totowa, New Jersey

© 1985 Morris Silver
First published in the USA 1986 by
Barnes & Noble Books
81 Adams Drive
Totowa, New Jersey, 07512

Library of Congress Cataloging in Publication Data

Silver, Morris.
    Economic structures of the ancient Near East.

    Bibliography: p.
    Includes index.
    1. Near East—economic conditions.   2. Near East—
history.   I. Title.
HC415.15.S55   1985   330.939′4   85-22859
ISBN 0-389-20596-6

Printed and bound in Great Britain

CONTENTS

74857

To my sturdy sons
Gerry and Ron

PREFACE

Admittedly it is unusual for the professional economist to be interested in the ancient world. Therefore let me state for the record that I am not now and never have been an antiquarian. My objective is much more ambitious. Almost sixty years have passed since the distinguished classical scholar Alfred Zimmern concluded that 'the book we need is a political economy of antiquity, embodying the universal conclusions of the theoretical economists and applying them to the interpretation of ancient life.' *Economic Structures of the Ancient Near East* is intended to meet this challenge. I have long been convinced that the study of ancient economies has much to teach us about economic growth and decline, and social change generally. The present work represents a step in a research programme beginning with my joint work with the late Dick Auster on *The State as a Firm: Economic Forces in Political Development* (1979) and continuing with *Affluence, Altruism, and Atrophy: The Decline of Welfare States* (1980) and *Prophets and Markets: The Political Economy of Ancient Israel* (1983).

In writing this book I have tried to say something new not only to economists and other social scientists but to historians and Near Eastern specialists. Hopefully, I have brought antiquity to the former and economic analysis to the latter. At the same time a strenuous effort was made so that the product would be interesting to the educated public. Needless to add, my contribution lies in bringing together a diffuse literature (including a great deal from Egyptian and Classical sources) and approaching this material from the viewpoint of an economist. For translations of the primary materials I have relied, judiciously, I trust, on the specialist literature. To ease the task of the non-specialist reader I have grouped references in topical notes at the end of chapters. References have been included in the body of the text only in the case of substantive quotations or in other special circumstances. Biblical citations refer to the Hebrew Bible. The translations of the Jewish Publication Society embody the latest scholarship and are highly recommended to the reader. For chronology, reliance has been placed on readily available standard works including Oates (1979) for Mesopotamia and Montet (1981) and J.A. Wilson (1951) for Egypt. It should be understood that all dates are approximate, debated, and subject to revision. The Appendix provides dates for the more important places and periods.

Morris Silver
Woodbury, New York

ACKNOWLEDGEMENTS

For their generous comments and suggestions I owe a deep debt of gratitude to many scholars of the ancient Near East, including J.A. Brinkman, Benjamin Foster, J.R. Kraus, Erica Reiner, Piotr Steinkeller, Norman Yoffee, and, most of all, Chris J. Eyre, Niels Peter Lemche, E. Lipiński, Marvin A. Powell, and Carlo Zaccagnini, with whom I have had useful exchanges of ideas. My colleague Jacob Stern was always willing to answer my questions about the Graeco-Roman world. Thanks are also due to Donald N. McCloskey, William H. McNeill, Douglass C. North, Stanley Page and Gordon Tullock. None of these fine scholars can be held responsible for my opinions and errors.

My research was greatly facilitated by a grant from a fund created by the will of the late Harry Schwager, a distinguished alumnus of the City College of New York, class of 1911, and by a Professional Staff Congress — City University of New York Research Award (Grant Number 664316). Financial support was also received from the Faculty Senate of City College.

Economic Structures of the Ancient Near East could not have been completed without the optimism, understanding, and good advice of my wife Sondra.

SYMBOLS AND SPECIAL CHARACTERS

[   ]   enclose restoration of material that is obliterated in an ancient text

(   )   in translations indicate additions for explanatory purposes

All terms taken from languages other than English, such as Akkadian, Sumerian, Egyptian, Ugaritic, Hebrew, Greek, Latin, German, and French, are printed in letter-spaced italic type.

Upper-case italic type is used for signs of uncertain value of Sumerian texts, Sumerograms in Akkadian texts, and Sumerograms and Akkadograms in Hittite texts. (Akkadograms and Sumerograms are Akkadian and Sumerian words written as such in, for instance, a Hittite tablet, but meant to be pronounced in Hittite translation.)

Conventionally, an *e* is intercalated between consonants in pronouncing ancient Egyptian words except where a *3* or a ^c, which are read *a*, are present.

In words treated as proper names *š*, *ḫ/ḥ*, and *ḳ* are usually transliterated as *sh*, *h*, and *k*, and ʿ and ʾ are omitted. These symbols are retained in words discussed as technical terms. Diacritics have been retained.

THE ANCIENT NEAR EAST
Map One

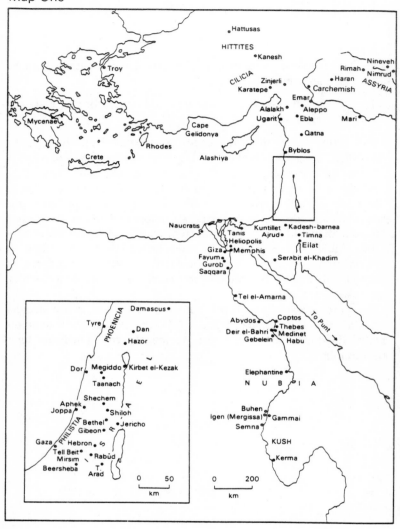

Hattusas

HITTITES

Kanesh

Troy

CILICIA

Zinjerli

Karatepe

Nineveh

Rimah
Nimrud

Haran

ASSYRIA

Carchemish

Emar

Alalakh
Aleppo

Ugarit
Ebla

Mari

Mycenae

Cape
Gelidonya

Qatna

Rhodes

Crete

Alashiya

Byblos

Naucratis

Tanis
Heliopolis

Kuntillet
Ajrud

Kadesh-barnea

Timna

Eilat

Giza
Memphis

Fayum
Gurob
Saqqara

Serabit el-Khadim

Tel el-Amarna

To Punt

Abydos

Coptos
Thebes

Deir el-Bahri
Gebelein

Medinet
Habu

Damascus

Tyre

PHOENICIA

Dan

Hazor

Dor

Megiddo

Kirbet el-Kezak

Taanach

Elephantine

N U B I A

Shechem

Aphek
Joppa

Shiloh

Bethel
Gibeon

Jericho

PHILISTIA

Buhen

Igen (Mergissa)

Gammai

Gaza

Hebron

Semna

Tell Beit
Mirsim

Rabûd

KUSH

Beersheba

T.
Arad

Kerma

0   50

km

0   200

km

Map Two

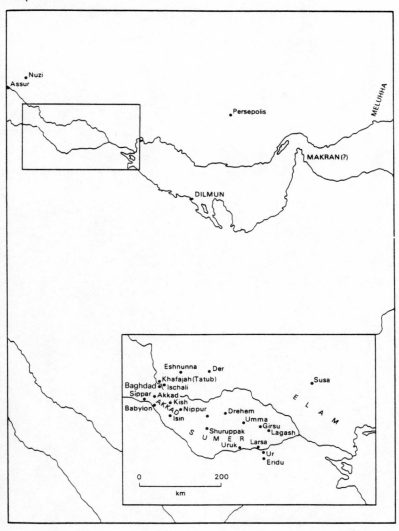

Nuzi
Assur
Persepolis
MELUHHA
MAKRAN(?)
DILMUN

Eshnunna
Der
Khafajah (Tatub)
Susa
Baghdad
Ischali
Sippar
Akkad
AKKAD
Kish
Babylon
Nippur
Isin
Drehem
Umma
Girsu
S U M E R
Shuruppak
Lagash
ELAM
Uruk
Larsa
Ur
Eridu

0   200
km

INTRODUCTION

Douglass C. North (1977) has suggested that an analysis of transaction costs — that is, the resources used up in exchanging ownership rights including costs of communication, acquiring and disseminating information, and designing and enforcing contracts — provides a useful framework for comparing ancient and modern economies. The proposal is attractive. Within such a research agenda the terms 'ancient' and 'modern' would acquire substantive content, instead of serving to disguise, as is so often the case, the trivial contrast between 'long ago' and 'now'. Indeed, illumination of private 'micro' choices of institutions is the major task of a newly emerging field, 'neoclassical institutional economics'. This term refers to the application of choice-theoretic models to transform structural characteristics from noneconomic givens into endogenous variables.[1] To illustrate, relatively high costs of communication in antiquity would have operated to reduce the degree of control over one's trading partners, agents, and employees while increasing the danger of monopolistic exploitation. Similarly, as North argues, the technological level of ancient society probably raised the cost of defining and enforcing property rights. A preference for self-sufficiency, reliance on storage, the important role played by temples of the gods, the substitution of memory, recitation, and symbolic gestures for general literacy, emphasis on professional standards in business relationships, the prominence of women in entrepreneurial roles, and the elevation of familial ties and other departures from impersonal economics in the markets for both goods and productive factors might be understood as major structural adaptations in ancient economic life to transaction costs.[2] These and other institutional characteristics of the ancient Near Eastern economy are explored in Part I of the study.

But, and here is the central question examined in Part II, is North (1977, p. 710) correct in stating that transaction costs 'would have been an insuperable barrier to price-making markets throughout most of history'?[3] In his premise we may detect the influence of the economic historian Karl Polanyi, who believed that markets became important only in the eighteenth and nineteenth centuries of the present era. Polanyi enjoys major support among anthropologists,

1

archaeologists, prehistorians, ethnohistorians, economic historians, institutional economists, and other social scientists (see, recently, Ortiz 1983, Part One). My conclusion from an extensive review of the literature is that, despite a distaste for theory and the coolness of Marxists, his influence among ancient Near Eastern specialists is far more pervasive than they admit or, perhaps, are aware. This influence become obvious in discussions of the markets for land and labour-power, or, rather, the absence of these markets in ancient economies. Sometimes the validity of one or another of Polanyi's positions is shifted to times and places outside the scholar's main area of expertise, most often to third-millennium Sumer and Pharaonic Egypt. This temptation towards displacement in time and space provides one good reason for a study treating the entire ancient Near East.

Part II carefully compares Polanyi's empirical propositions or assertions with the available evidence. In the case of Polanyi the form of a polemic contributes a sharp focus on the key technical/operative aspects of ancient markets — Polanyi deserves credit for this — while providing ample scope for an overall evaluation of the Near Eastern economy. As pointed out by Gledhill and Larsen (p. 198):

> The investigation of Polanyi's theories is ultimately of more fundamental significance than proving Polanyi right or wrong in a special case. Advancing alternative accounts of the empirical data of necessity leads to problems of theory and conceptualization, and our observation must both underpin and be selected by an alternative analytical framework.

In the course of providing this alternative analytical framework critical attention is given to the economic views of the Assyriologists I.M. Diakonoff, W.F. Leemans, and Mario Liverani and of the Egyptologist Jacob J. Janssen. In-depth consideration is given to several key questions, including whether 'ports of trade' served to economise on the costs of tax collection, the part played by contractual slavery in credit markets, adverse selection in the slave market, individual versus communal land ownership, the importance of capital accumulation and trade, markets versus temple and palace hierarchies, and the resort to legal fictions to circumvent government regulations.

An analysis of the ancient economy even when directed mainly at the Near East must comprehend a great deal of material in terms of both space and time. Apparently disparate data must be placed side by side on account of their inner analytical unity. A danger of the most inclusive perspective is that the resulting picture may be misleadingly uniform and static in composition. A contributory factor here is, of course, the sporadic nature of the surviving evidence itself which forces Assyriologists to comprehend history by means of case studies. Such objections are real, but to give in to them would make progress toward a scientific synthesis impossible. A deliberate effort has been made to avoid a telescoped perspective by calling attention to the causes and effects of changes in living standards and by taking account of geographic diversity, including differences in natural resource endowments and proximity to trade routes and urban centres. More importantly, Part III copes with the impact on the ancient Near Eastern economy of changes in economic incentives and of changes in economic policy. It takes a major step towards lifting the veil over the variety of concrete historical situations and correcting an image of outstanding uniformity. It becomes evident that ancient economies were capable of making profound alterations in order to take advantage of new economic opportunities. We also see that the ancient Near East experienced periods of pervasive economic regulation by the state interspersed with lengthy periods of relatively unfettered market activity. There were also 'Dark Ages', in which household economy increased in importance relative to both markets and hierarchies, including temple and palace. Of course, the final test of my ambitious pudding is in the eating.

Notes

1. Recent studies exploring the impact of economic variables on legal, social and political institutions include Auster and Silver (1979), Ekelund and Tollison (1981), North and Thomas (1973), and Silver (1980, 1983a).

2. For a useful introduction to personal economics, see Ben-Porath (1980).

3. More recently, North (1984, p. 262) maintained that: 'In the premodern world, economies were simple, uncomplicated organizational structures. Exchange was, for most individuals, a supplement to a largely self-sufficient life.'

PART ONE

STRUCTURAL CHARACTERISTICS OF THE
ANCIENT ECONOMY

GODS AS INPUTS AND OUTPUTS OF THE ANCIENT ECONOMY

The Contribution of Gods to Economic Growth

Temples as Centres and Protectors of Trade

It is well known that as the gods offered safe and honest dealing — an implicit surety or guarantee — the temples of the ancient Near East and the Graeco-Roman world served as places of worship and centres of intercity and international commerce. This participation and invitation to foreigners is illustrated in Mesopotamia (roughly modern Iraq) by a literary tale ('Enki and the World Order') of the later third millennium from Sumer (southern Mesopotamia — that is, south of the city of Nippur): 'Let the boats from Magan (probably the Oman peninsula) carry a treasure, the *magillu*-boats from Meluhha (probably the region of the Indus civilisation) trade in gold and silver. Let them bring (all that) to Nippur, to Enlil' (Civil 1983, p. 236). Indeed, Enlil, that centrally located city's chief god, bore the epithet 'trader of the wide world', while his wife, consistently as we shall see with the entrepreneurial role played by upper-class Near Eastern women, was 'merchant of the world'. Interestingly, the cultic *múrub*-festival coincided with the falling due of loans. A similar theme is found in a poem from Ugarit, a major north Syrian port in the fourteenth to thirteenth centuries, in which the god Baal 'calls a caravan into his sanctuary (or "calls out a trade route in his house"), a trading company into his temple' (Albright 1934, pp. 124-5, and van Zijl 1972, p. 120).[1] Archaeological excavations at several Near Eastern sites reveal the presence, beginning in the second half of the fourth millennium, of large-scale storage facilities in close proximity to or within what are believed to be temple precincts.

Excavations of the Athenian Agora reveal that during the prosperous, trade-oriented classical period a significant development of craftmanship and small industrial establishments took place in the immediate vicinity of the temple shared by the patron god and goddess of the crafts, Hephaestus (the fashioner of Achilles' armour) and Athena Ergane ('Patroness of Toil'). Revealingly, *panegyris* came to mean 'religious festival' and 'market' (Nilsson 1949, p. 259). Similarly, in the fifth century at Memphis, a major port in Egypt, the

Phoenician trading colony from the city of Tyre surrounded the temple of Aphrodite the Stranger which lay close to Hephaestus' temple. With respect to the Roman empire, MacMullen (1970, pp. 336-7) is struck by the coincidence of holy days of the gods with market days and the conjunction of the archaeological remains of shrines and temples with those of shops: 'Pilgrims first paid homage to the god and then silver to the shopkeeper, all in the sacred precincts of Jove in Damascus, of Dionysus in Troy, of Venus in Rome.' Archaeologists have uncovered special buildings in the commercial town of Ostia where the crafts met and worshipped. Along the same line, in mediaeval Lucca the moneychangers who wished to set up shop in the square of the cathedral of San Martino had to swear to commit 'no theft, nor trick, nor falsification' (Blomquist 1979, p. 55).[2]

There is scattered evidence indicating that some Near Eastern deities combatted opportunism (self-interest pursued with guile) and lowered transaction costs by actively inculcating professional standards. We find, for example, in an Egyptian tomb scene of the middle of the third millennium a smelter telling his partner that 'Sloth is abominable to Sokaris', the god of metal smelting and protector of metal workers (Hodjash and Berlev 1980, pp. 36-7). 'Supreme leader of handicraft' is the title accorded to the priests of the god Ptah, who was very early identified with Sokaris. Apparently, the Egyptians saw craftsmen (or their overseers) as priests of their patron gods, so that their work took on the character of a sacred act. In the Bible the master craftsmen responsible for the construction of the Tabernacle and its furnishing were chosen by Yahweh and 'filled with the Spirit of God' (Exodus 35: 31, 34-5). The mythological literature of Ugarit shows that the divine craftsman Kothar ('Adroit') constructed the ornaments of the high god El's tent and built an innovative temple for Baal. Cults were created around real or mythic master technologists, for example, Egypt's great builder Imhotep and the Levantines Kothar and Chusor, the discoverer of iron and the method of working it. Indeed, metals and metal ores, especially iron, were deified.

It cannot be denied, of course, that the very religious imperatives binding craftsmen to performance standards and thereby contributing to the production of the public good — 'trust' — simultaneously facilitated monopolistic practices by lowering their cost of collusion. Note in support of this position the colophon of Mesopotamian technical texts: 'Let the initiate show the initiate; the non-initiate shall not see it. It belongs to the tabooed things of the great gods' (Saggs

1962, p. 471). This taboo does not constitute a conflict between religion and technical innovation, but quite obviously it slowed the diffusion of technical knowledge and retarded entry into the crafts. On balance, however, the technical secrecy mandated by the gods may have promoted technical progress and economic growth by anticipating patent laws (see further section 5, Chapter 2 p. 41). In any event, the divine sanction surely inhibited the individual crafsman from seeking to increase his profit by lowering quality or engaging in other forms of cheating so prominent in and destructive of ordinary business cartels (see Ekelund and Tollison 1981, pp. 115-19). But by the end of the sixth century the religious sanction had evidently weakened, for the goldsmiths and other skilled craftsmen employed within a major temple precinct in Babylonia (the Eanna in the city of Uruk) frequently embezzled or misallocated materials despite legally binding exclusive work contracts and the possibility of heavy fines.[3]

The protection enjoyed by visitors to marketplaces was extended to Greek, Italian, and Philistine harbours by means of a nearby temple. At Cyprus, a centre for the production and export of copper (see 'The Supply Response' under Assertion 7 in Chapter 5), several metalworking shops were excavated next to a temple at Kition, a major port on the south coast probably founded by the Phoenicians in about 800 BCE. The Bible makes no mention of a Yahwistic temple at Dor, the main port of Israel in the eighth century, but the presence of one is hinted by the finding of a seal whose inscription identifies the owner, an individual with the Israelite name Zekharyau, as 'Priest of Dor.' Ugarit's harbour was called Mihd (or Mahd), a name Astour (1981a, p. 17) links with Akkadian *maḫāzu*, meaning 'a market and cult city' (see further the discussion of Assertion 8 in Chapter 6). A temple of Ptah and the worship of Syrian gods are attested at Memphis in the mid-second millenium.

Commerce was also facilitated by the construction of temples at international borders. The name 'Carchemish', a city located on the major crossing point of the Upper Euphrates near the present Turko-Syrian frontier which appears in the Eblaite commercial texts of the mid-third millennium and possibly was founded by that north Syrian state, means 'the trading center of the god Chamish (or Chemosh)'; (Dahood 1981, p. 307; Pettinato 1981, p. 226; compare the discussion of Assertion 8 in Chapter 6). Ur-Nanshe (2494-2465) of Lagash built the temple Tirasha on the border of Umma, a neighbouring Sumerian state. A later text of Naram-Sin (2254-2218) mentions the presence of a temple where three states met.

No later than the beginning of the second millennium the Egyptians erected a temple in the eastern Delta at the 'mouth of the two ways', meaning, no doubt, the fork in the roads to Israel and the mines of Sinai. Egypt's Seti I (1302-1290), reflecting upon his parched route to the Red Sea mines, discovered a source of water and then resolved to found a town 'in whose august midst shall be a resting-place, a settlement, with a temple' (after Badawy 1967, p. 107). All the Egyptian god Seth's cult places were located, it appears, at the origin of caravan routes, for example Ombos or Newbet, 'gold-town'. For the Hittites in the fifteenth to thirteenth centuries, hints of the location of temples at international borders can, perhaps, be found in the obligation of 'border lords' to see that temples were maintained in good order and in mentions of 'cities of god', one of which at least was situated on a river. Also note the discovery of another temple not mentioned in the Bible at tenth- to seventh-century Arad, a fortress and trading station located in Judah's far south on the border of the Sinai desert, and the excavation of an eighth-century altar 20 miles to the west at Beer-Sheba. Both of these sites were on an important international trade route. Aharoni and Amiran (1964, p. 51) report the finding in Arad's Israelite strata of 'industrial installations' probably connected with metalworking and perfume distilling and Hebrew inscriptions written in ink on potsherds (ostraca), including 'fragments of dockets and business documents'. Pottery kilns were discovered near the entrance to the temple courtyard. Artifacts excavated there, including a significant proportion of First Dynasty kitchenware, reveals that Arad, at this time a relatively large town, served as a centre of trade relations with Egypt as early as the beginning of the third millennium.

The Bible does inform us that Israel established a temple in its extreme north at Dan, the city closest to the border with Damascus, whose Israelite remains have been studied by archaeologists, and another at Bethel in the south near Israel's border with its sister-state Judah. Bethel was located on an important north-south road linking, for instance, Bethlehem, Jerusalem, Shechem, and Samaria. Dan was linked to Hazor in the south and the Orontes River in the north and, to the west, to Tyre. Neutron activation analysis indicates that cylindrical storage jars (for oil?) found in large numbers at Tyre were produced in Israel, where similar jars have been found at various northern sites, including Hazor. The remains of a tenth- to ninth-century 'installation' at the far end of a room or courtyard of Dan's 'sacred precinct' have been identified as an olive press. These facts, taken together with the classic formula of Israelite settlement 'from Dan to Beer-Sheba' (2 Samuel 24:2 and elsewhere), lend support to the hypothesis that temples were erected in places where they would have facilitated international trade. Note also the excavation of several olive presses, spindle whorls, and more than sixty large clay 'doughnuts', now identified as loom weights, in the tenth-century 'cultic structure' at Taanach, a city five miles to the southwest of Megiddo on one of the passes of the major highway (Via Maris) across the Carmel ridge. Even more interesting is the discovery of loom weights and numerous textile fragments (linen, wool, and a linen-wool mixture) at the ninth- to eighth-century Israelite caravan-serai 'shrine' at Kuntillet Ajrud in eastern Sinai at the intersection of three desert trade routes.

Shrines located at boundaries are also known from the classical sources. According to Oliver (1907, pp. 22-3):

> The shrines of Feronia served both Latins and Sabines as a common meeting place not only for worship but also for the exchange of commodities ... while the concourse of the Latins, Hernicans, Romans, and Volscians at the Latin festival of Jupiter Latiares tended to foster a brisk trade.

Norman Brown (1947, p. 40) adds that: 'Certain Greek festivals in which a plurality of communities participated were known as "amphictyonies", or festivals of the "dwellers-around".' These *panegyreis* had a cultic foundation, but in historical times the accompanying fair was a major attraction. Indeed, Delphi and Olympia minted coins for their festivals. Among the early Greeks and Romans the stone heaps and pillars serving as boundary markers and ominous warnings not to trespass also became sacred sites of intercommunity gatherings and commercial contacts.[4] The Greek Hermes and the Roman Janus and Silvanus, who were closely associated with boundaries, became gods of trade and the crafts.[5] At late sixth-century Athens stone pillars (*horoi*) inscribed 'I am the boundary of the Agora' were apparently distributed around the central square, especially where streets entered. Additional evidence is provided by the prophet Isaiah's (19:19) oracle that a 'pillar' dedicated to Yahweh would be set up at Egypt's border. Interestingly, Isaiah continues in verse 23: 'In that day there shall be a highway out of Egypt to Assyria, the Assyrian shall come into Egypt, and the

Egyptian into Assyria; and the Egyptians shall worship with the Assyrians.'[6]

Syncretism as an Investment in Trust

Quite consistently with Isaiah's oracle, Nakata (1971, p. 97) has stressed the importance of the 'patronage of an impartial deity who was not limited to any locality or any interest group' in smoothing the path of trade between distant communities. Indeed, it is possible, without reducing religion to the status of economic epiphenomenon, to find in Nakata's observation an incentive for communities to reduce transaction costs by investing in the creation of common religious practices. This would include the identification of one group's god with that of the other and the formation of pantheons. With respect to pantheons the remarks of W.R. Smith (1889, p. 39) should be considered:

> A pantheon, or organized commonwealth of gods, such as we find in the state religion of Egypt or in the Homeric poems, is not the primitive type of heathenism, and little trace of it appears in the oldest documents of the religion of the smaller Semitic communities . . . Each group had its own god, or perhaps a god and goddess, to whom other gods bore no relation whatever. It was only as the small groups coalesced into larger unities, that a society and kinship began to be formed, as the model of the alliance or fusion of their respective worshippers.

The syncretistic process so often noted and condemned both in the Bible and by modern commentators may, at least in part, be understood in terms of the creation of a new public capital good, 'trust'. This effort may well be the underlying theme of Genesis 34, which raises the possibility of mutually beneficial exchange relations between the hill-dwelling Israelites with their herds and flocks and the grain-growing 'Canaanites' in the plain. The local ruler (of Shechem) tells his townspeople that the patriarch Jacob is peaceable, 'therefore let him dwell in the land and trade therein' (34: 21).[7] To this end it is decided that all the Canaanites will be circumcised in order to cement relations with the Israelites.[8]

Another example to which we shall return in Chapter 7 is the elaborate myth of the god Osiris and the corresponding rituals that served to solidify trade relations between Egypt and Byblos, a port in the Levant, as early as the middle of the third millennium. The constructive elaboration (or creation) of myth — that is, sacred applied fictional stories (see Burkert 1979, Chapter 1) — was made possible in the first instance by what might be called occupational specialisation of gods. Thorkild Jacobsen (1976, pp. 25-6) explains:

> The various city gods in whom the early [Mesopotamian] settlers trusted appear to be powers in the basic economic characteristic of the region in which their cities were situated . . . It is understandable that numinous experience in situations connected with basic life-sustaining activities would assume special significance and call for special allegiance. Thus the earliest form of Messopotamian religion was the worship of fertility and yield . . . In actual fact [the] full pattern is not to be found in any single cult; rather the figure of the god tends on closer view to divide into different aspects, each with the power in a particular basic economy emphasized.[9]

According to the story, the chest in which Osiris, an Egyptian fertility god identified with grain and flax and who was patron of the agricultural arts, had been shut up and cast into the Nile by his brother Seth was searched for and found within a tree by the goddess Isis at Byblos. Lumber, it should be noted, was Egypt's main import from Lebanon. It appears that the Egyptian Osiris, Seth, and Isis were identified with the 'Phoenician' Adonis (the Greek name), Baal, and Astarte.[10] There is evidence from classical times that Byblos marked the opening of navigation in early March with laments for the dead god Adonis, who was 'born of the fir tree', and the launching of a boat on which Isis, the patroness of navigation, had placed the chest containing the body of Osiris. It appears that a papyrus 'head' of Osiris voyaged annually from Egypt to Byblos.[11]

Another interesting example of syncretistic investment is provided by the Sumerian epic 'Enmerkar and the Lord of Aratta' (see further Chapter 7). This tale is set in the earlier third millennium, when 'the mountain land (of) Tilmun (probably Bahrain in the Persian Gulf) was not yet', when 'traffic was not engaged in', when 'the commissioning of merchants was not practiced'. Enmerkar, the ruler of Uruk, took grain from the storehouse and poured it into sacks which were then loaded onto 'transporting donkeys' and forwarded to Aratta, probably in Afghanistan (S. Cohen 1973, p. 112; see also Kramer 1952). After various tests of will and tribulations, Aratta agreed to export semi-precious stones in return for Sumerian grain. The central core of historical truth in the explanation of this trade pattern is that both cities worshipped or came to worship the same goddess, Inanna. Analysis of the Osiris and Enmerkar myths not only permits us to see how religious feelings can be made to serve material ends but also lends support to the Hungarian Assyriologist Komoróczy's (1976, p. 37) conclusion that 'the mythology of the Ancient Orient can be utilized . . . as a historical source of unparalleled value.'

Additional evidence of syncretistic investment can be discovered in the Eblaite texts of the mid-third millennium. These texts mention about 500 gods and include lists equating the gods of Ebla with those of Mesopotamia, a region with which Ebla enjoyed extensive trade relations. Again, it appears that in the early second millennium the god Shamash was worshipped or came to be worshipped not only by southern Mesopotamians but by their trading partners on the island Tilmun. Egypt's southern trade provides several useful illustrations (see further the discussion of Assertion 7 in Chapter 5). Together with more conventional commodities, early third-millennium Egypt may have imported the god Min. This suspicion is based primarily on the inclusion in a prayer to Min of 'words of the Nubian (*nhsyw*)' and Min's role as protector of travellers on the deserts of 'the God's Land' (probably Arabia, see further p. 24). Later and more concretely, during the flourishing nineteenth-century trade with Upper Nubia (Sudan), Pharaoh Sesostris III founded in this region a well-endowed temple dedicated to the Nubian god Dedun. Reportedly, the latter was incorporated into the Egyptian pantheon and worshipped in the standard pattern.

Much later, the special trading relationship in the sixth century between the 'Dorians of Rhodes' and Egypt was reinforced by the myth that Athena's temple at Rhodes had been established by a daughter of Danaus, the eponymous ancestor of the Danaans and brother of Aegyptus, the eponymous ancester of Pharaoh Amasis' kingdom (see also the discussion of the Greek trading station at Naucratis, a leading centre of the international grain trade, under Assertion 1, p. 76).[12]

Business Transactions under Divine Auspices

During the earlier second millennium it was standard practice for the merchants of Babylonia to settle accounts in the temple of Shamash. This is attested in a series of legal formulas, including 'When they have returned from the safely completed journey, they shall render their accounts in the presence of Shamash' (Hallo 1965, p. 199). Paragraph 98 of Hammurabi's Code, which dates from the eighteenth century, calls for partners to divide the profit or loss 'in the presence of god'. One internatiional merchant wrote to another accusing him of violating the terms of the contract ('sealed document') they had deposited in the temple. We also know that partnerships were dissolved in Shamash's temple. In Assyria (basically, the land along the middle Tigris in northern Mesopotamia) a business dispute led one merchant to summon another to 'the gate of the god' (see further below), where the latter 'seized the sword of (the god) Assur' to indicate that he would abide by the terms of a mediated agreement. We hear of 'tablets of the gate of the god' and of merchants taking oaths in a temple area called *hamrum*. There are even Babylonian loan contracts which list various gods as witnesses to the transaction. Gods figured as witnesses and sometimes offered testimony in Elamite trials. In a revealing text of the late twelfth century, Babylon's god Marduk explains that during his 24 year sojourn in Hittite Anatolia he 'established within it the caravan trade of the Babylonians' (after Rykle Borger cited in Miller and Roberts 1977, p. 12; apparently, the occasion for Marduk's 'business trip' was the capture of his idol in c. 1600). But in the later sixth century, when, as we saw earlier, craftsmen were embezzling materials belonging to the Eanna temple precinct, a number of loan tablets included the clause: 'If [the debtor] does not give (the debt to the temple), a sin against the *king* (or his representative) he will commit' (Martirossian 1983, p. 129; italics added).[13]

The Bible informs us that Joshua apportioned land among the Israelites by casting lots 'before the Lord' at Shiloh (Joshua 18: 8-10), a city in which 1 Samuel 3:3 locates a temple and the ark of God. In the classical world, the Delphi inscriptions dating from 201 BCE to 100 CE show us a ritual conducted beside the altar before the god Apollo, priests, and witnesses in which slaves purchased their freedom, and, as I interpret the texts, free persons sold themselves into slavery for a stated period, occasionally for the remainder of the purchaser's life (see the discussion of self-sale in Chapter 5, p. 91).[14]

Third millennium Egypt knew a goddess named 'Truth' (Maat), whose priests were judges and viziers. Mesopotamia appears to have possessed several specialised oath-goddesses, and eighteenth-century Ur, a southern city, had a 'House of (the goddess) Truth'. Along the same line, the Greeks introduced a god named 'Oath' (Horkos), and, in about 254 BCE, the Romans erected a temple to Good Faith. Oaths were sworn before divine symbols. Indeed, the literature hints that in Babylonia, Ugarit, and Hittite Anatolia contracts were drawn up and settled in front of a temple window through which the statue of a god or goddess was visible.[15] More concretely, a Neo-Hittite inscription of the earlier first millennium from Carchemish reports on the installation of the god Atarsuha (the seated statue of a god) in a gatehouse; a pictogram illustrates a gatehouse with a second-floor window. In the bilingual inscriptions of Karatepe (southern Turkey) a similar type of structure is represented in hieroglyphic Luwian, a language related to Hittite, by a pictogram described as a 'fence'. Early second-millennium Assur (in Assyria) had a religious festival called 'the week of (the goddess) Tashmetum-of-the-open-window' (Larsen 1976, p. 356). Note in this connection a clause in early second-millennium Babylonian loan contracts calling for payment to a priestess 'at the opening of the lattice' (Harris 1964, pp. 130-1) and, more generally, the persistence of the 'lady at the window' theme in ancient art and architecture. Interestingly, the Greek word *horkos*, usually translated as 'oath', and its cognate *herkos* share the basic meaning 'that which restrains from doing a thing'.

Several Sumerian hymns to gods denounce contract violators. At early second-millennium Mari, a north Syrian centre of the east-west transit trade located on the middle Euphrates, legal documents go so far as to equate failure to honour a contract for the sale of land with 'eating the *assakku*' — i.e. violating sacred property (emblem?) (Malamat 1966, pp. 40-1). Apparently, accountants worked in a courtyard close to a 'chapel' (literally, 'kitchen') called the *bīt papaḥi* in which there stood a statue of a god. Similarly, in Elam (in Iran on the Mesopotamian border) those who violated contracts might forfeit the god's protective power (*kiten*, Akkadian *kidennu*). This is expressed by the formula: 'He has touched the *kiten* of Inshushinak,' meaning, Hinz suggests, that the defaulter was brought into contact with the emblem of the god. The seriousness with which divine oaths might be taken is attested to by the stela of an Egyptian draughtsman named Neferabu who lived in the second half of the second millennium: 'I am a man who swore falsely by Ptah the Lord of Truth, and he caused me to behold darkness by day' (Sandman-Holmberg 1946, pp. 70-1). (The god Ptah shares many attributes with the Greek Hephaestus.) Wilson (1948, p. 156) explains that while oaths naming the gods did not guarantee performance, they nevertheless played an effective role in contract enforcement:

The chief sanction was, of course, implicit within the oath, which called upon the name of a god or upon the god-king [in Egypt], and which, therefore assumed very serious obligations vis-à-vis a force of far-reaching intelligence and penalizing power. An age which took its gods seriously would not be likely to treat the oath lightly.[16]

The efficacy of divine oaths sworn in property transfers and litigations (as well as in criminal matters, of course) was enhanced by reliance on standard and, therefore, potent formulas. An especially interesting example is provided by Papyrus Gurob II of the middle of the second millennium, which shows Egyptian employees and labour contractors swearing to render proper service before the judges in the 'House of Osiris'. (Note medieval London's related procedure of requiring workers unloading and carting casks of wine to swear an oath on the Bible that they would serve faithfully.)

The role played by oaths in international commerce is well illustrated by an agreement between two Syrian states, Carchemish and Ugarit, providing that if a merchant of one king were to be murdered in the territory of the other who then failed to apprehend the culprits, the latter would dispatch representatives who would swear an oath: 'We do not know their killers, and their goods, their chattels, of these merchants have been lost' (Yaron 1969a, p. 75). The rulers bound themselves to all the provisions of the treaty by means of mutual oaths naming several gods. In nineteenth-century Anatolia, transporters from Assyria who claimed to be exempt from transit taxes might be made to swear an oath to the dagger of the god Assur. Paragraph 103 of Hammurabi's Code insists that a merchant claiming to have been robbed on the road must so affirm 'by god' and then those whose merchandise he was carrying would have no claim against him. Along the same line, the somewhat earlier Laws of Eshnunna (located about fifty miles northeast of Baghdad) require (Paragraph 37) that if a depository claimed that his house had been burglarised, he would be free of responsibility toward the depositors only after swearing an oath in the name of Eshnunna'a main god. A quite similar legal clause is found in Exodus 22:6-7: 'If a man deliver to his neighbour money or stuff to keep, and it is stolen out of the man's house . . . If the thief is not found, then the master of the house shall come near unto God to see whether he has not put his hand unto his neighbour's property' (see also Exodus 22:10).[17]

It was not always necessary for litigants to undertake a costly journey to a distant temple in order to swear an oath. In the earlier second millennium, duplicate divine emblems were available at various Babylonian locations from which, upon payment of a fee, they might be carried by priests. One very suggestive legal text translated by Harris (1965, pp. 218-20) shows that an individual 'circum-ambulated the orchard, carrying the axe of the god . . . and established (his ownership) and regained possession of it.'[18]

A letter of the early second millennium demonstrates that Assyrian merchants stored valuables in the temple under the charge of a category of priest: 'Take the bundle of gold with my seal into the Assur temple in the capital and ask the *kumrum*-priest[19] for the sack which is deposited together with the bundles under my seal' (Larsen 1977b, p. 95). It is convenient to note here that the placement of clay seals on the mouths of jars and on the knots of bundles was a major Near Eastern innovation serving to strengthen property rights and thereby facilitate specialisation and trade. Excavations of a Hittite temple at Hattusas revealed extensive storage facilities, including multistoreyed warehouses. The latter contained several hundred large jars with a combined minimum capacity of either 62,000 or 119,000 gallons. An Egyptian papyrus (British Museum 10383) mentions a mast in the possession of a merchant lying in the open court at the rear of the temple at Medinet Habu.

In fourteenth-century Babylonia the 'boundary stones' (*kudurru*'s) recording royal land grants were sometimes stored in temples. Similarly, a round-topped stela of the nineteenth century excavated in a temple in Egypt's eastern Delta apparently records the grant of royal land to a town. In the eleventh century, a legally validated marriage settlement was duly recorded on the roll of the temple of Rameses III. A frequent phrase in Assyrian contracts of the first millennium that a price or gift should be 'bound to the foot' of a god may conceivably refer to a registration fee or, alternatively, an escrow deposit (compare the discussion of the sources of women's business capital in Chapter 2, p. 47). Consistent with the above evidence, a Sumerian hymn of the early second millennium identifies the goddess of Isin by the epithet 'the exalted land registrar' (M. Cohen 1981, p. 100).

In addition to mitigating shirking problems and providing a sanctuary for private traders and their goods, it appears that Near Eastern temples, including, for example, the 'House of (the goddess) Truth' in Ur, lowered transaction costs by issuing letters of credit and coins (see Assertion 9 in Chapter 6, pp. 128-9).[20]

Temples as Business Enterprises

The trust enabling gods to issue coinage also permitted them to function as relatively efficient financial intermediaries or banks and thereby to improve the allocation of resources in their societies. On the one hand, the temples were able to supplement tithes, donations, rents, and other sources of income by attracting private deposits at relatively low (possibly zero) interest cost, while, on the other hand, the natural reluctance of debtors to default on loans given by gods or priests operated to lower both contracting costs and interest rates. The evidence regarding the loan business and banking is taken up under Assertions 4 and 5 in Chapter 5.

Ancient temples often played an important role in agricultural and industrial production and trade. The agricultural role of Sumerian temples, for example, is illustrated in Chapter 7. Egyptian temples of the second half of the second millennium are known to have sold garments which may well have been produced in their own workshops and, more generally, the temples were not infrequently linked with merchants. The direct management of temple estates (by agents called *rwḏw*) is also well attested for this era. Already in the early third millennium temples are mentioned on oil-jar labels. A second-millennium text from Susa in Elam notes that: 'In town and country, for business in silver and gold, Nahhunte (the sun god) and Lord Arad-Kubi are partners, just as his father before him' (Hinz 1973b, p. 61). An excavated Hittite temple possessed a 'House of Work Achievement' but its exact status and function are unclear.[21] The business participation of temples, like that of palaces, was due largely to a limited supply of entrepreneurs, as is explained in Chapter 3.

The economic importance of temples also owed much to a factor quite familiar to economists of modern times, namely tax exemptions and exclusive franchises. Most famous in this connection is Genesis 47:26 wherein Joseph, the royal advisor, 'made a statute concerning the land of Egypt . . . that Pharaoh should have a fifth (of the harvest); only the land of the priests alone became not Pharaoh's.' In fact, royal decrees granting tax exemption to this or another temple or priest are known from all periods of Egyptian history. An outstanding illustration is provided by a decree of Pepi II (2275-2185) from the temple of Min at Coptos. Pepi's decree not only exempted 'Min-makes-the-foundation-of-Neferkare-to-flourish' from various requisitions and corvées but even forbade officials to issue or receive orders referring to the personnel or activities of this foundation. A later example is the Nauri decree of Seti I which richly endowed a 'House' of Osiris in Nubia where it might collect the coveted southern products and which prohibited 'interference' with its people, goods, and land. Its personnel might not be transported outside the district for corvée and its ships might not be 'stopped' by patrols, probably to collect duties. (Note that in his lawcode the Sumerian ruler Ur-Nammu mentions in the context of taxation that he 'detained' ships of Magan traders at the 'registry place'; see the discussion of ports of trade under Assertion 1 in Chapter 5). Temple-owned goods were exempted from certain transit taxes in the nineteenth-century Assyrian trade with Cappadocia. That Babylonian rulers favoured selected priests with tax exemptions in the second half of the second millennium is confirmed by the *kudurru*'s. Hittite rulers of the seventeenth and thirteenth centuries exempted the goddesses Arinna and Ishtar of Shamaha from taxes and corvée. Documents of ninth-century Assyria allude to royal decrees granting tax exemptions to temples.[22] Governmental tax policies, biased in favor of temples (or priests) operated to increase the share of temple- (or priest-)operated enterprises in total production either by raising their marginal revenue curves (or lowering their marginal cost curves) relative to those of independent firms when taxes varied with output or by driving marginal private competitors out of business, in the case of lump-sum taxes. Both types of tax were well known in the ancient Near East.[23]

In addition, it seems quite likely that the use of temples as tax-shelters operated to increase their share in total asset ownership and income. The evidence is fullest in the second century BCE, when, as is well known, selected Egyptian temples enjoyed exemptions from various taxes, including compulsory labour. Interestingly, there are contracts from this period (the Tebtynis Papyri of 195 to 137) in which individuals dedicated themselves and their families to the gods. These 'slaves' or 'servants' of gods agreed to pay the god a monthly fee in return for protection from assorted supernatural dangers. It has been suggested that the main demon they sought to evade was the royal tax collector. The Rosetta stone of 196 BCE shows Ptolemy Epiphanes 'freeing the temples of (the tax of) the artaba for every aroura of sacred land' (Gardiner 1948, p. 303). The Tebtynis decrees issued in 118 BCE by Euergetes II after a lengthy period of civil war confirmed temple revenues, including tax exemptions for property dedicated to the gods. Presumably, these fee-paying servants went about their private business activities in much the same way as previously, although they technically belonged to the gods.[24]

A final point is that in the Egypt of the Pharaohs and Ptolemies there are hints that temples were granted exclusive franchises for the production of fine linen and oil. Prostitution may, perhaps, be added to the list of legal monopolies not only in Egypt but in Corinth in the second half of the seventh century.[25]

2. Contribution of Economic Growth to Gods: An Application of Behavioural Economics

If it is true that by lowering transaction costs the gods served economic growth, it is also the case that economic growth reciprocated by permitting worshippers to better serve the gods. There is much to be said in favour of an observation made in 1965 by the noted Assyriologist I.J. Gelb that the 'daily bread of the people' determines the 'nectar of the gods'. In the first place, this service took the form of what I called cultic luxury consumption in *Prophets and Markets* (1983). The relationship between the affluence enjoyed by the Israelites and the demand for cultic consumption is well summarised by the eighth-century prophet Hosea (10:1): 'When his fruit was plentiful, he made altars aplenty; when his land was bountiful, cult pillars abounded.' A similar pattern has been noted among the Greeks during the period when they were experiencing what Chester Starr, (1977, p. 4) describes with a great deal of justification as 'the most remarkable example of economic growth and structural alteration in western history' (see also Silver 1980, Chapter 7). Starr's conservative estimate of about 3:1 for the physical resources committed to material cultic consumption (new temples, bronze tripods, cauldrons, figurines, and large-sized statues) in the sixth as against the seventh century greatly exceeds the most optimistic estimates of population growth during the sixth century.

There are hints that Egypt followed the same path during the era of affluence culminating in the reign of Rameses III in the later twelfth century. The monuments he erected across Egypt found their epitome in the magnificent temple at Medinet Habu and, like his immediate predecessors. Rameses III endowed temples quite liberally. At this time, Bleeker (1967, p. 32) reports: 'The religious festivals became . . . more and more numerous. The temple at Medinet Habu provides definite evidence for this phenomenon. During the reign of Rameses III celebrations were held on 162 days, in other words the number of days which together covered nearly six months of the year.' Bleeker adds that the records of a group of workmen in the cemetery at Thebes reveal as many holidays as working days. C. J. Eyre (personal correspondence) cautions me that many temple holidays were of little economic significance and that one quarter is a better estimate of the number of holidays than one-half.[26]

Israel's prophet Isaiah (1:11) knew that the Lord was 'sated with the burnt offerings of rams', and Amos (5:21-4) told them in no uncertain terms: 'I loath, I spurn your festivals, I am not appeased by your solemn assemblies. If you offer Me burnt offerings — or your meal offerings — I will not accept them . . . Spare Me the sound of your hymns . . . But let justice well up like an unfailing stream.' What the Lord desired from the affluent Israelites, Hosea (6:6) explained, was 'goodness not sacrifice'. For Amos, Hosea, Isaiah, Micah, Jeremiah, Zephaniah, and Ezekiel, Yahweh is no longer the national god and protector but a god of social justice who threatens personal and national destruction primarily because the poor are being oppressed. This prophetic revolution is reflected in the 'Admission Torah' (Psalms 15): 'Lord, who shall sojourn in Thy Tabernacle? . . . He that walks uprightly, works righteousness, and speaks truth in his heart . . . who has never lent money at interest or accepted a bribe against the innocent.' But while the response of the Israelite cult to affluence is the best attested example, it is not unique.

A hymn dedicated to Nanshe, the goddess of the city Lagash in Sumer, appears to deny participation in the New Year's Day ritual to persons guilty of social injustice. Heimpel has dated the hymn to the later years of the Ur III Dynasty (2112-2004), an era of relatively high living standards. Again, during the Third and Fourth Dynasties (2780-2560) of Egypt's Old Kingdom (2780-2260), the rich erected splendid tombs, but in the Fifth and Sixth Dynasties they built smaller ones and inscribed them with solemn declarations that they had lived moral, socially just lives. The inscription of a certain Sheshi, for instance, maintains that he rescued the weak and gave food to the hungry. The later Ramesside age is one of personal piety in which the deity is visualised as the protector of the poor.

In affluent classical Greece the term *philanthropia*, originally signifying the love of gods for men, came to mean the love of men for each other. In much the same way, in the earlier stages of Roman affluence in the later first century BCE and first century CE one's chances of pleasing the gods depended primarily on the proper performance of traditional rituals. But such characteristics as 'holiness of mind', 'purity of heart', and 'innocence' assumed importance in the second century, when affluence had peaked.

Many gods found themselves unable to adjust to the desires of affluent worshippers. Perhaps they were overly identified with special socioeconomic groups or with physical representations and mythologies that had become obsolete or even distasteful. As an economist might put it, their fixed capital had become obsolete. In third-millennium Egypt, the rise to prominence of the god Osiris was apparently associated with a phenomenon Egyptologists refer to as the 'democratisation of mortuary beliefs'. That is, the general populace appropriated texts capable of providing immortality which previously had been monopolised by Pharaoh. This can, of course, be linked with the increased ability of Egyptians to afford tombs and elaborate coffins and to create endowments for the provision of the vital food and drink offerings on various festival days.[27]

3. Gods Shape Economic Policy

The views of the gods on economic problems as expressed by their cultic spokespersons and others doubtlessly influenced ancient public policy just as in later times. For instance, a number of accounts of early Greek colonial foundations begin with the consultation of the oracle of Apollo at Delphi. This consultation and the tradition that the god gave the colonists precise geographical directions leads Snodgrass (1981, p. 63) to theorise that Delphi was or became a repository of geographic knowledge. He remarks that 'it was [not] only colonial voyages for which divine approval was sought and thank offerings made in the event of success; we hear of several commercial undertakings that had such backing'. Phoenician oracles probably played a similar role. In the early second millennium, when, after a lapse of about a century, southern Babylonia resumed trade relations with Tilmun, returning merchants, according to both Leemans and Oppenheim, presented a 'tithe' (*zag*-10) to the temple of the goddess Ningal. We do not hear of geographic guidance in this connection, but it is possible that the traders received more from Ningal than a safe journey. The term *zag*-10 suggests to Leemans (1960a, p. 31) that 'gifts were made according to a fixed rate based on custom or regulation'. (Butz suggests that the Ningal temple received 'tithes' from the Nanna temple.) Indeed, the hypothesis that temples served as repositories of economically valuable geographic information finds support in the Egyptian evidence. First of all, there is the god Amon's oracle to Queen Hatshepsut concerning the status of Egypt's incense trade in the early fifteenth century:

> (Formerly) the God's Land had never been trodden (and?) the *'ntyw*-terraces (possibly frankincense) were not known to the people (of Egypt). It had been heard of from mouth to mouth in the accounts of the ancestors ... The marvels brought thence under thy fathers, the Kings of Lower Egypt, were transmitted from one to another, and since the age of the forefathers of the Kings of Upper Egypt who were before, in return for heavy expenses. Nobody had reached them save the *śmntyw* (uncertain, possibly meaning overland carriers). Henceforth I will cause your troops to tread (on them). (Saleh 1973, p. 370)

An engraved list of twenty-seven mining regions in a Luxor temple of the thirteenth century is also suggestive of a repository role. It describes Cyprus, for instance, as producing copper 'in millions'. The 'Famine Stela', purporting to be the decree of a Third Dynasty ruler but dated by most scholars to the Ptolemaic period (323-30), portrays the king, distressed over Egypt's seven-year famine, consulting a priest of Imhotep, who then departs to consult the sacred books (the 'Souls of Re') in the temple's 'House of Life', where the clergy received their higher education, and returns to deliver a detailed lesson on economic geography.[28]

But did the gods possess a formalised or constitutional role in shaping public policy? Hinz (1973a, pp. 101-4) has shown that second-millennium Elam possessed legally binding 'paths of justice established by the god Inshushinak and the goddess Ishmekarab' concerning property transfers, loans, and other economic matters. Of course, the joint participation of kings and gods in establishing law codes is well-known not only in Elam but elsewhere (e.g. Hammurabi's stela). Less concretely but more generally, it appears that in Mesopotamia the governmental structures of humans and gods had to be congruent. One of the gods, the 'divine counsellor', advised the gods, and his priest ('father', or *apkallu* (*NUN.ME*) or *ummânu*) advised the king.[29] For example, the Sumerian god of wisdom Enki (or Ea) is termed '*apkallu* of the gods' and is represented by an 'incantation priest' whose mythical(?) exemplar is the royal advisor Adapa. Egypt knew groupings of gods called 'ennead' or, earlier, 'corporation' (*ḫt*). In a mythological text of the third millennium,

Thoth, a god of writing and wisdom, is titled 'vizier', and, later on, in the second half of the second millennium, Thoth is 'messenger' or 'representative' of the creator god Re. In epics we discover the 'chief lector priest and scribe' and the 'vizier' as royal advisors who, as early as the middle of the third millennium, addressed moralistic 'prophecies', 'instructions', and 'admonitions' to the pharaohs. Goedicke (1977, p. 62) reports that 'cult affiliations of lector priests are attested in the Old Kingdom as $\underline{hry}$-hbt n $\underline{it}$ and in the Middle Kingdom [2160-1785] in connection with specific cults.' In the time of Rameses III a hymn to the god Min is headed 'Rituals(?) of Min' and, below a priest is identified as 'the chief lector priest reading aloud the ritual(?)' (Hayes 1946, p. 19).[30] Several viziers are called 'father to God' (i.e. pharaoh's intercessor), and in at least one instance the holder of this title is addressed as a priest. Along the same lines, an inscription of the Twenty-second Dynasty (945-745) calls for a prayer to be recited by the 'father of the gods' and '*sem*-priests'. Interestingly, the biblical Joseph, an arguably cultic figure, who advised Pharaoh with respect to grain storage and taxation (Genesis 41:28-36) is called 'father to Pharaoh' in Genesis 45:8. During the Eighteenth Dynasty (fifteenth through fourteenth centuries), 'father to Pharaoh' was the designation of the crown prince's tutor. In Greece, religious figures like Epimenides and Onomacritus advised Solon and the Pisistratids.[31]

With respect to Israelite practices, we know, first of all, the prophet Samuel's warning that a king would 'take a tenth part of your grain and give it to his eunuchs and courtiers' and that he 'told the people the manner of the kingdom and wrote it in a book and laid it before the Lord' (1 Samuel 8:15, 10:25). When, in 2 Samuel 24, King David conducts a census, no doubt as a prelude to imposing taxes, he is opposed by 'the prophet Gad, David's seer' (24:11). (Note that in Exodus 30:12-16 the census is the occasion for the payment by all adults of a poll-tax equal to 'a half-shekel by the sanctuary weight', termed 'expiation money', for the 'service of the Tent of Meeting' — that is, the cult.) Deuteronomy 17:14-15 permits the Israelites to establish a monarchy, but the king must be one 'whom the Lord thy God shall choose'. Clearly, a cultic input is demanded. While the Bible includes references to a divine council (see, for example, the 'prologue' to the Book of Job and Psalms 82), there is no reasonably clear reference to an office of 'divine counsellor'. (It appears to some scholars that El advises Yahweh in Isaiah 40:12-26.) Nevertheless, the reflections of a priest and royal advisor at the Israelite court are numerous and unmistakable. In *Prophets and Markets* (1983a) I survey this evidence and find it not unreasonable that Isaiah, who composed royal records, spent part of his career as a royal advisor, while Amos as least sought to occupy this office.

Obviously, the problems raised in this chapter require far more extensive research. I hope that it demonstrates that it is possible for historical economists and students of spiritual culture to talk to one another. Indeed, with more effort on both sides, a fruitful dialogue can be initiated.

Notes

1. Gibson (1977, p. 61) renders the passage: 'Call a caravan into your mansion, (building) wares within your palace.' Ginsberg (1969 p. 133) translates: 'Summon *weeds* into thy house, *herbs* into the midst of thy palace.' Possibly the reference is to building materials for Baal's temple.

2. Sources on concentration of trade around temples: Albright (1934, pp. 124-5); Blomquist (1979, p. 55); Civil (1983, p. 236); Hopper (1979, p. 50); Katzenstein (1979, pp. 29-30); Kraay (1976, pp. 103, 121); Kramer (1969c, p. 576); Mackaay (1983, pp. 3-4); MacMullen (1970, pp. 336-7); Nilsson (1940, p. 100; 1949, p. 259); and Oppenheim (1948, p. 42).

3. Sources on deity-inculcated professional standards: Hodjash and Berlev (1980, pp. 36-7), J. Lewy (1955), Mullen (1980, p. 134), Renger (1971), Saggs (1962, p. 471), and Sandman-Holmberg (1946, pp. 49-50).

4. On the phallic symbolism of boundary pillars, see Brown (1947, pp. 33-7), Chittenden (1947), and, especially, Burkert (1979, pp. 39-41), who sees in it not fertility, but an easily understood message of potency, namely that the community beyond the boundary does not consist solely of helpless women and children.

5. Furley (1981, pp. 59-60) suggests that Hermes' 'role of supervising terrestrial boundaries grew into that of metaphysical boundaries, in particular those between men and gods ... and between life and death ...' Thus the boundary stone marks the location of graves and witnesses the sacrifice of animals. Babylon knew a *bel kudurru*, 'lord of boundary pillars' in the second half of the second millennium.

6. Sources on temples, shrines, and pillars at harbours and boundaries: Aharoni (1968, p. 21; 1974; 1982, pp. 67-9, 228-33), Aharoni and Amiran (1964, pp. 51-3), Astour (1981a, p. 17), Avigad (1975); Biran (1980, pp. 172-9), Bleeker (1966, p. 84), Borowski (1982), N. Brown (1947, pp. 38-40), R. Cohen (1981), Colini (1980), Dahood (1981, p. 307), Dever (1983, p. 573), Geva (1982), Glotz (1967, pp. 113-14), Gophna (1976), Graesser (1972), Helck (1970), Jacobsen (1979, pp. 6-7), Klengel (1975, pp. 196-8), Mazar (1973), Ogilvie (1969, pp. 14-15), Oliver (1907, pp. 22-3), Pettinato (1981, p. 226), Sheffer (1981), van Seters (1966, p. 93), Silver (1983a, pp. 88-9), Stager and Wolff (1981, pp. 95-9), Vanstiphout (1970, pp. 10-11), Velde (1977, pp. 116-17), Weill (1940, pp. 32-3), Wheeler *et al.* (1979, p. 141), and Wycherly (1978, p. 33).

Stone pillars or traces of them have been found within the temple precincts of Israelite Arad and Dan. In Genesis 31:52, Laban the Aramean tells Jacob that 'this stone-heap (*gal*) and this pillar (*maṣṣēbāh*) shall be witness that I am not to cross to you past this heap, and that you are not to cross to me past this pillar with hostile intent.' They swear to uphold the treaty by their ancestral deities and then sacrifice. In connection with possible Israelite 'amphictyonies' and pillars, Shechem, the principal road junction of central Israel, comes first to mind. Here Joshua gathered 'all the tribes of Israel' (Joshua 23:1) and placed a great stone near the sanctuary 'to be a witness against you lest you deny your God' (Joshua 24:27-8; see also Deuteronomy 27). A very large broken stone slab was excavated at Shechem in the court of a temple dated to the second half of the second millennium.

It is also tempting to recall Gilgal, where, according to Joshua 4, the Israelites placed 'twelve stones' after crossing the Jordan (see also Joshua 22). Again, the name Kadesh (or Kedesh), meaning 'holy place', allegedly occurs in a Ugaritic text: 'Give birth, then, to Sib)ani, O wife of Etrah. He shall build Ashod and set up the *ad* ("raised stone") in the midst of the desert of Kadesh' (Weill 1940, p. 32). Kadesh with its central role in Israel's Exodus tradition and close associations with the 'tribe' of Levi is identified in the Bible as an oasis in the steppe to the south of Canaan at the Midian-Kenite-Amalek boundary (Genesis 14:6-7, 16:14; Numbers 13, 14, 20; Deuteronomy 1; Joshua 15:3). (In Exodus 24:4 'twelve pillars' are erected.) Kadesh is generally identified with Tell el-Qudeirat, located at the intersection of two major ancient desert routes: 'The Way of Shur' leading from Egypt past Beer-Sheba and Hebron and a road leading south of the central Negev to Eilat.

7. The translation of Genesis 34:21 is disputed philologically and, more importantly, is controversial on ideological grounds (see Silver 1983a, note 3, p. 8). Conceivably, Genesis 34 reflects events in the last part of the second millennium. N.P. Lemche (personal correspondence) properly cautious that the Bible as a narrative does not provide the same kind of historical evidence as, say, a contract from the time of Hammurabi. On the other hand, the 'hard' data are often terse and difficult to interpret. Literary sources can provide a better feeling for the human atmosphere of the economy and, at the least, provide insights into the economic conditions and ideology prevailing when the narrative was composed.

Note that the trade pattern visualised in the narrative is quite realistic. Archives of the late third millennium, for example, show the urbanised Sumerians trading for sheep with the pastoral Mardu people. The hymn to Ishme Dagan (1953-1935) adds: 'May the Mardu, who does not know a house, who does not know a city . . . who dwells in the steppes reach me with *A.LUM* (sheep) and (fat tailed) *kungal* sheep' (Lieberman 1969, p. 58).

8. The religious significance of circumcision is explained in Genesis 17 wherein God (El Shaddai) tells the patriarch Abraham: 'Such shall be the covenant, which you shall keep, between Me and you and your offspring to follow: every male among you shall be circumcised' (17:8). On the other hand, circumcision might, perhaps, be viewed as a ceremony for instituting a fictitious blood relationship with the Shechemites. Given, however, the known Semitic practice of referring to the gods in terms of kinship ('father, mother, brother',: see Jacobsen 1976, pp. 157-60), it would be difficult and probably unnecessary to disentangle these alternative modes of establishing *commercium*.

9. With respect to the worship of fertility and yield, note Goedicke's (1975b, note 16, p. 211) observation that 'It seems indicative that the Egyptian term for "time" (*tr*) is derived from the word for "agricultural season", while the word for "year" (*rnpt*) is a derivative of "to grow" (*rnp*).' Note also the 'Ingot God and Goddess' and votive ingots at twelfth-century Cyprus.

10. In the second half of the second millennium, according to Velde (1977, p. 12): 'From the hieroglyphic way of writing Baal, one can already deduce that the god is a form in which Seth manifests himself. The divine name Baal is determined with the Seth animal.' Both gods are storm gods and controllers of the seas (Velde 1977, pp. 122-3, 128). Adonis is identical with the Phoenician word)*adōn*, 'lord'. Possibly he can be identified with the god Dagan who in Ugaritic myth is 'the father of Baal'. According to Judges 17:21-3 and 1 Samuel 5:1-2, 'Dagon' was worshipped by the Philistines living on the coast of Israel at Ashdod and Gaza (see Ringgren 1973, pp. 135-6). Earlier, in the second half of the third millennium, an inscription of Akkad's (the region south of

Baghdad) King Sargon (2334-2279) records that 'the god Dagan gave him the upper region' of Syria — i.e. the cedar forests of the Amanus Mountains on the Syro-Turkish border (Lloyd 1978, p. 138). Most importantly, texts dating from the middle of the third millennium from Ebla, a north Syrian commercial centre located in the Orontes Valley about 42 miles from Aleppo, refer to Dagan as 'lord' or 'lord of the gods' or 'lord of Canaan' or 'the Canaanite'; Baal is also mentioned (see Dahood 1981, p. 307; Pettinato 1981, pp. 245-7). Isis, the mother of Horus, overlaps with the goddess Hathor ('Lady of Byblos'), whose name means 'House of Horus'. At Ebla, Dagan's companion is called *belatu*, meaning 'lady' (see Pettinato 1981, p. 246). Bleeker (1973, p. 73) suggests that 'the relationship between Hathor and the goddess of Byblos indicates early trading connections between Egypt and Syria which fell under the patronage of Hathor and which led to the said identification of the two goddesses' (see also Weill 1940, pp. 61-4, 67).

Note that in the fifteenth century Hatshepsut's 'messengers' to Punt carried 'all sorts of good things . . . for Hathor, Lady of Punt' (Liverani 1979a, p. 24). In dismissing Hatshepsut's claim as a 'fictitious procedure' designed to inflate the importance of Egyptian gods, Liverani (1979b, p. 25) overlooks the role of syncretism in reducing transaction costs.

11. Sources on the Osiris-Byblos connection: Griffiths (1970, pp. 321-3), Robertson (1982, pp. 331-2) and Witt (1971, p. 166). See also Part Three, Chapter 7, pp. 150-63.

Related themes are observable in the Mesopotamian cults of 'Dumuzi of the Grain' and 'Damu the Child' who 'seems to represent the power in the rising sap [and] appears to have had his original home among orchard growers on the lower Euphrates' (Jacobsen 1976, pp. 27, 63-73).

12. Sources on syncretistic investment at Ebla, Babylonia-Tilmun, and Egypt: Bleeker (1973, p. 73), During-Caspars (1979, p. 124), Erman (1971, pp. 23, 65-6, 502-3, 506), Francis and Vickers (1984), Leemans (1960b, p. 92) and Pettinato (1981, pp. 226, 245-50). See Erman (1971, pp. 260-1) for a useful discussion of the identification of the gods of Egypt's nomes (local districts).

13. Sources on temples and merchants in the early second millennium: Hallo (1965, p. 199), Harris (1960, p. 129), Hinz (1973b, p. 107); Leemans (1960a, p. 40), Martirossian (1983, p. 128), Oppenheim (1954, p. 12), Potts (1983, p. 128), and R.D. Ward (1973, pp. 110-11, 268-9).

14. The self-sale transaction is usually referred to as the *paramone*, 'obligation to remain' agreement. As the slave did not possess the appropriate legal status, both manumission and self-sale took the legal form of a sale to Apollo who served as trustworthy broker and protector of the slave. In the case of manumission, it appears that the money passed from slave to priest to owner. In the self-sale or *paramone* contract, it seems that the money passed from purchaser to priest to slave, or, perhaps, Apollo held the sale price in safekeeping for the slave until he or she had completed the stipulated term of service. Sources: Finley (1982, p. 143), Hopkins (1978, pp. 136-45), Samuel (1965), Westermann (1955, pp. 45-6), and Wiedemann (1981, pp. 45-9).

15. The temple window would, perhaps, correspond to the state window, well known in Egypt, in which the pharaoh showed himself on ceremonial occasions.

16. Sources on oath-deities, divine symbols, and breach of contract: Balkan (1967, pp. 409-10), Erman (1971, pp. 82, 139), Harris (1964, pp. 130-1), Hawkins (1979, p. 158), Hinz (1973b, pp. 49-50, 104-5), Hornung (1982, note 32, p. 75), Kramer (1963, pp. 120, 125), Larsen (1976, p. 356), Lichtheim (1976, I, pp. 109-10), Maidman (1981, p. 235), Malamat (1966, pp. 40-1), Matouš (1974), Oliver (1907, p. 22), Plescia (1970, pp. 1-3), Robertson (1982, pp. 315-21), Sandman-Holmberg (1946, pp. 70-1), van Selms (1958, pp. 197-8), Singer (1975, pp. 96-9), Stol (1982, p. 151), Tsevat (1978, p. 151), and J.A. Wilson (1948, pp. 154-6).

It appears that migratory peoples seeking entrance into the territory of Mari deposited their sacred objects with government officials as a guarantee for good behaviour. This inference is based on a letter written by a district governor in which he reports: 'The *sugāgū* ("chiefs, mayors, foremen"?) of the district have questioned me concerning their gods, which are collected in Sagaratum and Dur-Yahdun-Lim, in these terms: "Relea[se] the sac[rificial] gods so that sacrifices can be [offer]ed to them in [their] temples"' (Matthews 1978, pp. 139-40). In Exodus 5:3 Moses and Aaron told Pharaoh: 'The God of the Hebrews has met with us. Please let us go three days' journey into the wilderness and sacrifice to the Lord our God.' Did Pharaoh, like the ruler of Mari, hold sacred securities? Interestingly, the Roman writers Cato and Columella warned masters against allowing their slaves to gather for sacrifices that might be used by omen readers and the like to stir up 'criminal activity'.

17. Sources on oath formulas and rituals: Frymer-Kensky (1981), Goetze (1969a, p. 163), Harris (1965, pp. 218-20), Meek (1969b, pp. 170-1), Mercer (1912, p. 13; 1914, pp. 197-202, 205), Thrupp (1977, p. 147), Veenhof (1972, pp. 274-8), J.A. Wilson (1948, pp. 145-9), and Yaron (1969a, p. 75). See also Bakir (1952, p. 91) for the use of the oath-formula in a slave sale contract and Goetze (1965, pp. 212-14) for oaths taken by Babylonian tax collectors.

18. The act of 'encircling' by the litigants in real estate disputes is also attested at Nuzi. One is reminded that the Lord gave Jericho to the Israelites after the priests had carried the ark of the Lord around the city (Joshua 6:12-16).

19. An early second-millennium transaction in which a father sold himself and his daughter into slavery is witnessed by a *kumrum*-priest (Balkan 1974, note 12, p. 30).

20. Sources on seals and temples as storage centres and depositories: Černý and Peet (1927, pp. 32-3), M. Cohen (1981, p. 100), Fischer (1961a), Klengel (1975, pp. 183-4), Larsen (1977b, p. 95), Mercer (1914, p. 205), Mettinger (1971, pp. 102-3), Peet (1930, p. 125), Shendge (1983), and Spencer (1984, pp. 6-7).

21. Sources on temple participation in production and trade: Butz (1979), Helck (1975, p. 52), Hinz (1973b, p. 61), J.J. Janssen (1961, pp. 100-4; 1975, pp. 160-2), Klengel (1975, pp. 184-5); Kruchten (1979), Lambert (1953), Leemans (1950a, p. 43), and Silver (1983a, p. 67). See also Zaccagnini's (1978, pp. 236-7) remarks on the part played by Babylonian temples in international trade during the seventh to sixth centuries.

22. Sources on tax exemptions for temples and priests: Brinkman (personal correspondence), van Driel (1970, pp. 168-9), Edgerton (1947), Gardiner (1948, pp. 201-4), Goedicke (1971-1972, note 1, p. 73), Griffith (1927), Hayes (1946, pp. 3-11), J.J. Janssen (1975a, p. 180), Klengel (1975, p. 197), Oppenheim and Reiner (1977, pp. 122-3), and Veenhof (1972, p. 418).

Sometimes, however, Egyptian temples did pay taxes (Baer 1962, p. 33) and, similarly, the Babylonian state taxed temples in the late seventh and sixth centuries (Oppenheim and Reiner 1977, p. 106).

23. In the early second millennium, Anatolian kings levied a tax on passing Assyrian caravans called *nishatum* amounting to five percent of the textiles carried and to two minas on every standard container of tin, or 2/65 of the tin carried (Larsen 1974, p. 475). Somewhat later in the second millennium, a *miksu*-impost on commercial activity was levied in the city of Ur at the rate of ten percent, and this rate was probably applied to the transit trade of Mari still later. During Hammurabi's era it is known that a *miksu*-impost was imposed on both commercial activity in agricultural goods and agricultural production. During the second half of the second millennium, the *kudurru*'s mention proportional taxes on crops and the increase of flocks. In Syria at this time *miksu*-imposts are found in Alalakh and Ugarit (M. de J. Ellis 1976, pp. 149-50, 162). An Assyrian text states with respect to a parcel of land: 'Its corn tax is one-tenth, its straw tax a quarter' (van Driel 1970, p. 171). The prophet Samuel (1 Samuel 8:15) warned the Israelites that a king would take a tenth part of their grain harvest. Taxes on

merchants, trade, and land are noted in 1 Kings 10:14-15 and Isaiah 33:8 (see Hillers 1971). Poll taxes were known in Israel and, according to M. de J. Ellis (1976, pp. 162-3), elsewhere in the ancient Near East. Compulsory labour service was commonplace. The law code of Lipit-Ishtar dating from the early second millennium fixes a maximum on compulsory labour for married men and single men at 70 and 120 days, respectively (Komoróczy 1976, p. 33). Note also the corvées of Kings Solomon and Rehoboam in 1 Kings 5:27-32 and 12:1-14.

24. Sources on 'slaves of the gods': Avi-Yonah (1978, p. 152), Evans (1961, pp. 197-8), and H. Thompson (1941). A document from eighth-century Assyria alludes to a royal decree establishing 'freedom' (from compulsory labour?) for 'servants' of the goddess Ishtar (van Driel 1970, p. 173). 'Servants of the gods' are also encountered holding land 'of' the *damos* (commune?, public?) in Mycenaean texts dating from the second millennium (Finley 1982, p. 231). The temples in this period of Greek history were quite wealthy; the case of the priestess Eritha who sought to evade paying taxes by claiming she held land of the god suggests that the temples were tax-exempt (see Mylonas 1966, p. 206). The *širkutu* and *arua*-people also come to mind in this connection (see Dougherty 1923 and Chapter 2 note 7).

It is of some interest to compare the use of ancient temples as tax-shelters with the relationship within Communist countries between public enterprises and family farms or 'semiprivate' industrial enterprises in which the former provide 'administrative protection' in return from monetary gains from the private firms (see Rupp 1983, pp. 14-17).

25. Sources on exclusive franchises: Evans (1961, p. 226) and Mireaux (1959, p. 225).

26. Sources on Egyptian cultic consumption: Bleeker (167, p. 32), Breasted (1909, pp. 486, 492; 1912, pp. 167-8, 177-8), and Montet (1968, p. 211).

27. Sources on evolution of cult — *Egypt*: Breasted (1912, pp. 276-85), Clark (1960, p. 124), Kanawati (1977), Lichtheim (1973, I, p. 17), Morenz (1973, p. 55); Pflüger (1947, pp. 130-1), and Williams (1981, p. 12); *Greece*: Downey (1955, p. 18); *Rome*: Ogilvie (1969, p. 18), Silver (1980, pp. 65-7); *Ur III Sumer*: Heimpel (1981, pp. 67-8), Limet (1960, pp. 239-40).

28. Sources on temples as repositories of geographic information: Butz (1979, pp. 362-3), Elayi (1981, pp. 19-20), Holmes (1975, p. 91), Leemans (1960a, pp. 31, 35), Lichtheim (1980, III, pp. 94-103), Liverani (1979), W.M. Müller (1910, II, pp. 84-94), Oppenheim (1954, p. 7), Saleh (1973, p. 370), Snodgrass (1981, p. 63) and de Vaux (1978, p. 304).

29. In *Prophets and Markets* (1983a, pp. 154-6) I cited a tablet with the modern title 'Advice to a Prince' in support of the proposition that the *apkallu*, a term applied to a type of priest, served as a royal advisor (see further, Lambert 1960, pp. 110-15; Langdon 1907, p. 150; Reiner 1961, p. 9). J.A. Brinkman and Erica Reiner have informed me in personal correspondence, however, that *apkallu* does not appear in 'Advice to a Prince'; this is a misreading for *rubêšu* (actually the Sumerogram *NIN.MEŠ-šú*), meaning 'high officials, princes, nobles' or the like, not 'advisor'. Nevertheless, the sense of lines 4 and 26 calls for 'advisor(s)'. In addition I am struck by the fact that 'Father Enki (or Ea), counsellor to An, advisor to the great mountain Enlil' is commonly referred to as 'lord, prince, noble' (see Green 1975, pp. 67, 78). Actually, the meaning of the Sumerian literary term *nun*, usually translated 'prince', is uncertain. Larsen (1976, pp. 122-3) observes that 'the correspondence *nun/rubūum* is in fact surprising, for the Akkadian word is derived from the root which means "big, great", and it would accordingly yield a very satisfactory translation of the Sumerian . . . *lùgal*, "big man"'. The word *nun* is found as a title or epithet of several Sumerian deities, but the linkage is strongest for Enki, 'the great *nun*'.

30. A spell on the coffin of a lector priest named Senenebnef who lived in the early second millennium calls in mythological terms for Egyptian sovereignty over the soil of Asia (see Goedicke 1969-70).

31. Sources on divine counsellors: Goedicke (1977, p. 62), Green (1975, pp. 58-62, 67, 105), Hallo (1970, p. 62), Hayes (1946, pp. 18-19), Hornung (1982, p. 51), Mettinger (1971, p. 153), Nel (1977, p. 65), Reiner (1961), Ringgren (1973, pp. 53, 78), Sandman-Holmberg (1946, p. 158), Silver (1983a, chapter 13, 18), and Vernant (1982, pp. 75-80).

Symbolic Action and Recitation in the Contractual Process

Today the handshake makes a modest contribution to enhancing trust between trading partners and lowering their transaction costs. But for ancient Near Easterners, sealing a bargain with a handshake ('doing hands') and other more elaborate rituals, including mutual anointing with oil or the sharing of a meal, must have played a major role in establishing a sense of community and confidence, a 'social contract', among contractors. For example, a Mari contract for the sale of land in the early second millennium closes with the statement: 'They (the contractors) have eaten from the (same) platter, drunk from the (same) goblet, and anointed each other with oil' (quoted in Mettinger 1976, p. 216). The witnesses might also partake of the meal at the ratification of an agreement, and, indeed, one Mesopotamian contract for the sale of a house in the middle of the second half of the third millennium records that no less than eighteen witnesses shared the meal with the contracting parties.

In addition, a variety of *publicly performed*, *conventional* gestures operated to lower the costs of making and enforcing commercial contracts. Some examples are (1) passing one's shoe (to surrender a claim or right; see Ruth 4: 7-8); (2) washing one's hands (to renounce an inheritance); (3) loosening one's hem (to acknowledge the return of stored property); (4) pouring of oil on the head (to manumit a slave); (5) breaking a lump of clay (to dissolve an adoption; see further below); (6) veiling a woman or tearing off the veil (to marry or divorce); (7) festive toasting (*kirrum*) with beer (to seal marriage, rental, and loan contracts); (8) boring a hole in a servant's ear at the door (to indicate his acceptance of lifetime servitude; see Exodus 21: 5-6); (9) striking the hand of the creditor or striking the forehead of the debtor (to enter into a suretyship contract; see Proverbs 11: 15, 17: 18, 22: 26; Job 17: 3); (10) ceremonial driving of a peg into a wall (to finalise the sale of fields, houses, and slaves in mid-third-millennium Lagash and to register a mortgage in early second-millennium Elam; (11) transfer of the *bukannum*, 'pestle' (to transfer a slave or a field, possibly a royal fief[1]). Perhaps the most famous public ceremony combining gestures and recitation in the transfer of property is the Roman *mancipatio*. Watson's (1970, pp. 50-1) description speaks for itself:

> For *mancipatio*, the transferor and the transferee appeared with the thing to be transferred (unless it were land which could be mancipated at a distance) before five witnesses who had to be male Roman citizens above the age of puberty and before a sixth person who had the same qualifications and who held a bronze scale. The transferee grasped the thing, for instance a slave, with his hand, struck the scales with a bronze (or copper) ingot, and said, 'I declare this man to be mine according to the law of the citizens and let him have been bought by me with this bronze and by these bronze scales.'[2]

The so-called 'I' form, a legal formula in which 'personal name said' is followed by the contents in direct speech in the first person is attested in sealed, witnessed Egyptian sale contracts beginning in the middle of the third millennium. Quite possibly, as Hammershaimb (1957, pp. 22-3) suggests, the contractual formula with direct speech originated in the era before written contracts and formal document registration when: 'Every kind of what we call civil cases . . . [were] conducted orally and it was the job of the witnesses, in the event of a later dispute, to testify what the agreement between the two parties had been.' (Compare the discussion of the slave market under Assertion 6, pp. 102-3.) Tucker's discussion of Abraham's purchase of a burial place for Sarah (Genesis 23) and of the seventh- to fifth-century Babylonian 'dialogue documents' is also relevant here. A reasonable facsimile of this type of contract is also found in the Middle Babylonian period (1595-1155), especially at Nippur, according to Greenfield (1982b), who cites the research of Herbert Petschow. Notice further the Assyro-Aramaic legal 'document of settlement' (*egirtu ša šulmu*) which requires, as Wiseman (1982, pp. 325-6) points out, 'a formal public statement by one party to the other before witnesses: "Here eat bread." The payment was then made and they "made peace (settlement) between them".' It is easy to imagine that the phrase 'my heart is satisfied', found in second- to first-millennium Egyptian contracts and in Babylonian sale documents of the early second millennium, was recited with accompanying gestures.[3] These brief remarks should suffice to demonstrate the richness of the problem termed 'exchange semiology' by Liverani (1979b, p. 17).

2. Code of the Merchant

In the early second millennium merchants engaged in long-distance trade made reference to the way an *awīlum* (gentleman?[4]) was supposed to behave, illustrating the importance, or at least the potential, of professional standards within a secular context. For example, in a letter cited in Chapter 1, p. 15, one Persian Gulf merchant complains to another that the latter had shown his agent low-quality copper and adds that this is not the way one gentleman is supposed to treat another. Similarly, two merchants in Assyria, finding themselves unable to collect a debt from three merchants in Anatolia, write that they should pay promptly or else the creditors could no longer act as gentlemen should. Elsewhere an agent is reminded that a gentleman carries out the instructions of his principal. Quite consistently, an Aramaic legal document of the seventh century employs ʾm, 'word', in the sense of 'settlement' (see Weinfeld 1982, p. 46).[5]

The importance to a firm's success of maintaining a good name or reputation (*šēm*) in a world of intensely personal trade relations is illustrated in Genesis 34 wherein Jacob's hopes of establishing trade relationships with the Shechemites (see the section on Syncretism as an Investment in Trust, p. 12) are dashed when his sons pillage that city. Jacob laments that they have ruined his reputation: 'You have brought trouble on me (or, you have muddied what was clear) making me odious among the inhabitants of the land' (34:30). Warnings to contract violators that they would be 'discredited' or 'brought into bad repute' attest to similar fears among the Assyrian merchants participating in the Anatolian trade. One is reminded here of the ancient Near East's preoccupation with the names of gods (see, for example, Exodus 3:13-18), including even, as Dahood has shown, the use of 'the Name' as a surrogate for or personification of deity.[6]

3. An Alternative Interpretation of 'Gift Trade'

Some ancient Near Eastern transactions classified under the rubric of gift trade and characterised as economically 'irrational' or as 'ceremonial' may in reality be mutually beneficial intertemporal barter exchanges to take advantage of unexpected opportunities or to satisfy unexpected needs. This practice arises when it is costly for the 'donor' to specify in advance the kinds of goods he desires to receive from the 'beneficiary' or for the latter to specify the kinds of 'gifts' he will be in a position to deliver in the future. The content of each gift is determined sequentially as events unfold within a framework of mutual trust. These considerations, it may be noted in passing, are operative not only in gifts amongst humans but in gifts to gods — i.e. 'sacrifices' — for which the deity later on rewards the donor with 'well-being' and 'peace'.[7]

As Breton and Wintrobe (1982, p. 72) explain, trust is a capital good whose stock can be increased by means of investment: '*A* has signalled his desire to produce trust jointly with *B* by offering to make a loan and . . . *B* has signalled a similar desire by repaying his loan. The asset produced [is] "*A* trusts *B*".' If 'gift' is substituted for 'loan', we have a framework that may very well apply to ancient gift trade. This fluidity, it may be noted, may very well explain why, as Zaccagnini (1983b, p. 217) observes, 'it is not always easy to trace a definite borderline between the two spheres (and "modes") of exchange (i.e. gift vs. "market" exchange).' Exchange relationships supported mainly by trust would tend to loom large in a world of slow communications and, especially, between trustworthy individuals including family members and neighbours and relatively long-lived enterprises such as royal houses and cults of deities. Note further in this connection that, *ceteris paribus*, the expected rate of return on investment in trust by means of intertemporal barter exchange would increase with the anticipated number of transactions.

Royal houses were in fact the main participants in the so-called gift trade. This is documented by the royal archives of Lagash and later of Mari, which reveal the names of about thirty kings who received and gave various gifts, and by the letters found at Amarna, Egypt's capital in the fourteenth century. The use of a fraternal style of address in correspondence served to enhance trust between the trading partners. It constituted a promise of counter-generosity, Zaccagnini explains. Thus, a Babylonian king whose gift had not been reciprocated by one pharaoh had reason to expect satisfaction from his successor. The difficulty of specifying return gifts in advance may be explained by the prevailing practice of giving rare objects, especially objects originating outside a ruler's boundaries. According to Oppenheim (1973, p. 264): 'The gifts exchanged consist typically of costly clothing, jewellery, precious metals, or household furnishings using rare woods.' Quite consistently, in the annals of Egypt's Thutmose III (1490-1436) some incoming goods are termed 'wonders' (*bi3t*) and others are 'production, trade goods' (*b3kw*). With respect to the origin of 'wonders' we find, for example, a ruler promising his counterpart at Mari that 'all the magnificent things which can be brought to me [from various sites in Anatolia], objects of art works, precious objects . . . I will have taken to you' (Gerstenblith 1983, p. 12). The king of Carchemish wrote to Mari's ruler: 'White horses for chariots are not available. I shall write so that they may deliver white horses from the place where they are available. Until that time I will send . . . red horses of Harsama' (Zaccagnini 1983b, p. 250). Mari's king, for his part, presented expensive Cretan objects to several Mesopotamian rulers. Again, Thutmose III received a silver bowl produced at Crete from the prince of Tinay in Cilicia. More generally, as Zaccagnini has noted, the documents show Syria and Cyprus exporting the products of other areas — ivory, tin, and lapis lazuli — to Egypt. A letter shows an official of Cyprus forwarding an elephant tusk as a gift to his Egyptian counterpart and requesting a return shipment (from the official? from Pharaoh?) of ivory (worked? for working in Kition's ivory workshops?). Aldred's (1970) review of the evidence has convinced him that the Asian 'tribute' or 'gifts' represented by pharaohs as a one-sided commerce was largely royal trading.

The Amarna letters reveal that every dispatch from a royal correspondent was accompanied by a gift, with the exception of one episode involving Babylon's Burnaburiash II (c. 1350). The term for 'gift' is *šulmanu*, an Akkadian word also used for payments to judges for judicial services and sacrificial offerings to gain the favour of gods. Sometimes a weaker ruler (e.g. Ugarit's king) obligated himself contractually to supply 'gifts' to a stronger one (e.g. the 'Great King' of the Hittites), probably in return for military protection (see Liverani 1979b, pp. 16–17). A letter from Mari records the king of Qatna's complaint 'regarding the insulting price of 20 minas of tin that he had been paid for two horses. He claims that in Qatna two horses cost 600 shekels of silver. At a tin/silver ratio of 14:1 he should have been paid 140 minas of tin . . .' (Muhly 1980, p. 39). In the Amarna letters the value of gifts given is stated more or less precisely (e.g. the amount of gold and silver used in making jewellery) and the donor expects a return gift of comparable value. A list of gifts given to the Babylonian king was in fact discovered among the documents. Burnaburiash states explicitly that he has nothing precious to send to Egypt's ruler because the latter's envoy had failed to bring him anything valuable. After recounting the small amount of gold dust he had received for chariots, white horses, and an artistic seal,

Burnaburiash exclaims: 'It is not even enough to pay my messengers for their trips to and fro!' (Grayson 1972, p. 48). Another Babylonian ruler protested when the carts bearing his gifts in the annual ceremonial parade before the Egyptian public were not separated from those of lesser rulers. However, Kadashman-Harbe I's complaint in the early fourteenth century that *Pharaoh* had not seen his donations separately may result from a premonition that, in addition to the insult, he would be injured by inadequate compensation (see Liverani 1979b, p. 15). Assyria's Assur-Uballit I (1365-1330) wrote that he needed gold to decorate his new palace and proposed to Akhenaten (1372-1354): 'If you are seriously disposed towards friendship (a significant term), send me much gold: . . . Write me what you need and it will be supplied. We are distant lands. Should our messengers keep running to and fro like this?' (Grayson 1972, pp. 48-9).

With respect to the above-mentioned 'messengers' note the early second-millennium references to the 'commissioning' of merchants in the epic 'Enmerkar and the Lord of Aratta' (see pp. 13-14) and, in private monuments, to Egyptians with 'commissions; (*wpwt*) who ventured into Kush in the Sudan and to Punt (probably the Somali coast), where, of course, they offered various Egyptian goods for incense. Several of Lagash's messengers to Elam, a centre of the cattle trade in the third millennium, are referred to as merchants (*dam-gàr's*), as is also the case later for messengers from Alashiya (Cyprus) and Babylonia in the Armarna correspondence. Indeed, in the thirteenth century an edict of Tudhaliya IV forbade the transfer of horses by messengers travelling between Hatti and Egypt and thereby, it would seem, prevented them from participating in a trade, attested in the reign of Rameses II, in which the Hittite ruler (apparently) exchanged horses for seaborne shipments of Egyptian grain. We know that in medieval Asia the 'tribute'- and 'gift'-bearing envoys of Chinese emperors and kings of nomads alike participated in the lucrative transfrontier trade.[8]

The pattern of intertemporal barter exchange also underlies the often long-lasting business 'friendship' or informal cooperative exchanges so prominent in the correspondence of international merchants. When, for instance, one mid-second-millennium trader in Ugarit reminds another that interest is not charged between gentlemen, he means that he is bound by the ethical code of the merchant to reciprocate, not that charging interest, an everyday practice, is undignified or immoral. This norm is stated compactly in a letter cited by Zaccagnini (1938b, p. 210): 'A gentleman, as long as he lives, will reciprocate a favour with a favour.' Thus the merchant Imdi-ilum sought to convince two lenders in Assur to forego collecting interest by offering to take care of their business in Anatolia 'doing my utmost over every shekel of silver' (Larsen 1982, p. 220). Similar considerations no doubt explain the references in the Assyrian texts to the rate of interest 'one brother charges to another' and the designation of some loans for business purposes as *tadmiqtu*, meaning 'favour, kindness, friendly word.' Garelli provides a number of reasons for believing that this type of loan was interest-free. It might be added, as Goitein has pointed out, that the readiness of traders to undertake obligations of mutual aid provided them with a substitute for the purchase of insurance in preserving adequate liquidity during a period of misfortune. The main advantage of business friendship, continuous relationships, native-place ties, and personal economics generally, however, was avoidance of the costs arising from periodic, detailed formal contracting. A concrete illustration of this is provided by linking Morrison's (1983, pp. 157, 159) remarks on the surprising brevity and simplicity of the standard Nuzi herding contract, a sealed list of livestock consigned to the herder by the owner, with her observation that 'individual herdsmen seem to have worked for only one livestock owner. Moreover, while the herdsmen were identified by . . . their family association — they were frequently further identified . . . by the name of the livestock owner for whom they worked . . .' On the other hand, protracted and costly negotiations might be necessary to initiate a trading relationship or to resume one after a hiatus. A case in point is provided by the negotiations between Egypt's Wenamon and the king of Byblos (see p. 136). The king, as Liverani perceives, was willing to send a sample of his lumber to Egypt, but he insisted upon being paid in full before completing delivery to the (now) suspect Egyptians.[9]

In a world of high information costs, the giving of gifts in the form of 'overpayments' for goods and services may be a rational practice. This is the case when the so-called 'overpayments' (prices or wages in excess of market-clearing levels) are premiums to compensate sellers for their investment in reputation formation and maintenance — i.e. for the preservation of 'quality' (see Shapiro 1983 and compare Posner 1981, p. 172), on 'barter friendship' and 'economic good measure').

4. Importance of Family Firms

The importance of family ties in ancient business life is attested to by the fact that Sumerian *é* and various Akkadian expressions, including *bītum*, *bīt* PN (personal name), and *bīt abim*, usually translated 'family' or 'household' can also be translated 'house' or '*firm*'. 'My house is your house' is a standard phrase in attempts to smooth out disputes between business partners. Large private firms (*bītum*) were prominent in later third-millennium Akkad. Several large 'houses' or firms were active in the Assyrian trade with Cappadocia in the early second-millennium (see further the discussion of Assertion 1, p. 24) and, somewhat later, in southern Babylonia at Nippur. In the middle of the second millennium the firm of Tehip-tilla played a major role in real estate transactions and other business activities in eastern Assyria at Nuzi. A list from Alalakh in northwest Syria dating from the same period refers to sixty-four firms (*bītātu*) in leatherworking, jewellery, and carpentry. A similar ambiguity in terminology is found in third- and second-millennium Egypt, where the word *pr* variously means 'house', 'family', 'institution', 'estate', and 'firm'. It is likely that the Greek *oikos* and Roman *familia* also include 'firm' among their meanings.[10]

There is more. The word for 'brother' can also mean 'business partner'. At Ugarit a certain Abirami wrote to his 'brother' about how a debt owed to merchants should be paid. Somewhat earlier at Nuzi, a partnership agreement might be termed a 'tablet of brothership'. Indeed, Zaccagnini cites a text of the earlier second millennium which shows two brothers concluding a pact of 'brotherhood' (*aḫḫūtum*). Similarly, *kinattu*, or *kinātu*, means both 'kinsman' and 'colleague', and *kinātūtu* has been translated 'colleagues' or 'business connections'. Again, the Sumerian word *dumu* might mean 'son' or 'servant' or 'agent'. Interestingly, an Egyptian priest against whom a claim had been lodged is described by a second priest as, *vis-à-vis* a third one, 'child of this merchant' (Reineke 1979, p. 14). Quite probably 'agent' or 'employee' is meant. Assyrian agents in the Cappadocian trade refer to their principals as 'fathers'. (We nevertheless hear of agents making illicit purchases with their 'fathers'' money.) Another indicator of the importance of familial ties in commerce is the West Semitic term *hibrum* (derived from *ḥbr*, 'unite, be joined') applied in the Mari documents to a 'tribal' unit (the clan?) and to a variety of artificial associations, including, apparently Syrian trading companies (*bt ḫbr*) of the mid-second millennium.[11]

The striking and well-documented overlap of terms denoting familial and business relationships is no doubt explained by the practice of recruiting managers and other personnel from among family and close friends in order to limit shirking, theft, and other forms of opportunistic behaviour abetted by slow and uncertain communications. As noted by J. and H. Lewy, the young Assyrian merchant, for instance, begins his career in Cappadocia under the general direction of family elders in distant Assur (on the Tigris in Assyria) and ends it in Assur supervising junior family members in Asia Minor. What today might be condemned as nepotism was a rational and quite pronounced feature of pre- and early-industrial economic life.[12] As explained by Niels Peter Lemche (personal correspondence):

> The use of family designations naturally ... emphasized the loyalty between the members of the 'house,' because even though the family ties were fictitious (as they indeed were in many cases) evidence of untrustworthiness would have been interpreted not as an economical crime, but as a social crime and the stigma on the transgressor would have been much more severe, because he had done wrong to the *paterfamilies* and not only an occasional manager.

The worship of exclusive ancestral gods served to reinforce adherence to the interests of the firm, as is amply demonstrated by the striking success of large Japanese firms in recent times.[13] When, as for example in a period of relatively rapid economic growth, employers had to resort to the general labour pool, their reliance on family connections or kin networks provided a relatively strong signal regarding the character and skill of prospective employees. At Nuzi several generations of a herding family did business with the same livestock-owning family.

'Paternalism' was, like 'nepotism', a rational adaptation to high information and contract enforcement costs. Both modes of personal economics raised the effectiveness of antiquity's limited stock of entrepreneurial talent by reducing its need to rely on the impersonal, and therefore untrustworthy, markets for management and labour so commonplace in the modern West. (Compare, however, the discussion of the free labour market under Assertion 6, pp. 104-7.)

5. Family Ties and Innovation

The family ties, natural or synthetic, that served to combat opportunistic behaviour within the firm must also have protected its trade secrets and thereby substituted for patent laws in encouraging innovation (see also section 1 of Chapter 1 and compare the remarks on innovation in Chapter 3). This is a factor deserving more weight than has hitherto been accorded it by scholars seeking to evaluate the economic growth potential of pre-industrial societies. In the ancient Near East we find, for example perfume recipes authorised by chemists (often women), formulae for coloured glasses, manuals for training chariot horses, and a stela describing how beekeeping was introduced by a provincial governor in eighth-century Assyria, who adds the significant point: 'I even understood how to separate the honey from the wax by boiling; *my gardeners also knew this*' (Oates 1979, p. 195; italics added). Admittedly, trade secrets were also protected by not committing them to writing or, as in the example of a sixteenth-century recipe for glaze-making, by writing them in cryptogram. Note also in connection with the ancient world's capacity for innovation Dorothy Crawford's interesting discussion of determined attempts by agriculturists in third-century-BCE Egypt to introduce new strains of garlic (with cloves) for the growing Greek market in Alexandria.[14]

6. Women as Entrepreneurs

The otherwise surprising prominence of highborn women in ancient Near Eastern business life — e.g. in production and sale of wool and textiles, lending, dealings in real estate and slaves — can be understood as a major element in a strategy to employ the family's managerial resources fully in order to cope with high transaction costs and to limit opportunistic behaviour within the firm.[15]

In Sumer during Lagash's great age of international trade and prosperity (see Chapter 7, 'New Markets and Land Consolidation'), a large fraction of the administrative texts of the reigns of Enentarzi, Lugalanda, and Urukagina (2364-2342) belonged to the *é-munus*, 'house of the wife (of the ruler.)' There is reason to believe that these records, including those of Urukagina's 'household of the goddess Bau' (the *é-munus* under his rule), reflect the private business activities of the royal house. Barnamtarra, the wife of Lugalanda, for example, sold imported copper in the neighbouring city of Umma. For her estates, which no doubt marketed milk products, she purchased choice cattle from Elam. The expression 'property (*ú-rum*) of Barnamtarra' is found on lists of people, animals, estates and various objects. A rather obscure text records the delivery of Urukagina's wife, Sasa, by the 'temple steward' of twenty-one shekels of pure silver of the '*bar duba*-obligation' (perhaps debt payments) at the time of 'combing full-grown sheep' (Stephens 1955, p. 129). She also exchanges barley for the wool of the 'people of distinction' in the temple. Other texts show these women selling fish to merchants (*dam-gàr*s). It is of interest in this connection that the Sumerian mythological poem 'Enki and the World Order' installs Nanshe, a goddess mentioned in the Lagash texts, as 'fishery inspector of the se[a]?' (Kramer 1963, p. 183). At roughly the same time the queen (*maliktum*) of Ebla acknowledged the receipt and delivery of goods and directed a textile enterprise ('house of wool'). In late third-millennium Sumer the wives of rulers and governors made loans, owned sheep, and participated in the clothing industry. The wife of King Shulgi, a *lukur*-priestess, played an important role in the administration of Drehem's sizeable livestock economy. Eighteenth-century documents from northern Mesopotamia (Tell al Rimah) reveal that the local ruler's wife, Iltani, operated a textile firm (*é*) employing twenty-five production workers. Shepherds and donkey-drivers are also mentioned as belonging to Iltani. Her textiles were distributed locally and were exported, with the assistance of her husband, to Babylon, Assyria, and Anatolia.[16] Iltani, moreover, had dealings with several women engaged in the textile business. At about the same time in Alalakh, the king's sister, Sumunnabi, participated in diverse business activities, including lending, exporting barley, and purchasing slaves, houses, and vineyards. At Ugarit the king's mother, Puduhepa, was familiar enough with the kinds of issues involved to render the verdict in a negligence suit concerning the wrecking of a cargo vessel. The inscription 'wine of the (house of the) great pharaoh's wife' has been found on fourteenth century jar-sealings at Buhen, a trading station in Lower Nubia (H.S. Smith 1976, p. 167).[17]

A woman did not, however, have to be a member of the royal household to succeed in the business world. Undoubtedly private documents from Lagash show women as buyers and sellers capable of owning garden lots and houses. Somewhat later in the third millennium, a Sumerian woman engaged in diverse commercial activities. Foster (1977, p. 33) reports that:

> Ama-é received extensive land allotments from the state, probably on a rental or other contractual basis, and dealt in real estate, metal, and grain. She invested her wealth with various agents. To one she entrusted food, aromatics, and wood, probably as an investment, and to another silver. Through another man she bought and sold wool in large quantities.

Foster adds to his summary the key point that 'there is no reason to believe her career was exceptional as women appear in other Sargonic texts.' In one of these, for instance, a merchant pays out silver to women who had consigned goods to him for trading. During the Ur III period a woman named Kubatum was a receiving agent for a certain Gazana, possibly a government agent, who dealt in substantial quantities of wool, grain, and goat's hair. Amat-Ningal, a woman of Ur in the early second millennium, gave a tenth part of goods imported from Tilmun to the temple of Ningal. Presumably, she, like the other givers of 'tithes', was a leading participant in the Persian Gulf trade (compare section 3, Chapter 1, p. 23). Larsen (1982, p. 220) points to several Assyrian businesswomen who 'were able to dispose over . . . very large funds which clearly constituted their private personal property'. The prominent position of women in Assur's business life is predictable once account is taken of that city's flourishing trade and the dispersal of many of its businessmen to the commercial stations of Anatolia and Syria and the connecting caravan routes (see the discussion of Assertion 1 in Chapter 5). The extent to which even married sisters are found actively participating with their brothers in business is also striking. Mention should also be made here of an early second-millennium text from Nippur in which a house plot belonging to a brother is sold by his priestess sister.

The excavators of Mari were rewarded by extensive palace archives dating to the eighteenth century, including receipts for taxes in kind (grain) from the firm of a woman named Addu-dūri. The latter may have held extensive palace lands in tenancy and is known to have served as a hearing officer in legal disputes concerning real estate and deposits of money. In another text of unknown provenience from this era the woman Amatum repaid a relatively large loan of one-half mina of silver. Women served as guarantors and sold land at Khafajah (Tutub) seven miles east of Baghdad. The business dealings of a number of women are prominent in the Nuzi texts, which reveal that women purchased land and gave loans. At Ugarit women participated in the market for agricultural property and, as in Babylonia, employed labour, as is suggested in literary texts by the term *agrtn*, 'our lady employer' (Muntingh 1967, note 15, p. 103). Little is known about commercial activity within Hittite Anatolia, but a text transfers two prisoners of war (?) from the queen to the houses of two women. The story of Joshua's conquest of Jericho hints that Canaanite women participated in the spinning business by noting the presence of stalks of flax in the 'house' or Rahab, who, we are told, 'dwelt in the midst of Israel unto this day' (Joshua 2: 1, 6:22-5). The description *'iššā zōnā* (Joshua 2:1) means that Rahab was an alien, not that she was a prostitute. For Israelite women we have the reference in Proverbs 31: 16-24 to the capable wife who purchases vineyards and fields and sells her woven products to the Canaanite (i.e. merchant).[18]

Metjen, a twenty-fourth-century Egyptian land consolidator (see Part Three, Chapter 7), inherited a landed estate from his mother. Along the same line, the late third-millennium tomb inscription of an Egyptian commoner records that he acquired livestock, a great field, a large and a small boat, and granaries. Qedes of Gebelein explains that he acquired these possessions in his father's household '(but) it was my mother Ibeb who acquired them for me' (Lichtheim 1973, I, p. 90). Texts dating from the middle of the second millennium show Egyptian women purchasing and selling land, paying harvest-taxes, hiring out or selling slaves, and receiving payment for weaving clothes. A difficult and fragmentary sixth-century papyrus from the cemetery at Memphis appears to deal with the business affairs of two transplanted Phoenician women.[19]

The prominent role of priestesses in the business life of the earlier second millennium is discussed under Assertion 4 in Chapter 5, p. 84. Therefore the present discussion is confined to a few noteworthy illustrations. A Mari woman, a governor's wife or a priestess or both, is described by Batto (1980, p. 237) as having 'engaged in vast commercial enterprises involving grain'. Queen Shibtu sent priestesses to the 'weaving house' (*bīt išparāti*). An *ugbabtum* (priestess) named Ishtar-lamassī participated in the clothing trade with the Assyrian commercial station in Anatolia, as did the priestess daughter of a well-known merchant. A text from Sippar in northern Babylonia shows a priestess (*nadītu*) by the name of Erishti-Shamash providing a borrower in one transaction a grand total of over four pounds of silver and two slaves. In the south at Larsa the princess Iltani, a *nadītu*, owned over 1,000 sheep.[20]

Indirect evidence that women played entrepreneurial roles in Near Eastern antiquity is provided by their possession of the seals used to validate contracts. The owner of one such seal in the later third millennium, Owen (1981, p. 181) surmises was possibly from a merchant family. To illustrate further, in Mari the previously mentioned Addu-dūri had her own seal, while that of Amadugga is imprinted on receipts for oil and cereals as well as a delivery of honey. Gordon names eight women whose seals are stamped on Nuzi tablets, including Puhumenni's for a large delivery of furniture. In addition to being transactors, women, especially in the third and second millennia, served as witnesses in business contracts, for which they may have received fees. During Hammurabi's era women served as scribes and possibly judges and engaged in legal disputes against husbands and brothers about the ownership of property. In the first half of the first millennium, seals inscribed in Hebrew with female names and the identification 'wife of' or 'daughter of' offer testimony that Israelite women, like their other Near Eastern sisters, participated in business affairs.[21]

We have already seen that Near Eastern women might command significant business capital. Thus it is not surprising that in the earlier second millennium a Mesopotamian wife proved that she had not authorised her husband to employ her personal assets in his business, and, in another case, a husband promised in writing not to lay claim to his divorced wife's estate. A certain Taribatum purchased a slave with money from her 'wardrobe'. An Elamite woman blocked her husband's attempt to gain control over an estate she had inherited from her father. Papyrus Brooklyn, a document of the eighteenth century, demonstrates the ownership by an Egyptian woman named Senebtisy of ninety-five slaves, including males and females, Egyptians and Asiatics. Egyptian texts refer to the 'woman of $s\langle nh$', meaning that she has property in her own right or under the terms of an endowment. Note also in this connection the prophet Ezekiel's (16:30) comparison of Judah to a woman who is *šalletet*, meaning, according to Greenfield (1982), 'in control of her property' or 'who possesses independent means'. Further attestation is provided by marriage contracts from Assur, Anatolia, and Alalakh giving husband and wife the right of divorce and specifying the same monetary penalty for whichever spouse was the initiating party. Two Anatolians agreed to own a house jointly and, more generally, to 'share poverty and wealth'. Early second millennium Babylonian marriages might also be quite egalitarian. A legally validated Egyptian marriage settlement (*shr*) of the eleventh century specifies that the wife is to receive a share of the wealth accumulated during the marriage. Mutual divorce rights with stipulated monetary penalties also occur in the fifth-century Jewish marriage contracts from Elephantine in Egypt.[22]

A judicial document (Papyrus Cairo 65739) of the second half of the second millennium records Erērnofre's testimony that she was able to purchase a slave after seven years of marriage in which 'I worked' and 'provided my dress' (Gardiner 1935, p. 141). Similarly, in a Nuzi will a husband stipulates that 'whatever oils and copper which Kirashe (the wife) has privately accumulated are given to her' (Greenberg 1951, p. 173). Another husband states: 'Whatever are the products of Shuhur-naya's labor ... (be it) grain, oxen, sheep, wool, oil, textiles, are given to her. Shuhur-naya will give them to whichever son she prefers, but she will not give them to a stranger' (Grosz 1981, note 38, p. 175). Inheritance was another source of business capital. An Elamite man left a field to his daughter, who passed it on to hers, who sold it. The Nuzi texts show that a daughter might be a principal heir, and, as one will demonstrates, she might be given the legal designation 'son': 'The entire inheritance share, in the city and in various cities, I have given to my daughter Shilwaturi, whom I have given the status of son' (Paradise 1980, p. 189). Interestingly, it appears that Job's three daughters received inheritances along with his seven sons (Job 42:15). A married woman might, of course, employ her dowry (Akkadian *šeriktu*) in business. We know, for example, that the *nadītu*, a priestess-businesswoman, typically received an ample dowry upon entering the 'cloister'. This might include personal control over as much as eleven pounds of silver 'ring-money' (see the discussion of Assertion 9 in Chapter 6, p. 124). There is also some rather ambiguous evidence of a Nuzi woman actually doing business with her *mulūgu*, apparently a type of dowry or gift from father to daughter. The evidence indicates, moreover, that a bride might employ in business not only resources originating in her own family and transferred to her, but also resources transferred from her husband or his family. I refer to the so-called 'brideprice' (Akkadian *terhatu*). These latter transfers are, however, better termed 'indirect dowry' following Goody.[23] Rainey (1965, p. 18) cites an Akkadian text from Ugarit about 'the money of (a widow's) *terhatu* which she took from her father's house'; this *terhatu* is parallel to 'the 80 shekels of silver which she brought in to ... her husband'. The widow was permitted to take the *terhatu* with her if she decided to quit her deceased husband's estate. Similarly, at Nuzi part (at least) of the *terhatu* was assigned to the bride. An early second-millennium Babylonian text states that the bride had received her *terhatu* and was satisfied. The *terhatu* paid by the cloister upon the initiation of a *naditu* remained largely or wholly in the hands of the priestess herself. Elsewhere, the binding of the *terhatu* in the 'hem' (*qannu*) is reported (see also 'Slave Market', p. 103). The eleventh-century Egyptian document referred to above includes the husband's statement that 'Pharaoh has said, let every woman's dowry(?) be given to her' (Černý and Peet 1927, p. 32). Another Egyptian document records a legal dispute in which the issue is whether a divorced wife had received property due her. In the fifth-century Aramaic marriage contracts from Elephantine the 'brideprice' (*mhr*), like the dowry (*ksp tkwnh*), is regarded as belonging to the bride. Note also in support of the position that the 'brideprice' belonged typically to the bride the complaint of Leah and Rachel in Genesis 31:15 that Laban their father had 'eaten' (consumed? made use of?) their price (*wy)kl)kl kspn*).[24]

It appears that the role of Greek women in business life was rather limited. However, it must not be forgotten that the sources are biased towards Athens and to the period beginning in the late fifth century. As Schaps (1979, p. 97) points out: 'When trying to gauge the direction in which Greek society was moving, it is important to remember that we know very little about the proto-Greek state of affairs. To what extent the principles of Athenian family organization were either innovation or archaism is, in the present state of our knowledge impossible to determine.' It does appear, however, that Greek women (Eirene, for example) played entrepreneurial roles in second century BCE Egypt. The Roman picture differs from the Greek. For instance, a socially prominent woman, Domitia Lucilla, who inherited the family brickyards in 106 CE not only operated these but launched a new branch factory. At the death of her daughter, also named Domitia Lucilla, some six years before her son Marcus Aurelius assumed the throne, forty-six men are known to have been employed in the kilns. The mother of the emperor Antoninus Pius was a leading producer of bricks. Roman women also operated dyeing establishments and firms producing lead pipes for carrying water.[25]

It appears that women played especially important entrepreneurial roles in the expanding economies of twenty-fourth-century Lagash, nineteenth-century Assur, eighteenth-century Babylonia and northern Syria, and, probably, second-century CE Rome (see further the discussion of Assertion 7 in Chapter 5, Chapter 7, and Silver 1980,

Chapter 5). The evidence for business participation by Greek women, on the other hand, refers to an era of relative economic stagnation (see Silver 1980, pp. 88-9). Depressed economic conditions would have reduced the pressure on the family's managerial resources and, consequently, its monetary incentive to allocate the services of its female members to entrepreneurial roles. One might say that the opportunity cost of household work and even of seclusion had declined.[26] Writing in 1914, Mercer (p. 197) who studied Babylonian sale contracts of the Kassite Dynasty in the second half of the second millennium, found that women appeared as witnesses to business contracts 'though not so frequently, in proportion, as in the earlier contracts' of the Hammurabi era. The Kassite period is generally regarded as a 'Dark Age' of economic retrogression (see p. 161). It remains to be seen, however, whether Mercer's findings will be confirmed by studies utilising up-to-date information, if and when they are undertaken. It is clear that the question of the ebb and flow of the participation of women in entrepreneurial roles deserves a more systematic treatment than is possible here.

7. Employment of Slaves and Adoptees

Another strategy widely utilised by ancient businesspersons to combat high transaction costs was to rely on slaves whose services might be more fully controlled and relied upon than those of free wage-workers or managers (see also the discussion of Assertion 6 in Chapter 5, pp. 102-4). Thus when the Ugaritian Ewr-kl established his house at Beirut, a centre of metalworking, he obtained a labour force by purchasing seven slaves from the Beirutis, including five members of the same family. To illustrate further, we find in the Bible that Abraham, who 'was very rich in cattle, silver, and in gold' (Genesis 13:2) was able to muster 318 slaves (persons 'born into his household') for a military action (Genesis 14:14). Again, the patriarch Isaac needed a 'great household' to tend his dispersed, and therefore difficult to police, flocks and herds (Genesis 26:13-14).[27] Finley (1965, p. 55) adds the interesting philological point that Homer's word *dmos*, 'slave', is linked with *doma* or *domos*, 'house'. The Greek slave belonged to the 'being' (*ousia*) of the *oikos*. In classical Athenian law the agency of slaves was recognised more clearly in matters of external trade than in internal commerce, in which, of course, detailed supervision by the owner was more feasible. The loyalty of Israelite and Roman slaves was enhanced by their incorporation into the household cult. The Israelite slave, houseborn or purchased, had to be circumcised (Genesis 17:12-13; see also Chapter 1, p. 12) and, moreover, unlike aliens and hired workers, was permitted to participate in the Passover feast (Exodus 12:43-5).[28]

The formal adoption or incorporation of free adults into the family, a practice well known in the Near East and found at seventh- to fifth-century Crete, also served to enhance the employee's loyalty and the ability of the employer to control his services. Among the Greeks and Romans the terms *oiketes* and *famulus* applied to slaves and free (adopted?) workers. In the second half of the second millennium Assyrian contracts of adoption explicitly obligated the adopted person to work for the adopter. One interesting adoption contract from Nuzi provides the adoptee with both a wife and a trade (Breneman 1971, p. 226):

> Hui-tilla son of Waratteia has given Naniia into sonship to Tirwiia servant of Enna-mati. And Tirwiia shall take (for) Naniia a wife, and shall teach him weaving. As long as Tirwiia lives, Naniia with his wife shall serve him. When Tirwiia dies Naniia may take his wife and go where he pleases.

Paragraph 199 of Hammurabi's Code protects the investment of the firm by providing that once an adopted child has been taught a trade, he might not be reclaimed by his biological family. The childless patriarch Abraham probably adopted his manager or steward (*bn byt*), Dammesek Eliezer, and made him his 'heir' (Genesis 15:2-3).[29] If the 'senior servant' (manager? slave?) in Genesis 24:2 can be identified with Eliezer, we find that he had Abraham's power of attorney. Individuals from among the 'ones listening to the call' (*sdmw ʿš*), apparently a class of dependent worker, played a similar role in private Egyptian households of the mid-second millennium. (Legal agency is recognised not only in Athenian law (see above) but in Paragraph 17 of the early second-millennium lawcode of Lipit-Ishtar.) Along the same line, in a Nuzi contract a woman has herself adopted as the sister of a man, making him responsible to 'manage my possessions' and 'be of assistance to me' (van Seters 1975, pp. 72-3).

Of course, adoption served other economic purposes and religious ones as well. It might be employed to provide the adopter with an annuity for his old age, as in contracts from Babylonia dating from the first half of the second millennium wherein an adopted son or daughter receives an inheritance and agrees to provide the parent with annual payments of grain, wool, and oil. As we shall see in the discussion of Assertion 14 in Chapter 6, legal adoption was also employed to disguise illegal land sales. For the childless, adoption provided an heir to make daily mortuary offerings for his deceased adoptive parents.[30]

8. Size of Firm and Versatility of Firm

Despite the various expedients employed by entrepreneurs to limit opportunism and to increase what organisation theorists call the 'span of control' the technological environment of antiquity operated to limit the importance of economies of scale and, consequently, the relative sizes of firms. This factor, however, should not be unduly magnified. Rather healthy firm sizes are indicated at various points in this study, especially in Chapter 3 and in the discussion of the textile industry under Assertion 7 in Chapter 5. The classical world also knew firms of respectable size.[31] On the other hand, it might be expected that the combination of high communication costs and a relatively limited pool of potential entrepreneurs (see Chapter 3) would have encouraged ancient Near Eastern firms to be more versatile, more diversified in their undertakings than modern firms.[32] Firms producing good or service X would tend to expand into upstream and downstream operations from X (vertical integration) as well as into good Y, an entirely different product (conglomerate or unrelated diversification). Analogies might be found in the participation of fourth-century Athenian international traders in making maritime loans,[33] in the 'development blocks' of European economic history, in the large family firms of thirteenth-century northern Italy, and in Japan's family-controlled *zaibatsu* combines. (The underlying theoretical issues are discussed in my *Enterprise and the Scope of the Firm*, especially Chapter 4.)

It is fair to say that many of the firms we have already met and will encounter in Part II fit this pattern. The point is well illustrated by the large commercial houses that flourished in Babylonia from the seventh- to the fourth-century. The House of Egibi, for example, bought and sold houses, fields, and slaves, took part in domestic and international trade, and participated in a wide variety of banking activities. Astour's (1972, p. 25) observation concerning the versatility of Ugarit's merchants as revealed by prosopography (that is, the attempt to identify specific individuals on the basis of personal names) merits quotation:

> Most of them were not tied to some specific field of profit-making but were active wherever there was an opportunity. Among their endeavours, beside export, import, and marketing the produce of the royal estates, one can mention exploitation of saltworks, production of copper and bronze ware, manufacture of purple fabrics (which included all stages of the process — murex fishing, extraction of purple dye, weaving, dyeing, and making a wide assortment of clothes), trade in horses and cattle, and a considerable role in collecting taxes.

Shilwa-teshup's firm at Nuzi employed about 80 shepherds to care for its livestock; sold hides, wool and hair; made large grain and metal loans; and engaged in real estate transactions. In late third-millennium Sumer the rulers and governors controlled vertically integrated firms that used the wool of the sheep they raised in their weaving workshops. At the same time an Umma businessman (-bureaucrat?) named Ur-e$_{11}$-e busied himself with manifold operations, including raising livestock, participating in transactions involving cheese, oil, leather, dead animals, wool, and the finishing and weaving of cloth, shipments by boat of fish and grain, and even the construction of boats. In addition Ur-e$_{11}$-e paid 'taxes' (or fees?) in regard to irrigation and fields (*maš a-šà-ga*).[34]

In addition to the opportunity to fill profitable market vacua created by economic change in a world with high communication costs and a limited supply of entrepreneurs, ancient firms undoubtedly were encouraged to select a diversified portfolio of business activities in order to pool the relatively high risks of the individual lines of investment. For several reasons, then, both the conglomerate and the multinational form of business enterprise were well known in Near Eastern antiquity. The 'houses' of antiquity were, of course, distinguished from modern corporations by their marked family orientation.

Notes

1. For a general discussion of the medieval European fief and its ancient Near Eastern counterpart, see 'Individual versus Communal Land Ownership' under Assertion 6 in Chapter 5. With respect to the transfer of the *bukannum*, 'pestle', note that during the medieval European investiture ceremony the lord presented his vessel with a symbolic object, a rod for example. Renunciation of a fief called for a reverse ceremony in which the vassal returned the symbolic object to the lord (Forquin 1976, pp. 137-8). It is tempting to assume that the 270 mortars, pestles, and plates of flinty green stone found in the fifth-century Persian royal treasury at Persepolis (see Naveh and Shaked 1973) were being held in readiness for investiture (or initiation) ceremonies.

2. Sources on symbolic actions in contracting: Breneman (1971, pp. 146-7); Cassin (1952); R.S. Ellis (1968, pp. 86-7); Frymer-Kensky (1981, pp. 125, 130-1); Greengus (1966, pp. 63-6); Hallo (1973, pp. 235-8); Harris (1955, pp. 92, 96-9); Kalluveetil (1982, pp. 20-1, 108-11); Kilmer (1974, pp. 177-83), Mendelsohn (1949, p. 36), Mettinger (1976, p. 216), Saggs (1960, p. 416), Speiser (1963, p. 70), Veenhof (1966, pp. 308-10) and Watson (1970, pp. 50-1).

3. Sources on recitations in contracting: Greenfield (1982b, pp. 473-4), Hammershaimb (1957, pp. 22-3), Tucker (1966), Wiseman (1982, pp. 325-6), and Yaron (1960, pp. 380-1).

4. Possibly *aṣḥāb*, 'colleague', was the corresponding term in the Mediterranean commerce of the eleventh century CE.

5. Sources on merchants as gentlemen: Leemans (1960a, p. 39), Nakata (1971, p. 95), Oppenheim (1967a, pp. 74-7), and Weinfeld (1982a, p. 46).

6. Sources on name and reputation: Dahood (1981, pp. 283, 309-10); Larsen (1976, pp. 133-4).

7. It is generally recognised that in ancient Near Eastern languages, many terms for sacrifice have as their underlying meaning the sense of 'gift, tribute, present', and the like (Levine 1974, p. 15). There is even a Mesopotamian deity named Shulmānu, 'gift' (Levine 1974, note 35, p. 16). Hittite rulers offered gifts to the gods (temples) in return for aid against external foes and for the grant of a long, healthy life (Klengel 1975, pp. 187-8).

The intertemporal barter exchange framework may also fit the sundry *arua* gifts — i.e. persons, animals, rings, millstones, boats, wool, and bitumen — given to temples by third-millennium Sumerians. Gelb (1972) renders *arua* as 'given *ex voto*', from, or in pursuance of, a vow.

8. Sources on royal gift trade: Aldred (1970, p. 111: 1978, p. 22), Astour (1973, p. 20), Gerstenblith (1983, p. 12), Grayson (1972, pp. 48-9), Kemp (1983, p. 132), Knapp (1983, p. 42), O. Lattimore (1962, pp. 482-3), Leemans (1950a, p. 43), Levine (1974, pp. 15-16), Liverani (1979a, pp. 3, 22-6, 28, 33; 1979b), Merrillees (1972, pp. 286-8), Muhly (1980, p. 39), Munn-Rankin (1956, pp. 97-8), Singer (1983, p. 4), Strange (1980, pp. 96-7), and Zaccagnini (1976, p. 161; 1983b, pp. 196-201, 205, 210, 217, 250).

9. Sources on business friendship: Garelli (1963, pp. 250-1), Goitein (1967, p. 204), Larsen (1982, p. 220), Liverani (1979b, pp. 20-3), Morrison (1983, pp. 157, 159), Oppenheim (1954, p. 10), and Oppenheim and Reiner (1977, pp. 88-90). For a variety of examples from the Assyria-Anatolia trade, see Balkan (1967). Goitein (1967, pp. 164-9) provides an excellent discussion of commercial cooperation or 'friendship' in the context of the Mediterranean region in the eleventh to thirteenth centuries CE (see also Udovitch 1977).

10. Sources on 'houses' as 'firms': Austin and Vidal-Naquet (1977, p. 41), J.J. Janssen (1961, p. 103), Larsen (1974, note 4, p. 469), Mauss (1967, p. 48), Oelsner (1976, p. 261), Spencer (1984, pp. 14-20), and Wiseman (1953, p. 79).

11. Sources on familial metaphors in business life: Balkan (1967, note 1, p. 407), Jones and Snyder (1961, note 83, pp. 278, 330), Leemans (1983, p. 62), Maisler (1946, p. 10), Malamat (1962, p. 144-5), Rainey (1965, p. 20), Reineke (1979, p. 14), T.L. Thompson (1974, p. 284), Weisberg (1967, note 53, p. 100), Westenholz (1983, pp. 226-8), and Zaccagnini (1983b, pp. 199, 208). In about the middle of the first millennium, according to Greenfield (1982b, pp. 477-8), 'Aramaic/Hebrew *šwtp*)/*šwtp* a loan-word from Akkadian *šutappu/šutāpu* ... replaced native *ḥbr/ḥbr* in all Aramaic dialects ... *Šutappu*, whatever its origins, was simply "partner" in this period.' Probably this substitution reflects an effort in the direction of terminological clarity rather than a substantive change in economic organisation.

12. Lewy and Lewy (1942-43, note 337, p. 82); see also Larsen's (1982, p. 227) remarks. On family firms in pre-industrial Europe, see Kocka (1971, pp. 138-9), Lane (1944), and Pollard (1965, pp. 63-4) who observes that: 'Among the ironmasters it was family relationships which allowed widely separated productive units to be combined in syndicates and managed in a coordinated manner by having'one member of the kinship group in charge at each furnace or forge . . .' For a more general perspective, see Becker (1981, pp. 11-12).

13. As late as 1900 family members of the Mitsui *zaibatsu* (see also Section 8 of this chapter) are found prostrating themselves before the ancestral tablets and vowing to work day and night for the welfare of the Mitsui House (Hirschmeier and Yui 1975, p. 208).

14. Sources on technical innovation in antiquity: Brinkman (1968, p. 219), D. Crawford (1973, especially pp. 351, 356-7), Komoróczy (1973, p. 128), Levey (1959, pp. 94-5, 142-3), Oates (1979, pp. 190, 195), Oppenheim (1973), and Saggs (1962, p. 472).

15. It is interesting to note in this connection a letter Watt wrote to Boulton in 1794 giving as the reason for the sale of the Madeley Wood Ironworks 'that many of the company are females who do not find it convenient to carry out such extensive concerns' (quoted in Pollard 1965, p. 65). On the other side of the coin, in sixteenth-century Cologne, a city where women vigorously took part in business life, a businessman recorded in his will that he had remarried 'for the sake of his children and for the sake of his business' (quoted in Wensky 1982, p. 631).

16. This is precisely the pattern of family specialisation advocated for the upper-class household in the fourth century BCE by Xenophon in his treatise on management, *Oeconomicus* (see Pomeroy 1975, pp. 72-3). In the export-oriented silk industry of late medieval Cologne the wife typically supervised production (mainly the weaving operation) and the husband took charge of acquiring raw materials and marketing the finished product (see Wensky 1982).

17. Sources on business participation by royal women: Dalley (1977), Fensham (1967, pp. 221-2), Hruška (1974, p. 158: 1976, p. 94), Kramer (1963, p. 183), Leemans (1950a, p. 41), Limet (1979, pp. 238, 242-3), Lutz (1932, pp. 554-5), Maekawa (1973-74, pp. 81-2), Pettinato (1981, p. 75), Sasson (1980, p. 457), H.S. Smith (1976, p. 169), and Stephens (1955, p. 129).

18. Sources on business participation by Mesopotamian, Syrian, and Canannite women: Batto (1980, p. 237), Breneman (1971, p. 288), Falkenstein (1974, p. 15), Foster (1977, p. 33), Hallo (1973, pp. 235-8), Harris (1960, p. 130), Klengel (1971b, p. 43; 1975, pp. 193-4), Larsen (1982, pp. 219-20, 229), Leemans (1960, p. 31), Muntingh (1967, note 15, p. 103), Sasson (1977, p. 107), Steinkeller (1982b), Stone (1982, p. 61), Veenhof (1972, pp. 102-23), and Wiseman (1953, pp. 43, 49-50, 117; 1964). On Babylonian women as innkeepers, see Finkelstein (1961, p. 99) and Wiseman (1964, pp. 8-9).

19. Sources on property ownership and business participation by Egyptian women: Gardiner (1948, pp. 55, 75-6), Hayes (1955, p. 127), Katzenstein (1979, p. 30), Lichtheim (1973, I, p. 90), Montet (1968, p. 16), and Pestman (1961, p. 88).

20. Sources on business participation by priestesses: Artzi and Malamat (1971, p. 83), Batto (1974, p. 61, note 9, p. 73), Leemans (1950a, note 25, p. 13: 1968, p. 179), and Veenhof (1972, note 178, pp. 103, 120-1).

21. Sources on women's seals and legal activity: Avigad (1977, pp. 39, 43), Batto (1974, pp. 71-2), Bohl (1920, pp. 11-12), Gordon (1936, pp. 165-6), and Owen (1981a, pp. 172-3, 181). Steinkeller (1982a, pp. 356-7, 366-7) cites a contract in which it seems that each (female) witness received a fee of oil and wool, while the (male) scribe received a garment and wool. The testimony of witnesses to the original transaction was a key part of Near Eastern legal procedure in the event of litigation (see Hinz 1973b, p. 107; R.D. Ward 1973, p. 93; and Section 1 of this chapter).

22. Sasson (1979, pp. 144-5) explains that the Hebrew Bible's 'levirate' marriage had a twofold purpose: (1) to provide shelter and care for a propertyless widow (or unmarried daughter?), and (2) to provide the unfortunate woman with children who would protect her in old age (see Deuteronomy 25:5-10; Genesis 38; Ruth; see also Numbers 27:1-11). Similarly, in archaic and classical Greece, according to Mireaux (1959, p. 108), 'the laws governing the epiclerate merely sought to protect the portionless daughter whom it obliged her nearest relative to marry and provide for.' A law attributed to Solon required the husband of the *epicleros* to fulfil his conjugal duties no less than three times per month. The charitable motive, I submit, and not some unique inability of Israelite women to inherit and transmit landed property underlies the duty of levirate marriage. For a contrary point of view, see Westbrook (1971, pp. 371-5), and compare Snaith (1966).

Under ancient Jewish law (the Mishna, c. 200 CE) the husband undertakes a written obligation (*ketûbāh*, 'writ of settlement') to provide a fixed sum of money to his wife if he divorces or predeceases her. The *ketûbāh* had the legal force of a prior lien operating retroactively on all the husband's real property (see Levine 1968, p. 280). Liebermann (1983, p. 519) illuminates the economic significance of the 'writ of settlement':

> Legally transferable to third parties, the *ketûbāh* is more than a passive insurance policy. It is a potentially active financial asset. Selling her *ketûbāh*, a woman may partially realize her financial rights prior to their actual maturity. The buyer of a *ketûbāh* will realize it . . . upon either divorce or the husband's death, provided the husband dies before his wife . . . Facing uncertainty, a *ketûbāh* buyer will always pay an amount lower than its nominal value.

23. In medieval Genoa women of the artisan and aristocrat groups received upon marriage a dowry and the husband's return gift, or *antefactum* (see D. Hughes 1975, pp. 127-30).

24. Sources on women's business capital: Bohl (1920, p. 12), Breneman (1971, p. 10), Burrows (1938, p. 46), Černý and Peet (1927, pp. 32, 36-9), Dalley (1980, pp. 53-5), Finkelstein (1962, p. 76), Fitzmyer (1971, pp. 137-41, 144-5, 157), Gardiner (1935, p. 141), Greenberg (1951, p. 173), Greenfield (1982a), Grosz (1981, pp. 175-8), Harris (1964, pp. 111-15), Hinz (1973b, pp. 108-9), Hoffner (1973 p. 208), Levine (1968, pp. 274-7), Paradise (1980, pp. 189-90, 205-6), Rainey (1965, pp. 18-19), Renger (1967, p. 161), H. Thompson (1934, note 8, p. 12), and Veenhof (1982, note 34, p. 159).

25. Sources on Greek and Roman women: Bloch (1941, p. 6), Loane (1938, pp. 76, 103-4, 110-11), MacMullen (1980), Pomeroy (1984, pp. 113-16, 158-60, 171-3), and Schaps (1979, p. 97).

26. In Genoa's great era of growing international trade from the mid-tenth to the mid-fourteenth century, aristocratic wives and, especially, widows played leading roles in commercial life. Genoa's liberal immigration and licensing policies reflected the pressure on its stock of managerial resources by permitting foreigners to found banks and to be taken as business partners. Interestingly, it appears that after the mid-

fourteenth century aristocratic women only rarely acted as business agents for their husbands. Sources: D. Hughes (1975, pp. 138-42) and Lopez (1964, pp. 445-7). In late thirteenth century Marseilles women frequently invested in commendae and in the example of a widow, Alazcie Carcassonne, the investments were substantial and personally directed (Pryor 1984, pp. 436-7).

27. N.P. Lemche (personal correspondence) calls my attention to the preference among today's nomadic peoples for employing family members as herdsmen rather than strangers. Among the market-oriented Komachi nomads of southern Iran, hired herdsmen are permitted to run their animals with their customer's herd but are contractually denied the right to own female breeding stock. Bradburd (1980) interprets this prohibition in a sinister light: the employing class seeks to alienate its proletariat from the means of production. A more reasonable explanation is that the denial of female breeding stock prevents theft of newly born animals and disputes over their ownership. Near Eastern herdsmen usually receive a share of the newborn animals as payment. A Babylonian contract of the early second millennium calls for the shepherd to keep twenty percent of the increase (Finkelstein 1968b, p. 33). For herding Laban's flock Jacob was to receive the newly born 'brown' sheep and variegated colour goats (Genesis 30:32-33); Jacob explained that under this innovative arrangement when Laban came to look over his hire 'every one that is not speckled and spotted among the goats, and dark among the sheep . . . shall be counted stolen.' Again, Hammurabi's Code and herding contracts of his era show that a variety of precautions were taken by owners to prevent thefts of livestock by shepherds (see Postgate 1975, pp. 6-7).

28. Sources on utilisation of slaves in the firm: Crook (1967, p. 98), Finley (1965, p. 55), Harrison (1968, pp. 174-6), Humphreys (1983, p. 10), Sasson (1966a, p. 135), Yaron (1960b). Humphreys (1983, p. 10) notes 'the almost total absence in Greece of free men willing to be [actually?] employed as foremen or managers', but her explanation 'that to be a permanent employee was too much like a slave's life' fails to come to grips with the control costs issue which lies behind the preference for slave labour on the part of employers. The Cairo Geniza documents of the eleventh-through fourteenth-centuries CE reveal, as Goitein (1967, p. 132) explains, that the importation and 'acquisition of a male slave was a great affair, on which a man was congratulated almost as if a son had been born to him. No wonder, for a slave fulfilled tasks similar to a son. He managed the affairs of his master, he travelled with him or for him, or he was in charge of his master's business, when the latter himself was out of town.'

29. This translation is controversial: see T.L. Thompson (1974, pp. 203-6). The Hebrew *bn byt* probably corresponds to the Babylonian *mār bītum*, 'son of the house'. The question is whether the latter term can be equated with the less equivocal *wilīd bītim*, 'houseborn slave' (see Mendelsohn 1949, p. 57). Crete's Gortyn Code, generally believed to have been inscribed in the fifth century BCE, provides that in the absence of kinsmen the succession devolves upon the *klaros* (slaves? adopted workers?) of the estate (see Willetts 1967, pp. 12, 15, 43).

30. Sources on adoption: Bayliss (1973, pp. 118-21), Bogoslowski (1977), Breneman (1971, p. 226), Kilmer (1974, pp. 177-8), Kramer (1969b, p. 160), Meek (1969b, pp. 173-4), Oppenheim and Reiner (1977, p. 7), Poebel (1909, pp. 29-30), Semenov (1974, p. 585), van Seters (1975, pp. 72-3), Sweet (1958, p. 43), Wiedemann (1981, p. 7), and Willetts (1967, pp. 30-1, 48, 76).

31. See Burford (1972, p. 79), Finley (1973, p. 74), and Pomeroy (1984, pp. 158, 169-70). An Athenian shield factory of the fourth century employed 120 slaves.

32. See in this connection Udovitch's (1979, pp. 271-3) perceptive discussion of business institutions in the medieval Near East.

33. Note in this connection the character in the Greek philosopher Theophrastus' (c. 372-287) *Characters* (VI, 3:9) who makes interest-bearing loans to small traders in the Agora and also acts as 'inn-keeper, brothel-keeper, and tax-farmer' and, indeed,

'does not reject any trade as beneath his dignity' (quoted in Millett 1983, p. 48).

34. Sources on versatility of ancient firms: Astour (1972, p. 25), Dandamayev (1971, pp. 77-8); Friedmann (1981, pp. 97-8), Jones and Synder (1961, pp. 322-44), and Limet (1979, p. 241).

3 THE REDISTRIBUTIONIST OR TEMPLE-STATE HYPOTHESIS

In the case of Sumer in about the middle of the third millennium the foundations of the redistributionist or temple-state hypothesis were laid by Deimel (1931) and Falkenstein (1974) and built upon by Polanyi (1981) and Finley (1973, p. 28). The already shaky premise, that most if not all agricultural land was owned by temples, has been further undermined if not demolished by reconsideration of the data on land ownership. Recent scholarship has demonstrated that temples and states (mainly the Ur III Dynasty) were in no way the sole owners of land. Deimel calculated from the Lagash documents that the total area of the temple estates amounted to some 77–116 square miles. Utilising essentially the same basic data and approach, Diakonoff estimated that the territory of Lagash comprised about 1,158 square miles, of which some 772 consisted of naturally irrigated land (see the discussion on pp. 148-9).[1] There are references to privately owned agricultural land in the Ur III texts. In addition, the $\check{s}e$-ur_5-ra texts show a temple farming a 'mortgaged field' and, apparently, lending out teams of plowmen and ox-drivers to independent field owners.[2] Very rough estimates of the land administered by Egyptian temples in the later second millennium range from one-sixth to nearly the total arable area.[3] In fact, as will be seen in the discussion of Assertion 6 in Chapter 5, there is ample evidence not only of private individual land ownership but of an active land market in most Near Eastern times and places.[4]

Nevertheless, as was pointed out in Chapter 1, it is not surprising that temple and palace officials should have played a direct role in production, especially in the introduction of new products for new markets. In practice, the entrepreneur or innovator is an individual who has acquired some familiarity with the needs and circumstances of relatively distant markets and has access to the capital necessary to implement his or her insights. In today's world a variety of social and economic roles provide individuals with the opportunity to implement economically valuable new ideas, but in antiquity the appropriate roles would have been more or less limited to officials of temple or palace, to aristocrats, and, of course, to merchants. Indeed, the translation of the tablets from Ebla raises the possibility that prominent merchants were elected to the rule (*en*-ship) several commercially orientated states.[5] Given the limited pool from which society drew its entrepreneurs, a major role for temple and palace is predictable.[6] The force of this line of argument with respect to agricultural innovation and land consolidation is illustrated in Chapter 7.

This is not to say that innovations introduced by the 'upper classes' failed to penetrate to the grass roots of ancient Near Eastern society. It appears, for instance, that in the middle of the second millennium a new northern Syrian technology for making opaque and coloured glass objects was diffused to the courts of Babylonia, Assyria, and Egypt. The excavation of glass objects all over Babylonia and Assyria is consistent with a downward percolation of the new technology. Oppenheim (1973, pp. 264-5) suggests that the combination of 'horizontal' and 'vertical' diffusion 'contributed towards a fast and effective spread of technical innovations and new ideas throughout the ancient Near East.' But according to Scott (1976, pp. 2-3), the fear of food shortages in most 'precapitalist peasant societies' gave rise to a 'subsistence ethic': 'The local tradition of seed varieties, planting techniques, and timing was designed over centuries of trial and error to produce the most stable and reliable yield possible under the circumstances. These were the *technical arrangements* evolved by the peasant to iron out the "ripples that might drown a man".' While Scott's position has merit, the importance of technical conservatism in ancient agriculture should not be exaggerated. In addition to the examples discussed in Parts II and III, note should be taken of the castration and nose-ringing of bulls to provide a nonhuman source of power and the evidence for experimentation, (seed selection, domestication, and the introduction of new plants from abroad) in Mesopotamia, Egypt, Israel, and Greece (compare Chapter 2, Section 5). An interesting example of the diffusion of an innovation is the chicken, which was called the 'bird from Meluhha' (the location of this region is disputed but it probably should be identified with the Indus civilisation and its adjacent areas) in Sumer and, in Syria, 'the Akkadian (i.e. Babylonian) bird'.[7]

Caution is also justified in interpreting the business activities of rulers, officials, and priests. For instance, a late third-millennium (Ur III Dynasty) text published by Grégoire reveals that the firm of the governor (*ensi*) of Umma and his wife and 'children' employed over 200 male and female workers (*gemé-arād*) who are not obviously government employees. Gelb's (1982, p. 94) assumption that this firm 'was under the indirect control of the state/crown' seems to be unfounded. Ur-e$_{11}$-e, the Umma businessman whose diverse activities were summarised earlier (see p. 51), finished cloth and produced garments with the aid of two agents. Note further in this connection Hallo's (1958, p. 83) observation that

> The archive of Umma was in no sense a bank, nor was it, like Drehem, the private domain of the king of Ur. Rather, Umma was an old city-state with an independent tradition. Many of the transactions recorded in its archive seem to have taken place among private individuals and the city administration . . . They were characterized by the use of the seal impression which, like the modern signature, is the symbol of private, or at least free, contractual relationships.[8]

Lagash's governor employed 40 to 50 permanent workers; another text shows him paying wages to hundreds of men and women (called *gir.sè-ga ensi.ka*) who are distinct from the employees (*sè.ga*) at his official residence. A similar distinction is observed in mid-second-millennium Egypt between a vizier's 'own people' and the 'ones listening to the call of the vizier' — i.e. those assigned to the office of the vizier. Of course, it is known that in the middle of the third millennium at Ebla and in the early second millennium at Mari, for example, rulers did control large workshops.

But surely such examples do not in themselves justify the identification of industrial enterprise with public enterprise. Carlo Zaccagnini (personal correspondence) generally supports this identification in the third and second millenniums, but he points to the 'exception here and there [of the] "textile industry".' More basically, Pettinato (1981, p. 190) has called attention to the discovery in Ebla's archives of a 'tribute' text 'which registers not only the tribute of the governors but also of some cities [and commercial centres] and, if the text is correctly understood, *of the king of Ebla himself*. This surprising element of the king's paying taxes . . . underscores the depersonalizing of the government offices' (italics added). Thus it would appear that even royal enterprise cannot automatically be identified with public enterprise, in which profitability tends to be supplanted by socio-political performance criteria. Given the uncertainties and disputes swirling about the Ebla texts, it is reassuring to note similar patterns in Assyrian and Roman economic history. In the early second millennium, Assur's ruler participated in but by no means dominated Assyria's trade with Cappadocia.

Similarly, during the period after the middle of the first century CE when brick production became a major Roman industry, the Emperor competed with the firms of other large landowners (many of whom were undoubtedly government officials) as a private citizen. Pettinato believes he has found evidence of private (i.e. nonroyal) industry in the Ebla texts.[9] Additional evidence of 'private' production and trade are presented elsewhere in this study, especially in the discussions of Assertions 7 and 11 in Part II.

Notes

1. Diakonoff's evidence is summarised and discussed by Kramer (1963, p. 76). Other key recent works dealing with this issue include Foster (1981), Gelb (1971), and Yoffee (1979).

2. Sources on privately owned land in Ur III: Gelb (1979, pp. 69-70), and Jones and Snyder (1961, pp. 253, 262, 269-70).

3. See the contribution by C.J. Eyre (in press) in a forthcoming volume edited by Marvin A. Powell.

4. According to J.P. Weinberg (1976), a 'citizen (*bürger*)-temple community' evolved in the Near East during the first millennium BCE as a result of the dissolution of the two sectors of the economy, namely state and private-communal. A common feature of these so-called 'citizen-temple communities' was the recognition of the god(s) as owner of the land. I must confess that I find it difficult to follow Weinberg's argument or to see the relevance of his evidence.

5. Pettinato's (1981, p. 72) hypothesis that the kings of Ebla were elected to seven-year terms would 'explain how at the time of Ebrium's term the preceding *en*, "kings", were still alive.' Similarly, according to Diakonoff (1969a, p. 184), Urukagina's predecessor Lugalanda 'continued to live peaceably in the city [of Lagash] after his deposition.' Urukagina, indeed, states in an inscription that he was 'chosen by the (god) Ningursu from among 36,000 individuals', that is, the population of Lagash (Vanstiphout 1970, p. 34). For additional evidence of elective kingship, see Saggs (1962, pp. 359-60) and 1 Kings 12:1. Perhaps more to the point is Isaiah's (23:8) prophecy about Tyre 'where merchants were princes'. According to Greek tradition, Solon made trading voyages prior to his appointment to the archonship (see J.K. Davies 1981, p. 39).

6. A leading entrepreneurial role for kings and their families has also been observed in less developed societies of the present era. See, for example, an excellent study by Dumett (1983, especially p. 671) of the Gold Coast's indigenous entrepreneurs in the second half of the nineteenth century.

7. Sources on innovation: Oppenheim (1973), Oppenheim and Reiner (1977, pp. 316-17), Rostovtzeff (1941, p. 1162), Schwabe (1984, p. 152), and Silver (1983a, pp. 20-1, 76-7).

8. In the first millennium, Assyrian firms maintained files of 'signature' seals (Morrison 1974, p. 440).

9. Sources on business activity by rulers and officials: Bloch (1941), Bogoslowski (1977, pp. 82-3), Grégoire (1970, pp. 120-1), Hallo (1958, p. 83), Jones and Snyder (1961, p. 338), Larsen (1976, pp. 129-43), Limet (1979, pp. 237-8), Pettinato (1981, pp. 165-6, 190, 264), and Renger (1979, pp. 252-3).

4 COMMERCIAL TRANSPORT, GAINS FROM TRADE AND STORAGE

The following remarks are hardly intended to be exhaustive. The evidence on long-distance land trade, for example, is massive and deserving of extensive treatment on its own. On the other hand, the data on storage and monopoly power are far from ample so far as I have been able to detect. This chapter is mainly intended to demonstrate the potential importance of traffic in staples along the trade routes of antiquity. The movement of luxury items is largely ignored (but see the section on the Gift Trade in Chapter 2, pp. 35-6).

1. Land Transport

By far the most complete documentation of overland transportation in Near Eastern antiquity comes from the archives of the Assyrian merchants operating at Kanesh in Anatolia in the early second millennium. Caravans of 'black donkeys' travelled the more than 700 miles from Assur to Cappadocia loaded with imported tin and woollen textiles, some of which originated in northern Babylonia. The return cargo was silver and, sometimes, gold. Larsen (1976, p. 89) offers as a conservative estimate that 'about 100,000 textiles [were shipped] from Assur over a period of about fifty years.' Given the rough accuracy of H. Lewy's calculation that each standard *kutânu*-cloth weighed about six pounds, this totals about 300 tons. Some 13,500 kilograms of tin, or 200 donkey loads, are also attested in the surviving texts. 'Again as a conservative estimate,' Larsen (1976, p. 89) writes, 'an export from Assyria over a period of fifty years of about eighty tons' is indicated. That this trade was characterised by venturing — i.e. the sale of goods after shipment — is indicative of its reliable, standardised nature. Most of the famous black donkeys were probably sold in Anatolia upon the arrival of a caravan. There is evidence that the Damascus region ('The Mountain of its Donkeys') specialised in breeding and the city itself ('The Town of its Donkeys') served as the market centre for the export of this special breed to Assyria and Babylonia.

Again, two tablets from Uruk of the years 551 and 550 record consignments to the merchant Nādin-ahi of metals (682 pounds for each tablet), dyes, wine, honey, purple-dyed wool, linen, and other merchandise from Egypt, Phoenicia, and various locations in Asia Minor. This raises the possibility of a regular and substantial commerce involving a lengthy overland journey even if use was also made of the Euphrates.

Another indication of trade regularity in the third millennium is the discovery in Egypt of Canaanite pottery, probably wine and oil containers, with specially designed handles to permit roping on both sides of a donkey. The overland movement of grain on a large scale is attested for Sumer in a letter from Ishbi-Erra to Ibbi-Sin of Ur (2028-2004) in which he reports that he has purchased and transported to the city of Isin over 72,000 bushels of grain. Qualitative evidence is provided by 'Enmerkar and the Lord of Aratta', a Sumerian epic set in the first half of the third millennium, in which the king of Uruk loads sacks on 'transporting donkeys' and sends them to Aratta (probably in Afghanistan) where the grain is 'piled up' (see pp. 13-14 and 148). At Moalla in upper Egypt, the late third-millennium inscription of the Egyptian administrator Ankhtyfy reveals the arrival during a famine of 'a trading caravan [which] brought the prize of Upper Egyptian grain' and adds 'I sold it, (so) (my) Upper Egyptian grain went southward as far as Wawat and north as far as the Thinite district' (Goedicke 1977, p. 28). A Mari tablet of the eighteenth century mentions the return, unladen, of a 3,000-donkey caravan from a journey to the north to acquire grain and wool. An epic of Hittite origin refers to the merchants of Ura, an important port in Cilicia, who 'will bring many *NAM.RA* people, cattle, sheep, horses, (and) asses in large numbers we will drive; barley and grapes(?) in large amounts we will keep at hand' (Hoffner 1968, p. 36). The importance of the overland transport of grain is also hinted by the Assyrian practice of measuring grain in 'assloads'.[1]

J. Lewy (1958a, p. 93), commenting on the Assyrian trade in Anatolia, notes that 'between some towns . . . copper was shipped in wagons a fact which attests the existence in Anatolia of real highways.' Similarly, a letter from about the same time mentions a caravan of donkeys with their harnesses and wagons carrying juniper wood from northern Syria into southern Babylonia. The term *eriggu* designated a type of wagon employed to haul long wooden beams. Much later, in the sixth century, a text çalls for wagons to carry 360 beams ranging in length from twelve to eighteen feet from Uruk to

Dilbat. Burnt-clay tiles were used to pave the roads at Buhen, a lower Nubian trading and industrial town. Archaeological evidence also points to the existence of at least partially paved roads in fifteenth-century Minoan Crete and in thirteenth-century Mycenaean Greece. Assyria possessed roads of sufficient permanence and importance to be mentioned as field boundaries in transfer documents. In the eighth and seventh centuries real highways appear to have linked Etruscan cities such as Caere to mining centres; paved road surfaces or cobbles have been discovered in urban areas or their immediate vicinity. Texts of the middle of the second millennium from Alalakh refer to tolls collected at bridges that probably were maintained by the government.

Pottery shards found in southern Israel dating from the earlier third millennium suggest to Helck the existence of watering stations for caravans. In any event, Egyptian tomb inscriptions in the Wadi Hammamat of as early as the beginning of the second millennium show Egyptian caravans making their way across desert areas without apparent difficulties. The trading expedition led by the 'chief treasurer' Henenu, for example, reportedly included numerous artisans, probably to construct or assemble 'prefabricated' ships and fashion heavy stone anchors upon the caravan's arrival, after a four-day journey, at the Red Sea, and some 3,000 soldiers, each of whom received a daily ration of two jugs of water and twenty cakes of bread. (A text of 90 CE records the payment of tolls on a mast and a yardarm carried across the desert on the Coptos-Red Sea road.) Another stela of this era found near the Red Sea refers to the safe return of ships from Punt. Recently, a port of the early twentieth century has been discovered on the shore of the Red Sea at Wadi Gewasis. Inscriptions of the later third to early second millennia found along the routes across Upper Egypt's eastern desert to the Red Sea mention naval titles. A representation on a (probably) fifteenth-century tomb shows a caravan returning from Punt, with asses laden with goods and live incense trees being carried on poles by pairs of men. The earliest documentary references to caravanserais, however, are found in a hymn to the Sumerian king Shulgi (2094-2047): 'I smoothed out (or enlarged) the paths, I put the roads of the land in order (or straightened the highways). I determined the danna's, built there (lodging-)houses, planted gardens by their side, established resting places, installed in those places experienced (men) (or friendly folk)'. (Frayne 1983, p. 743; compare Kramer 1969c, p. 585). In an Egyptian inscription of the early second millennium, the officer

Seanch relates his activities along the desert route to the God's Land: 'I transformed its valleys into gardens of herbs and its heights into tanks of water and provided it with children throughout its whole extent' (Erman 1971, pp. 506-7; see further the discussion of Assertion 7 in Chapter 5, p. 111).

Specialised caravan leaders, *imy-r ʿw*, literally, according to Faulkner, 'overseer of dragomans', and *htmw ntr* (or *sd3wty ntr*), literally 'sealbearer of the god', played key roles in Egypt's southern trade in the late third millennium. Along the same line, metal payments are received by an 'overseer of dragomans' (*rabi targumanni*) in a nineteenth-century Cappadocian text and by a 'dragoman' (*ta-ar-ga-ma-an-num*) in an eighteenth-century text listing tin consignments sent from Mari to various western states, including Ugarit. The tin had been transported to Mari by caravan from Eshnunna.[2]

With respect to the cost of overland transport, Larsen (1977a, p. 136) estimates that the shipment of woollen cloths some 700 miles from Assur to Anatolia raised the cost by no more than 25 percent. Using the *entire* difference between Garelli's (1963, p. 280) average sale and purchase prices to represent transport cost, the shipment of tin from Assur to Anatolia raised the cost by *at most* 93 percent. Beyond these scanty Near Eastern data, there are Roman figures. In the time of Cato the Elder (234-149), taking a disassembled mill (an oil-crusher weighing as much as 3,000 pounds) by ox-team wagon from Pompeii to Cato's farm some hundred miles away nearly doubled the cost of the mill. Information provided by Diocletian's Edict (301 CE) permits several very rough cost calculations. For example, transporting wheat by ox-wagon for one hundred miles raised its cost by 75 percent, but transport by pack animal was significantly cheaper. Calculations based on Leighton's data indicate that the carriage of wheat by donkey or camel increased its cost by no more than 60 percent of the original purchase price.[3] W.H. McNeill (personal correspondence) explains that the possibilities of overland trade should not be underestimated 'in landscapes where grass grew naturally and so offered a fuel for transport that was in effect without cost — analogous to the wind that propelled sailing ships'.[4]

2. Water Transport

Commercial water transport — by canal, river, along the coast, or by sea — and there was much of this in the ancient Near East, was very much cheaper than overland transport. References to this trade will be encountered in Part II, especially in the discussions of Assertions 7 and 10–12. An indication of magnitude is provided by an early second-millennium letter in which an official reports his intention to rent ten boats from merchants and send roughly 300 metric tons of grain along the Euphrates from the port of Emar to Mari. (Grain shipments are attested for nearly the entire year.) Another Mari letter concerns two ships carrying some 1,600 gallons of wine, and a juridical document reveals a single shipment of 1,100 gallons. (The Mari tablets also show the transport of millstones and bitumen.) A letter of the thirteenth century from Ugarit's 'prefect' to the Egyptian governor in Canannite Aphek concerns a wheat transaction at Joppa, a Canaanite port controlled by Egypt at the time. The 15 metric tons of wheat mentioned were probably supposed to be shipped north along the coast to Ugarit. Perhaps the wheat originated in Egypt, or, alternatively, may have been grown in Canaan and transported to Joppa for export. In view of the well-documented coastwise traffic involving Ugarit, Joppa, and many other ports and, in addition, a text attesting to a cargo of grain sent from Cyprus to Ugarit, there is little reason to assume with Singer (1983, p. 4) that the transaction in question 'must have been the result of unusual circumstances'. Certainly nothing in the letter itself suggests any sort of emergency. (See further the discussion of Egyptian wheat and linen exports to Byblos in Chapter 7, pp. 150-2.) An Egyptian text (Papyrus Louvre E 3226) of the second half of the second millennium attests to a substantial and regular internal waterborne traffic in grain and dates.

According to data from Diocletian's Edict, carrying wheat from Alexandria to Rome, for example, raised the cost by only 16 percent, or about 1.4 percent per hundred miles. An Egyptian papyrus gives the rate for transporting grain by river in 42 CE as 5.9 percent per hundred miles. In the third century BCE, transporting marble by water some twenty miles from Paros to Naxos added 25 percent to the cost. Hoisting machines for loading and unloading heavy cargo were used at least as early as the classical Greek period.

Yeo (1946, pp. 231-2) points out that 'It was not until the building of the Yankee Clipper . . . that sailing ships of the modern era, even with an improved type of steering gear, surpassed the speed of ancient ships.' A speed of 30 to 35 kilometres per day downstream was not atypical for cargo boats even in the late third millennium, Hallo adds.

(This speed may have involved towing the vessel.) The documents also indicate an upstream speed of 9 to 10 kilometres per day. Nor should the size of ancient cargo vessels be underestimated. A twelfth-century letter in which the Hittite king urgently requests a grain shipment from Ugarit appears to credit that port with vessels capable of carrying 500 metric tons. Archaeological evidence for ships of this size is provided by the recovery of stone anchors weighing about half a ton, indicating, according to expert testimony, that one or two freighters would have no difficulty carrying 500 tons of grain. In the middle of the third millennium, Egypt possessed vessels some 170 feet in length. The ancient Near East also appears to have known a variety of purpose-built freighters, including Egypt's 'Byblos-ships' and 'Keftiu (Crete)-ships', Ugarit's 'ships of the land of Ur' or of the land of Mari', Sumer's 'Tilmun-ships', Babylonia's 'grain-boats' (*má-sĕ*), and, very probably, Israel's 'Tarshish-ships' (1 Kings 22:49). There is some evidence that in the eighteenth century Ur produced ships for export.[5]

3. Differences in Comparative Advantage, Storage and Monopoly Power

The transport data summarised above confirm that while turnover costs were high by modern standards, they were far from prohibitive and, as we have seen, did not prevent an extensive regular commerce in staples. At the same time, in order to shed risk while economising on relatively high costs of search and transport, the ancient Near East held 'excess ' stocks of staples against fluctuations in supply. High physical transfer and search costs also operated to lengthen the transaction period or optimal trading interval of ancient firms and households. That is, they encouraged storage by outweighing the advantages of holding smaller stocks and inventories and making more frequent trips to the marketplace. (The set-up costs of marketing also encouraged traders to undertake multi-purpose trips and to arrange for deliveries and receipts in several successive time periods.) The characterisation 'storage economy' (see the discussion of Assertion 3 in Chapter 5) is therefore understandable, but, especially in the presence of an active loan market (see the discussion of Assertion 4 in Chapter 5), it is hardly indicative of an exotic, centralised 'redistributive economy'. In fact, not much hard data has been brought together on the sizes of stocks and even less on the size of the carryover of, say, grain from one year to the next. Nine domed structures of the later third millennium capable of holding an estimated 500 to 700 tons of grain were excavated (together with a number of ovens) at Khirbet el-Kerak, a city located at the tip of the Sea of Galilee where two major trade routes intersected, one leading from Syria into the Jordan Valley and the other from Damascus towards the Mediterranean coast. With respect to carryover of barley stored in various Sumerian granaries in 2047, a text cited by Parpola *et al.* mentions *še sumun*, 'old barley'.[6]

The diversity of natural resources in the Near East provided a firm foundation for regularised inter-regional trade. The Mediterranean region, for example, contains seacoast, plain, scrub uplands, valleys, and mountains within relatively compact areas. Israel-Syria had timber, good clay for pottery, and the capacity to produce high-quality wine and olive oil. Cyprus and Oman were rich in copper ore. Mesopotamia consists of a series of subzones differing markedly in their ecological characteristics. Broadly speaking, this region was seriously deficient in wood, stone, and metals but well-suited to the production of barley, sesame (or linseed), and wool, and, especially in the swampy south, to the growing of date palms. Iran, on the other hand, had plentiful stone. Egypt, like Mesopotamia, was poor in good construction timber and was a high-cost producer of wine and oil, but it had gold and opportunities to produce flax and wheat. Islands in the seas and passes through the mountains mitigated the severity of communication problems within the region. Therefore, despite relatively high transaction and transport costs, the above and other differences in productive factor endowments must have ensured significant gains from regional specialisation and exchange. These gains were, of course, supplemented by those resulting from local entrepreneurial and technical innovations and traditions of craftsmanship.

There is little information on which to base estimates of the importance of monopoly power in the ancient Near Eastern economy. Sumerian texts of about the middle of the third millennium hint that it may not have been great. The seller is 'he who gives, who delivers, who consumes the purchase price' while the buyer is 'he who measures out the purchase price for good X' (*lú.X.sa$_{10}$*) or 'he who makes or fixes the purchase price' (*lú.sa$_{10}$.ak*).[7] Probably this terminology implies that the seller is typically a price-taker not that the buyer is typically a price-maker. It must be admitted, however, that these questions of commercial terminology are philologically difficult for Assyriologists. In the case of new products marketed by temple and palace (see Chapter 3 and Chapter 7 on 'New Markets and Land Consolidation'), price-making behaviour is to be expected.

Notes

1. Sources on overland transport: Adams (1974, p. 247), Albright (1968, note 43, p. 72), Bell *et al.* (1984, pp. 31, 40-2), Bietak (1979, pp. 127-8), Frayne (1983, p. 743), Goedicke (1977, p. 28), Von Hagen (1967, pp. 360-1), Helck (1975, p. 269; 1979, pp. 360-1), Hoffner (1968, p. 36), Kitchen (1971, pp. 190-9), Kramer (1963, p. 70), Larsen (1976, pp. 86, 89), Leemans (1960a, pp. 98-9, 134), H. Lewy (1964, pp. 181, 183), J. Lewy (1961, pp. 71-4), Oppenheim (1967b, pp. 238-9, 253), and Veenhof (1972, p. 2).

2. Sources on highways and caravan stations: Astour (1973, p. 21), Erman (1971, pp. 506-7), Faulkner (1953, p. 34), Gelb (1968), Grant (1980, pp. 20, 25), Helck (1979, p. 362), Kramer (1969c, p. 585), Lewis (1960), J. Lewy (1958a, p. 93), W. McDonald (1964, p. 236), Macnamara (1973, p. 144), Malamat (1971, especially pp. 34, 37-8), Mallowan (1965a, pp. 20-1), Michell (1957, pp. 249-50), *New York Times*, September 6, 1981, Saggs (1984, p. 197), Säve-Söderbergh (1946, pp. 13-15, 22-3), Sayed (1978), Spar (1972, pp. 55-8), Tsevat (1958, p. 122), and Vermeule (1964, p. 263).

3. Hopkins (1983, pp. 102-5) is justly sceptical about the extent to which Diocletian's Edict provides a reliable guide to actual transport charges. His criticisms are, however, somewhat exaggerated. For example, in disputing the estimate that overland transport of wheat for 300 Roman miles roughly doubled its cost, Hopkins (p. 105) reasons as follows:

> To judge from scattered Roman evidence and much comparative data, twice the normal price or more was common in famines. [Then] wheat could have been sent overland to relieve a local famine within a radius of 300 Roman miles (444 km.) But during a serious famine at Antioch in AD 362/3 this did not happen, or not until the emperor Julian intervened personally to secure large quantities of wheat from two towns only 50 and 100 km. distant by land from Antioch.

Hopkins, like Finley (1973, p. 127) before him, takes no account of the fact that, despite the enlightened protests of Libanius and others, Julian had responded to rising grain prices in Antioch with an edict of maximum prices and other well-meant but counterproductive measures that discouraged and misdirected grain imports (see Downey 1951, pp. 315-19).

4. Sources on cost of land transport: Garelli (1963, p. 280), Larsen (1977a, p. 136), O. Lattimore (1962, p. 481), Leighton (1972, pp. 157-60), and Silver (1983a, pp. 45-6). O. Lattimore (1962, p. 481) adds that Chinese grain was carried by camel as far as 800 miles to the Mongol frontier and sold at a profit.

5. Sources on water transport: Burke (1964, p. 70), Butz (1979, p. 371), Duncan-Jones (1974, p. 368), Gardiner (1941, p. 47), de Graeve (1981, pp. 151-2), Hallo (1964, p. 84), Helck (1975, pp. 268-9), Heltzer (1978a, pp. 150-2, note 27; p. 154), Knapp (1983, pp. 42-3), Megally (1977, pp. 256-7), Owen (1981b), Rougé (1981, p. 74), Sasson (1966b, p. 172; 1968, p. 53), Schaeffer (1939, p. 39), Silver (1983, pp. 46-7), Singer (1983a, pp. 3-4), Strange (1980, pp. 74-5), and Yeo (1946, pp. 231-5).

6. Sources on storage: Makkay (1983, pp. 3-4) and Parpola *et al.* (1977, pp. 136-7). Sources on economics of storage: Alchian (1969), Clower (1969, pp. 8-9), Fenoaltea (1976, pp. 134-41), and McCloskey and Nash (1984).

7. Sources on monopoly power: Contenau (1966, p. 76) and Veenhof (1972, p. 360).

PART TWO

MARKETS IN THE ANCIENT NEAR EAST:
The Challenge of the Evidence

Part Two challenges Karl Polanyi's position that the ancient Near East did not know market activity by confronting his factual assertions with the available evidence. The ground rules for the contest reflect Polanyi's two-pronged strategy, combining direct denials of the existence of markets with subsidiary arguments casting further doubt on them.

Reliance has been placed on Karl Polanyi's posthumously published manuscript entitled *The Livelihood of Man* (1981). The editor of this volume, Harry W. Pearson, has included material on Polanyi's life and has contributed a useful introduction citing Polanyi's major publications and placing his thought in persepective. Extensive references and criticisms of both his theory and evidence are provided by Douglass C. North (1981) in *Structure and Change in Economic History*.

This part of the study is a major expansion and deepening of an article that appeared in the *Journal of Economic History* (Silver 1983c).

5 THE EXISTENCE OF MARKETS

Assertion 1

Indeed, as late as the opening of the seventh century, no sign of market development was forthcoming in Greece. For at least a thousand years before that time, the continental empires of Mesopotamia, Asia Minor, Syria, and Egypt and the seafarers of Ugarit and Crete carried on large-scale trade without . . . the market as the regulator of supply and demand . . . The so-called 'Cappadocian' trading colony . . . lacked price making markets. (Polanyi 1981, pp. xli, 146)

Price Formation at Ports of Trade

The primary focus of Assertion 1 is on foreign trade, which, according to Polanyi, was conducted at 'ports of trade', where prices were determined by treaty, not by supply and demand (1981, pp. 78-9, 94-5). It should be made clear at the outset that the specification of prices in advance — as opposed to determining them by spot transactions at the point of exchange — does not mean that forces of supply and demand are absent or irrelevant. The specification of prices in private long-term contracts serves to limit uncertainty and opportunism and to fill gaps in markets. Governmental treaties, a form of contract, might also be employed, yet would still acknowledge forces of supply and demand. (Note that an Akkadian technical term for treaty, *riksu*, often is applied to commercial contracts, e.g. for hiring shepherds and fieldworkers.)

There is ample evidence of commercial treaties and of royal correspondence dealing with matters of trade. The rulers of Ebla and another state, for example, agreed in the mid-third millennium on the taxes to be paid by merchants of each state at a newly founded commercial centre. To take an example mentioned by Polanyi, letters excavated in Cappadocia in central Anatolia reveal that in the early second millennium local rulers provided security along the caravan routes from Assyria. The Assyrian merchants paid taxes on the goods they carried in return for this service. During the second half of the second millennium, Ugarit, the important north Syrian port mentioned by Polanyi, signed a treaty with a neighbouring state legalising citizens' partnerships (*tappūtu*) for commercial expeditions to Egypt. Another treaty laid down several provisions concerning the murder of a merchant of one state in the territory of the other. Again, the king of Tyre wrote to Ugarit's ruler about the grounding of a merchant vessel and the related salvage operations, and Pharaoh was sent a letter by the ruler of Cyprus requesting payment for a shipment of lumber. Two north Syrian states entered into an agreement requiring merchants seeking to sell grain or oil to obtain royal authorisation, but nothing is said concerning prices. Treaties were also signed concerning the capture and extradition of fugitive slaves. In the ninth century Ben-hadad the king of Aram conceded to Israel's Ahab the right to 'have (commercial) streets in Damascus, as my father made in Samaria (the capital of Israel)' (1 Kings 20:34; see also the discussion of Assertion 8 in Chapter 6). More generally, the palace archives at Ugarit, in Egypt, and elsewhere show that kings participated in international trade but not that they sought to set prices by treaty. This royal participation is well illustrated by the joint trading ventures undertaken in the tenth century by Solomon and Hiram of Tyre (1 Kings 9:26-8) and in the ninth century by Ahaziah and Jehoshaphat, the kings of Israel and Judah (2 Chronicles 20:35-6).[1]

The evidence on price formation at the Assyrian trading station in Anatolia is fully consistent with the operation of market forces of the usual kind. The thousands of business documents from the station refer to changes in the demand or supply of the main import goods, tin and textiles, and the effects of seasonality and emergency, and record price changes. The price changes, including a change of more than 20 per cent in the price of tin over a short period, are inconsistent with Polanyi's position. So also are a merchant's instruction that 'if over there the market is deficient, let my merchandise travel on to Geographic Name, so that at least one mina of silver will turn up for me' and a report from an agent that Babylonian textiles are very expensive now, 'if it is possible to make a purchase which allows you a profit, we will buy for you' (Veenhof 1972, pp. 376-7). Along the same line, a merchant in Anatolia informs a business associate that the price of copper (in terms of silver) has been driven up by the arrival from Ebla of numerous copper-seeking merchants. He adds: 'Within the next ten days they will have exhausted its (the palace's) copper. I shall then buy silver (that is, sell copper) and send it to you' (Kienast 1960, p. 47). A text dating from the time of Hammurabi (1792-1750) in Babylonia consigns a large shipment of paint for sale in a neighbouring Mesopotamian kingdom 'according to the market value (or equivalent)' and another from Nuzi specifies that a merchant will bring back the 'price' of the merchandise he sells. The evidence for Ugarit is scanty, but even in documents from palace archives presumably concerning imported and domestically produced goods sold or purchased by royal stores, price fluctuations are noticeable. In the case of raw wool ($\check{s}\varsigma rt$), for example, the tablets show prices of 2, 4 and 7 shekels per talent.[2]

Ports of Trade as Centres of Tax Collection

The 'ports of trade' and segregated districts for foreign merchants may well have been intended by pharaohs and other rulers not so much as a 'wall of contact' or barrier against alien subversion of their alleged 'redistributive economies', but rather to facilitate the collection from traders of 'gifts' and 'tribute' that actually amounted to quite ordinary tolls, customs duties, payments for monopolistic trading privileges, and the like. Thus in the *Iliad* we find Euneos, the ruler of Lemnos, a large island near Troy, and the son of Jason who pursued the 'Golden Fleece,' giving wine to the Achaian kings before selling the main part of his cargo: 'Apart to the sons of Atreus, Agamemnon, and Menelauos, Jason's son had given wine as a gift, a thousand measures; and thence the rest of the flowing-haired Achaians bought wine' (7:470-3; R. Lattimore 1951, pp. 180). Turning to ancient Egypt, we find that before Harkuf's completion of a successful trading mission to Nubia in the third millennium (see further the section on 'Investment in Capital Goods,' pp. 110-11) he first '*shtp*-ed (the ruler) until he praised all the gods for the sake of the Sovereign' (Kadish 1966, p. 29). The verb *shtp* generally means 'to cause to be at peace, to appease, to cause to be satisfied.' Thus it appears reasonable to assume that Harkuf bribed the Nubian leader with 'gifts' so that he 'thanked Pharaoh', that is, permitted trade to take place. (Note in support of this interpretation a tomb inscription in which artisans praise the god after being *shtp*-ed by Idu, the tomb's owner.) Harkuf, moreover, was not the only commercial agent who boasted of having *shtp*-ed a foreign ruler in pharaoh's behalf. But the price might be too high. In the sixteenth century, the pharaoh Kamose in seeking to win support for an attack on the occupying Hyksos spoke to his Council as follows: 'I shall not be able to pass him (the Hyksos) as far as Memphis (or?) the water(?) of Egypt, for he is in possession of Hermopolis, and no man can alight, shorn (as he is) by the imposts of the *Styw*' (H.S. and A. Smith 1976, p. 59).

There is, to continue, little reason to doubt that in the sixth century when Amasis forbade ships to trade outside Naucratis, a depot this ruler had given to the Greeks on the westernmost mouth of the Nile, his objective was, in good royal fashion, to lower the cost of collecting taxes. According to Herodotus: 'Anyone who brought a ship into any of the other mouths of the Nile was bound to state an oath that he did so of necessity, and then proceed to the Canopic mouth; should contrary winds prevent him from doing so, he had to carry his freight to Naucratis by barges' (de Selincourt 1972, p. 200). Sais, the capital of Egypt at this time, was not on the Nile, and Naucratis served as its port. In the fourth century Nectanebo I granted the temple of Neith one-tenth of the royal taxes collected on seaborne imports to Naucratis.

Similarly, in the nineteenth century, Sesostris III required Nubian traders to halt at Heh (modern Semna) or, alternatively, to leave their boats behind and continue overland some thirty miles to the trading station at Iqen (Mergissa; see further, the section on 'Investment in Capital Goods', p. 110). Lorton (1974, note 4, p. 114) provides a text from the reign of Thutmoses III in which the taxation of Egyptians is compared to obligations of Nubian traders 'bearing all (kinds of) good deliveries which are brought as wonders of the south, obligated with (the procurement of) trade goods ($b3kw$) every year, like all the subjects ($mi\ n\underline{d}t\ nbt$) of my majesty.' There are also ambiguous texts cited by Lorton (1974, pp. 139-44) stating that Thutmose III supplied ports with 'every (sort of) good thing, according to their stipulation(s)' and attesting to his peaceful receipt of goods from distant lands (e.g. Hittite Anatolia and Crete) in return for the 'breath of life' ($\underline{t}3w\ n\langle nh$). After exchanging incense for various Egyptian goods (or permitting this trade), the rulers of Punt asked Hatshepsut's 'messengers' whether they (probably their 'messengers') might 'come to his majesty, so that we could live by the breath of life he gives' (Liverani 1979b, p. 26). In the fourteenth century Akhenaten granted the 'breath of life' after receiving the goods of 'Syria, Nubia, the West, and the East' (Montet 1968, p. 144). Obviously, Liverani is correct in characterising this peculiar terminology as Egyptocentric ideology, but this cannot be the whole story. We may also infer that the grant of Egypt's air is the grant of trading rights. To use Liverani's terms, these rights and not 'exclusively ideological recompense' were the 'real thing' sought by the rulers of Punt.

There are indications that the 'House of the Great Green' was Egypt's Bureau of Customs in the first half of the first millennium. A

Sumerian inscription informs us that 'Tilmun-ships' brought wood to Ur-Nanshe (2494-2465), Lagash's ruler as 'tribute'. But Vanstiphout (1970, pp. 17-18) notes that in one text Ur-Nanshe 'mentions his wood shipments immediately after his constructions in Erinkimar', Lagash's seaport, and he then suggests: 'The mention of the wood as tribute should be taken with a pinch of salt: it was obviously a business transaction set up presumably by a guild of specialized merchant venturers, working under a royal privilege — somewhat like the European East India companies in later times.' Concrete evidence that Mesopotamian 'ports of trade' served as tax collection centres comes from the reign of Ur-Nammu (2112-2095), who in law and inscription refers to the 'detaining' of ships of the Magan traders at the 'registry place' (*ki-sar-ra*) (Jacobsen 1960, pp. 184-5). The legal reference, it should be noted, occurs in the context of taxation. Note also the reference to duties at Ugarit under Assertion 3. In the eighth century the Assyrians established an institution known as the *bīt kāri* at ports and inland trading stations. The fiscal function of the *bīt kāri* is illustrated by an agreement in which the Tyrians were permitted to 'enter and leave the quay stations ... (and) sell and buy' — that is, they did not have to pay customs on their lumber — but were forbidden 'to sell it to the Egyptians and Philistines' (Elat 1978, p. 27). Somewhat later the Assyrians opened the 'sealed' *kāri* of Egypt.[3]

Assertion 2

The peril to solidarity involved in making a selfish gain at the expense of the food of one's brother had ... to be removed ... That was achieved through the declaration of equivalencies in the name of the representative of the godhead itself [that is, the ruler] ... At the gates a few main staples — necessaries that keep — are both received and handed out ... Simple quantitative equivalencies for grain, oil, wine, and wool allow the staples to be substituted for each other ... Although food is distributed, this is no food market, since there is no 'meeting of supply and demand crowds'. (Polanyi 1981, pp. 61, 134)

Variability in Grain Prices

In fact, the evidence does not suggest that Near Eastern governments as a general rule controlled the price of grain. There is evidence of a grain market (see the discussion of Assertion 3) and of the operation of market forces. Third-millennium documents of sale reveal steep variations in barley prices. Piotr Steinkeller (personal correspondence) has called my attention to texts in which one shekel of silver purchased 10 or 20 or 120 quarts of barley. He also informs me that sale documents for barley, oil, and dates 'distinguish between the prices of the good year (Sumerian *mu-ḫé-ĝal-la*) and the prices of the bad year (*mu-nu-ĝal-la*).' In the very late third millennium an official reports to his king that he has purchased a substantial quantity of grain for shipment to the capital city but now the price has doubled (see further Section 1, Chapter 4 p. 62, and the discussion of inflation under Assertion 9, p. 130). The balanced silver accounts (see the discussion of Assertion 11, pp. 133-4) show that the range in the price of grain (presumably barley) equals 65 percent of the median price. A literary document from about the same time speaks in proverbial terms of 'The merchant — how he has reduced prices! How he has reduced the oil and barley!' Kramer's (1981, p. 266) interpretation is that the merchant 'presumably reduced prices to attract customers, and then reduced the weight of the merchandise on the sly'. The proverb certainly conveys the impression of market behaviour. In Assyrian texts from Cappadocia, wheat and barley typically sell for about 5 and 3 shekels per sack, respectively. However, prices of 7.5 and 10 are noted for wheat, and barley sells for 5.3 shekels per sack in one tablet. Another text orders the sale of grain because its price is high (*kurrum batiq še⟩ am dināma*; Veenhof 1972, note 510, p. 383). Some Assyrian contracts of the eighth and seventh centuries stipulate that the sale took place in a year of hardship as measured by the high price of grain. A letter to the Assyrian king Assurbanipal informing him about current grain prices in three provinces includes the expression 'good prices' (*maḫiru damqu*). His predecessor Esarhaddon was assured by a prominent priest of good climatic conditions and 'good prices'.[4]

Response of Grain Prices to Changes in Supply and Demand

Texts from seventh-century Babylonia and twelfth-century Egypt show sharp changes in grain prices due to political disorder or the initiation or lifting of sieges. Thus in the 'Tomb Robbery Papyri', an Egyptian woman cross-examined by the court scribe concerning gold found in her home explains: 'We got it by selling barley during the year of the hyenas, when people went hungry' (Montet 1981, pp. 74-5). An interesting example is found in 2 Kings 7:1, where the ninth-century prophet Elisha announces that a Syrian siege will be lifted, and 'Tomorrow about this time a measure of *soleth* (fine wheat flour) shall be sold for one shekel, and two measures of barley for a shekel in the gates of Samaria.' Earlier (2 Kings 6:25), it is reported that the head of a donkey sold for eighty shekels and 'one-quarter *kab*' of 'doves dung' (possibly a popular term for carob-pods) for five shekels. In short, Elisha recognises that an increase in the supply of grain will lower market prices. Similarly, a Sumerian literary text of as early as 2000 with the modern title 'The Curse of Agade' links the breakdown of land and sea communications and drought with exorbitant prices of grain, oil, wool, and fish. The latter commodities were bought up as eagerly as 'good words'. In an inscription from the middle of the nineteenth century the king of Uruk boasts in set phrases about the low prices during his reign of barley, wool, copper, and sesame oil. But he attributes the low prices to 'abundance', not price controls.[5]

There is, in addition, evidence of seasonal variations in grain prices in Mesopotamia and, possibly, in Egypt. The seasonal pattern is, of course, the result of shifts in the supply curve of grain due to positive storage costs. The magnitude of seasonal variation in prices is at least roughly reflected in late third- to early second-millennium Mesopotamian loan contracts in which the interest rate on grain loans (33⅓ percent) is 13⅓ percentage points higher than on loans of silver. To understand this, note first of all that grain loans were usually taken out before harvest (at sowing time or later) when prices were relatively high, and repaid immediately after the harvest when prices were relatively low. Consequently, in a free loan market the interest rate on barley would exceed the rate charged on silver. More concretely, assume an interest rate of 20 percent on silver, set the price of one unit of barley at sowing time at one unit of silver, and let X be the seasonal fractional decline in the price of barley. Then, a loan of one unit of silver would (upon repayment) increase the lender's command over barley by $100[(1.20/1-X)-1]$ percent. If X equals 0.10 — which, to judge by an eighteenth-century BCE Babylonian seasonal price change provided by Leemans (and, for that matter, by seventeenth-century CE price changes in England and Belgium), is not totally unreasonable — a silver loan at 20 percent would increase the lender's command over barley by 33⅓ percent. To do as well, the lender would have to charge 13⅓ percentage points of interest more on a barley loan than on silver. Similar forces are reflected in a late nineteenth-century loan contract in which an individual who borrowed one mina of silver to buy barley just before the harvest is obligated to repay not a fixed physical quantity of barley, but one mina's worth just after the harvest.[6]

Assertion 3

It was in the framework of the planned transfer and investment of staples stored on a gigantic scale that the accounting devices were developed that characterized the redistributive empires over long periods of time ... Goods passed on as payment [taxes or rent] to the center are passed out again as payments, and fall out of circulation. (Polanyi 1981, p. 115)

Middlemen in the Grain Market

The importance of storage of staples was noted and discussed in Chapter 4 (pp. 66-7). Here attention is directed at Polanyi's elimination, for all intents and purposes, of a role for market exchanges with food producers and middlemen. That Polanyi had in mind mainly the ancient Near East is demonstrated by his references to 'the Sumerian city states and their enormously enlarged replica, the Pharaonic empire' and to the 'storage-cum-redistribution methods practiced by early Sumeria and its Mesopotamian successors' (1981, pp. 59, 65, 134). Staples, at least beyond the subsistence requirements of the direct producers, are allocated by governmental authority and not by the market mechanism. To this extent, ancient Near Eastern economies are portrayed as large, hierarchically organised firms (see Chapter 2, p. 50, and Chapter 3).

A scholar of similar bent, S.C. Humphreys (1978, p. 56), probably had Rome in mind when she attributed 'most of the corn trade in the ancient world' to the 'collection of corn as tax or tribute'. But Hopkins compared estimated total grain exports from Egypt and elsewhere in Africa to Rome in the first century CE with the total tribute grain, concluding that as much as two-thirds of the total export was available for purchase by private businessmen and government. Indeed, wax tablets of 40 CE from a suburb of Pompeii show two freedmen dealing in grain imported from Egypt and demonstrate that private businessmen were very much involved in grain storage and speculation. In one tablet, a trader pledges 45 tons of wheat as collateral for a loan.

For Mesopotamia there is ample early evidence of private ownership of land and of a land market (see the discussion of Assertion 6, pp. 92-6) and, as we have seen, grain sales. It is difficult, however, to isolate the commercial roles of producers and middlemen. As Foster explains, it is usually impossible to tell whether the record of a grain shipment represents a commercial venture, a payment of taxes, or something else. Nevertheless, Foster does cite a tablet from the middle of the second half of the third millennium conveying barley to a merchant, and he mentions a female entrepreneur named Ama-é as well as a certain Gininu and his associate Sunitum who dealt in grain. Foster (1977, p. 38) also calls attention to

> ship manifests that contain such a varied cargo that . . . commercial enterprises seems the best explanation for them. A single such shipment includes jars of oil, animal hides, brewing ingredients, legumes, spices, sea fish, fatted animals, barley and flour, under the charge of a slave or servant of an untitled person. The grain and flour are measured with the standard metrology one often finds in commercial texts.

A receipt from the same period found at Gasur (later Nuzi) states that someone named Zuzu gave Ate, the merchant, barley which was to be sold in a nearby district. Other third-millennium texts refer to the Sumerian *lù še-sá-sá* who roasted grain and sold it on the market. Barley is commonly listed among goods on hand in the balanced silver accounts of merchants in the twenty-first century (see further the discussion of Assertion 11 pp. 133-4). Veenhof cites a document from the Assyrian commercial station in Cappadocia attesting to the purchase by traders of substantial quantities of barley and wheat resold at a profit. Another text confirms that private merchants stored grain in granaries; one of these merchants owned 1,500 sacks of wheat.

Babylonian texts of this era reveal granaries stated to be privately owned, or at least with no apparent connection to temple or palace, doing business with the general public. That private individuals stored grain in private granaries is confirmed by paragraphs 120 and 121 of Hammurabi's Code, legislating default and storage charges. We learn from an eighteenth-century tablet the price paid for a large quantity of barley by someone termed 'the Tilmunite', probably a merchant who exported grain to Tilmun (Bahrain). During the same century texts from Mari show us a businesswoman who, according to Batto, pursued extensive commercial activities in grain. Grain loans were frequently made by individuals described as 'merchants' (although the meaning of the word is a subject of dispute — see the discussion of Assertion 11, p. 132). Recall the contract mentioned above, a loan of one mina of silver to be repaid after the harvest by one mina's worth of barley. Leemans (1954) suggests that the business of the borrower was to purchase barley from farmers in the countryside, whereas the lender was possibly an urban dealer in grain. Consistent with this interpretation, Edzard cites several texts in which loans of silver are to be repaid by rather substantial quantities of barley. Several tablets from Nuzi advance gold to be repaid in barley after the harvest.[7] The retail sale of bread in the earlier second millennium is attested in a Babylonian letter: 'I have no hired man who would grind the barley (for me) so we have been eating bought bread' (Oppenheim and Reiner 1977, note 3, p. 385).

A Nuzi tablet of the middle of the second millennium refers to people journeying to the 'community of merchants' (*dimtu tamkarḫe*) to purchase barley. In the fourteenth century, temple granaries at Nippur accepted private deposits of grain kept in compartments under a store intendant. Assyria in the thirteenth century possessed at least one firm owning large quantities of grain and making grain loans. A letter excavated at Ugarit deals with the transport of 500 metric tons of grain purchased by the Hittite king at Mukish (see also Section 2 of Chapter 4, p. 65). In a tablet of the mid-thirteenth century the king declares that Sinaranu the son of Siginu, an individual involved in international trade, is 'exempt from duty. His grain(?), his beer, his oil shall not enter the palace' (Strange 1980, p. 102; note the reference to customs duties at this 'port of trade'). The epic Hittite text cited in Chapter 4 (p. 62) portrays a caravan of merchants bringing 'large amounts' of barley. (Interestingly, the Hittite term for inn (*arzana* house) is derived from the name of a porridge made from barley groats.) The Bible, again, provides evidence of grain merchants in eighth-century Israel: 'Listen to this you who devour the needy . . . saying, "If only the new moon were over, so that we could sell grain; the Sabbath, so that we could offer wheat for sale . . ."' (Amos 8:4–5). Private speculation in grain is indicated in Proverbs 11:26 (one of the 'Proverbs of Solomon'): 'He that withholds grain, the people shall curse him; but blessing shall be upon the head of him that sells it.'[8]

The Case of Egypt

Pharaonic Egypt is allegedly the epitome of a redistributional society.

This 'model' is compactly described by Jacob J. Janssen (1982, p. 253):

> Egypt's economic structure as a whole can best be described as organized on the principle of redistribution, which means that the surplus of the peasant households was collected by the authorities, state and temple, in order to be redistributed among particular sections of society: officials, priests, the army, necropolis workmen, and so on. The redistribution system which was probably concentrated in the cities and towns, rested as a superstructure upon a 'peasant society', consisting of households that were largely self-sufficient as far as the necessities of life were concerned. The goods which they did not produce themselves (e.g. salt, copper, particular types of trinkets, and other luxuries), or which did not come to them through redistribution, they acquired by direct barter from their neighbors, or, to a minor extent, on the market. In such a society markets, if present at all, would have played a peripheral role only.

In an earlier article, Janssen (1975a, pp. 131, 185) maintained that 'profound knowledge of modern market-directed economy proves to be of little value to the egyptologist and may even be obnoxious.' But he admitted that the evidence is so scanty that 'for the present, a study of the redistributional system in all its aspects seems the only possibility.'

It is known, however, that private ownership, as well as sale and leasing of land, is found throughout Egyptian history. Lorton points out that third-millennium texts recording grain loans (*t3bt*) designate the creditor as 'its possessor'. Also in the third millennium, the inscription of a commoner, Qedes of Gebelein, mentions his ownership of boats and granaries of Upper Egyptian barley. A farmer's letter of about 2000 BCE (see p. 138) refers to the sale of emmer and to interest-bearing grain loans. Grain loans made by Egyptian merchants (*šwty* is the basic word but the Canaanite loanword *mkr* also appears) to 'peasants' are noted in Papyrus Lansing, which dates to the later second millennium. In the mention of merchants connected with high officials, Janssen (1975a) himself finds a hint of grain sales by large estates in the same period. A 'prophetic' Egyptian text[9] with the modern title 'The Admonitions of Ipuwer' includes the complaint: 'Behold he who had no grain is (now) the owner of granaries. He who took grain on loan issues it'

(Lichtheim 1976, II, p. 170). There would be little point in this example of the reversal of fortune if Egypt had known grain distribution only as a Pharaonic monopoly. The papyrus dates from between 1350 and 1100 but, reportedly, the language and orthography may indicate an original in the second half of the third millennium.[10]

Assertion 4

In the archaic state, temple and palace are the chief providers of harvest credit. (Polanyi 1981, p. 141)

As noted in Chapter 1, the temples of the ancient Near East served as places of worship and centres of commerce. Glotz's (1967, p. 304) suggestion that 'finance was born in the shade of sanctity' is oversimplified but insightful. Nevertheless, Piotr Steinkeller (personal correspondence) maintains that practically all loan documents from the middle to the end of the third millennium concern loans made by private persons. Fish provides examples from late third-millennium Nippur in which the usual interest rate is 33⅓ per cent, but rates of 30⅓ and, in one tablet, 20 per cent are also found. Note also the references under Assertion 3 above to private grain loans in Pharaonic Egypt. Egyptian texts (the Gurob fragments) of the second half of the second millennium raise the possibility that the pharaoh made interest-bearing seed loans or, alternatively, charged interest on overdue harvest taxes.

The evidence regarding grain loans is fullest, however, for Babylonia in the earlier second millennium. The documents show that both private persons and temples loaned out barley. But this rather oversimplifies the situation, because, as Leemans explains, there were three variants of the temple loan: loans made by private persons and the deity; loans made by *nadītu*'s (priestesses); loans made by the deity alone. At Sippar, at least, priestesses appear to have made the largest percentage of the barley loans. But the exact relationship between the temples and these women, the daughters of wealthy families and royalty, is obscure. Quite possibly, they were private lenders and dealers in real estate and slaves. Only in the case of loans 'by the deity' do interest rates seem lower than those charged by private lenders.

The royal granaries, used mainly to provision soldiers and the like, also gave out loans of barley. The Babylonian evidence for palace loans, however, appears to be confined to the period after the reign of Hammurabi, who is known to have instituted various reforms, including maximum interest rates on barley loans (see Chapter 8, p. 160).[11]

Assertion 5

With the emergence of price-making markets ... credit take[s] on functions of a new character ... Modern banking, far from making markets unnecessary, as archaic banking did, is a means of expanding the market system beyond any simple exchange of goods in hand ... Neo-Babylonian merchant bankers dealt directly with farming ... Only in the late Middle Ages did wholesale trading over long distances provide a source of capital that sought employment in the more speculative channels. (Polanyi 1981, pp. 141-2; the neo-Babylonian period dates from 626 to 539)

Credit and Investment Market

Assertion 5 is obscure, to say the least. If Polanyi means to deny the existence of Mesopotamian firms providing nonagricultural business loans, he is mistaken. It is true that the evidence for very early periods is thin and ambiguous. For example, Sumerian tablets dating from about the middle of the second half of the third millennium record barley loans to individuals of various professional categories, including stock raiser, dealer in tar, tradesman, courier, and business traveller. In one instance, it appears that the borrower's purpose was to purchase a house. It is not really clear, however, whether the loans bore interest; nor is it known whether the lender(s?) 'Amarezem' was acting as a palace employee or as a private businessman. We do know, however, the names and a good deal about the affairs of several important members of a class of professional money lenders, that operated in Mesopotamia, despite high transaction costs, for many centuries — from the late third millennium through the first half of the second millennium. One late third-millennium text from Nippur is a loan of silver 'for partnership'; another reports a loan of silver to a baker. There is also an interest-bearing loan for the barley rations of the 'female mill worker's'. Indeed, the early part of the second millennium provides numerous lending contracts of an entirely commercial nature. A woman of Ur, for example, lends three partners barley and silver for hiring a crew and boats for a trading venture. Temple loans made jointly by a private person and the deity (temple) sometimes expressly state that the loan is for business purposes; in many other cases the purpose is unstated, but the amount of silver seems too large for consumption purposes. (This is not to say that small loans were necessarily for consumption.)

Garelli informs us that the recorded purpose of loans to Assyrians in Cappadocia corresponded to commercial objectives, including purchases of merchandise and business trips. A tablet translated by Oppenheim (1974, p. 232) provides that when the borrower returns from Cappadocia and repays his loan 'he may retain one mina of it and "do business" with it on two (more) overland journeys.' So well established were the trade patterns that travelling merchants often repaid loans to representatives of the creditor who drew up quittances and forwarded them to the debtor's representatives for presentation to the creditor. Eighteenth-century tablets from Alalakh deal with loans of silver for 'capital' (for trading purposes?). A particularly interesting source of information is the seventeenth-century Edict of Ammisaduqa, the tenth ruler of the Hammurabi Dynasty in Babylon. The Edict legislates against attempts to disguise interest-bearing loans as advances for the purchase of merchandise or as merchandise for a business trip or as a commercial partnership. The Edict, it should be understood, cancelled debt obligations.

Documents from Nuzi demonstrate that private lenders gave merchants interest-bearing loans for 'business ventures'. Much later seventh-century contracts excavated in Assyria rarely specify the purpose of a loan, but in one case the purchase of donkeys is involved and in another the borrower appears to be a caravan leader trading in grain. Babylonian documents from about the same time not only record business loans but often specify the kind of business to be engaged in, for instance, a trading venture. Note in this connection the phrase 'to lend money for overland business activities' (Oppenheim 1947, note 3, p. 119).[12]

The presumed absence of limited liability on equity shares (see further below) does not raise an insuperable barrier to risk sharing and the pooling by entrepreneurs of large amounts of capital. It must not be overlooked that ordinary debt (nonresidual claims) carries limited liability. That highly leveraged owner-managers are tempted to behave opportunistically, for example, by gambling with the money of the creditors is, of course, quite true. However, bond holders can restrain such behaviour by monitoring (e.g. conducting periodic audits, as we seem to find in the Ur III Dynasty) and reserving the right to call in loans on demand (see further below). A lender experienced in the borrower's line of business ordinarily makes a more effective monitor. Thus, in discussing Athenian maritime loans Millett (1983, p. 52) notes perceptively that 'the indications are that the complexity of maritime credit made it an unsuitable field for casual lenders without practical experience in trading.' It is possible to deal with the problem of free-riding among creditor-monitors by assigning specific collateralised assets to secured creditors.[13]

Call loans were known in earlier second-millennium Babylonia, as is demonstrated by the clause 'as soon as he will ask for this (silver)' in temple, palace, and private loans at Sippar (Stol 1982, p. 148). Note in this connection an especially interesting text in which an individual lends out one of the five shekels of silver he had previously borrowed from a certain Sin-ishmeanni and the god Nanna with repayment 'when the god Nanna and Sin-ishmeanni ask for the money' (Harris 1960, p. 30). Besides providing a powerful weapon against debtor misbehaviour and altering the distribution of liquidity, a system whereby loans are automatically renewed in the absence of positive action by one party reduces the administrative costs associated with frequent renewals of short-term commercial loans.[14]

Texts from as early as the second half of the second millennium use the Akkadian word *lapātu* (Sumerian *TAG*), with the meaning 'book to one's credit' (Foster 1977, p. 32). Quradum, a merchant who dealt in a wide variety of commodities, had more than a dozen credit accounts. Credit sales of oil, wool, and other goods took place in the early second millennium. There is also evidence of purchases of real estate, animals, and slaves on credit, with a receipt given each time a portion of the debt was repaid.

Ugaritic *harranāti* ('caravans' or 'commercial firms') established in Hittite Anatolia a *bīt ṭuppašši* ('house of tabletship' or 'accounting house'), which, according to Sasson functioned as a bank. Indeed, the 'house of tabletship' sent gold to the Hittite ruler in lieu of providing military forces. Tablets from the nineteenth-century Assyrian commercial stations in Anatolia show the *bīt kārim* paying 15 percent interest on loans while charging borrowers rates of 30 and 40 percent (see also the section on 'Evidence for Coinage', p. 126). In connection with deposit banking, Oppenheim (1969a) calls attention to cuneiform sources of the first half of the second millennium and the seventh to sixth centuries referring to sealed bags of silver (*kaspum kankum*) deposited with persons who used the silver in various transactions (compare the discussion of Assertion 9, p. 126). With respect to the productive use of deposits, note should be made here of the rather imprecise maxim of the Egyptian scribe named Any at the beginning of the first millennium or, perhaps, as early as the middle of the second millennium: 'If wealth is placed where it bears interest it comes back to you redoubled' (Lichtheim 1976, II, p. 135). Note also in this connection the eighteenth-century Syrian woman who wrote to a man, evidently a banker, demanding the silver belonging to her sister: 'Whatever was entrusted to you to be given, give (now)! It is (her) private capital (*sikkum*)' (Tsevat 1958, p. 113). The evidence shows that long-distance payments or transfers might be expedited by the use of the cheque of letter of credit (and, possibly, the bill of exchange). For example, an eighteenth-century tablet originating in a Babylonian temple calls for payment fifteen days later of lead deposited with the priestess of an Assyrian temple. At Assur in the thirteenth century, a businesswoman paid for an order of bricks with a letter of credit involving wool. That earlier second-millennium Babylonia knew negotiable loans of a two-party promissory-note type is suggested by numbers of surviving loan documents specifying repayment not to the creditor but to the 'bearer of this tablet' (*ana nâš kanikišu*). In fourteenth-century Assyria deed tablets were bought and sold on the market, and in the seventh century a debt was settled by means of 'a document applying to fields, ... (documents?) applying to a house, and two documents applying to silver' (Finkelstein 1956, pp. 141-2).

During the nineteenth century, Babylonian investors (private individuals and temples) provided funds to merchants participating in the Persian Gulf trade. Similarly, the merchant houses or firms involved in the Assyrian trade with Anatolia were financed by means of long-term partnerships called *naruqqu*, literally 'sack'. The one complete contract so far discovered shows that the capital involved amounted to the very substantial sum of 33 pounds of gold. It would appear that the trader or manager of the sack was himself entitled to one-third of the profit (*nēmulum*) earned during the twelve-year life of the agreement and the other contributors were to receive the remainder of the profit. The manager of the sack also had to 'stand' for one-third (of the losses? put up one-third of the capital?). The investors were denied a share in the profit of the venture if they withdrew their funds prior to the expiration of the contract, but, on the other hand, their liquidity was increased by the right to sell their share of the sack to third parties. The *naruqqum* vividly reveals risk sharing and the 'separation of security ownership from control' in an ancient context. The sack-managers' reputational and financial interest in the profitability of the venture (both serving as 'coinsurance') combined to reduce his incentive to misbehave and, consequently, reduced the monitoring costs that had to be borne by shareholders. Possibly the shareholders reserved the right to dissolve the contract in the event of unsatisfactory managerial performance. (In the seventh to sixth centuries Babylonian investors stipulated the maximum amount of their capital that might be used for travelling expenses and prohibited managers from doing business on the side.) The contract does not make clear, however, whether the shares of the venture possessed the limited-liability feature of corporate equity shares. Another tablet conveys silver to an Anatolian for making profits of which two-thirds will belong to the Assyrian investor. The question of limited liability also remains open for the *aširuma* or groups of ten (foreign?) businessmen (or military personnel?) attested to in Ugarit's palace archives (see the discussion of Assertion 11, p. 133). A tablet from Ugarit refers to an individual about to undertake a 'voyage to Egypt' with four backers. An Assyrian contract of the seventh century in which three men borrow four minas of silver provides, somewhat obscurely, that 'if Qāllaya (an individual not named among the borrowers) withdraws from this *nadabāku* (meaning the same as *natbāku*, literally "a place where corn(?) is heaped up") he shall bear the liability for the four minas of silver' (Postgate 1976, p. 46).

Besides credit, banking houses, and negotiability, the commercial loan market widened by resorting to suretyship or third-party guarantee of repayment. Biblical references to surety include Genesis 43:9; 44:32; Job 17:3; and Proverbs 11:15; 17:18; 20:16; and 22:26. Contracts of suretyship are well known in Mesopotamia during the seventh to fourth centuries but are also found much earlier — in the second millennium at Ugarit, Nuzi, and Khafajah (Tutub) and in Anatolia and in the third millennium at Lagash. Note the Sumerian proverb (c. 2500): 'Do not guarantee (for someone), that man will have a hold on you' (Alster 1974, p. 15).[15]

Contractual Slavery

The credit market also widened by resorting to contractual slavery. Generally speaking, an individual had the right to pledge himself or a family member as security for a loan. In the event of default the pledged individual was legally obligated to 'enter the house' of the creditor and serve him. Sometimes, as in early second-millennium

Anatolia, the obligation was made quite explicit in the loan contract: 'They (i.e. Babbala and Palhasia) will pay (their debt) at harvest; if they have not paid they will enter the house of (the creditor) Enashru' (Balkan 1974, note 12, p. 30). In other cases this obligation was assumed under state law. For instance, paragraph 117 of Hammurabi's Code requires defaulting debtors to enter the house of the creditor (or purchaser) and serve him for three years. A poignant illustration is provided by a letter translated by Oppenheim (1967) informing a man that a creditor has seized his wife and daughter and urging him to return from his trip before his family dies from the constant work of grinding the creditor's barley. (According to Paragraph 151 of Hammurabi's Code, one spouse might not be distrained for debts contracted by the other prior to their marriage.) Texts from eighteenth-century Mari and elsewhere refer to the 'prisoner for debt' (*niputûm*). An edict addressed to the king of Ugarit by the Hittite ruler concerning the activities there of merchants from Ura provides that 'if silver of the sons of Ura is with the sons of Ugarit, and they are unable to pay, and (then) the king of Ugarit this man (meaning the debtor), with his wife, with his sons, into the hands of the sons of Ura, the merchants, he shall give them' (Yaron 1969a, p. 72).

In an epic Hittite text cited earlier, a caravan of Ura merchants carries ample stocks of various merchandise including 'many *NAM.RA* people' apparently meaning 'seized people, conquered people, supported people' (Hoffner 1968, pp. 36, 39; see also Gelb 1973, pp. 77, 92). 'Houses' of *NAM.RA* people were donated to Hittite temples by private individuals, a 'head wood tablet writer', a king and a queen of the thirteenth century, and a foreign ruler. Their previous occupations include cow- and horse-herd, weaver, soldier(?), maker of 'long weapons', and even 'priest since long ago (Klengel 1975, pp. 193-6). The donation documents show that these *NAM.RA* people originated outside Hatti. Perhaps these *NAM.RA* people are related to the *NIM* people of the late third-millennium 'messenger texts' from Girsu who are sometimes described as 'seized' and, apparently, are under military supervision. (The logogram *NIM* meaning 'up' was used for Elam by the Sumerians.) It is important to add that ancient terms translated 'seize', for example the Akkadian term *ṣabatum*, may also have the sense of 'purchase'. Thus the Hittite edict mentioned above states with respect to the Ura merchants: 'And houses, fields, for their silver they shall not seize' (Yaron 1969a, p. 72; see also Astour 1970, pp. 116-19). Several texts from Ugarit warn debtors that to be sold into slavery in Egypt is the penalty for default. Recall the biblical story of Joseph.

Paragaph 117 of Hammurabi's Code also shows that an individual might sell himself or a family member into slavery. Indeed, an Anatolian text cited by Balkan shows a man named Habia selling himself and his family to a certain Hahua. Again, service might be for a limited time, indeterminate, or permanent. Self-sale contracts are available from the late third-millennium to the earlier second-millennium in Sumer and Babylonia, in early second-millennium Anatolia, mid-second-millennium Nuzi, and seventh- to sixth-century Egypt.[16]

The economic importance of contractual slavery arises from the provision to the lender (or purchaser) of fuller control over the debtor's (seller's) productive services and consumption pattern than would otherwise be possible. Instead of a wage (Sumerian *á*) in money to be spent (or a wage-in-kind which might be sold, then spent) at his discretion, the contractual slave received a 'barley ration' (Sumerian *sě-ba*) consisting of the basic necessities to maintain him as an effective worker. (The daily grain ration per man was about two quarts of barley.) As Gelb notes in stressing the difference in meaning between 'barley ration' and 'wage', the 'barley ration' is issued to infants, animals, and semi-free workers alike. The slave might also be made to work a longer and more intense day with fewer amenities and to adopt a healthier life style (e.g. a nutritious diet, avoidance of pregnancy and child birth) than would be chosen by a self-owned worker. The right to contract into slavery makes the borrower eligible for a larger consumption or production loan than could otherwise be expected because the severe limitations placed on the debtor's permitted range of behaviour enhances the expected productivity of his labour services.[17] Production loans include those for training, migration, and other types of human capital as well as those for material capital. Evidence for investment in training is discussed below (p. 112). At this point some evidence on investment in migration is considered. With respect to investment in migration we can find a hint in immigrant craftsmen who may be placed within the Homeric *demioergoi*, 'public workers' (*Odyssey 17:382-5)*, and the biblical *gerîm*, 'resident aliens' (Exodus 22:20; 2 Samuel 4:3; and elsewhere). In connection with the *demioergoi*, note the references in Mycenaean economic texts to the personal/ethnic names Kuprious and Gublious, derived from Cyprus and Byblos, respectively. Also relevant are the many foreign craftsmen at early second millennium Mari, the Hurrian names in Babylonian ration lists of the late second millennium, the skilled Levantines who worked in Egypt's dockyard near Memphis in the mid-second millennium (see Chapter 7, 'New Markets and Land Consolidation') and, in the seventh century, tended the vines at Gemeten in Upper Nubia, and, finally, the foreign craftsmen found in the cities of Iran in the late sixth and earlier fifth centuries. Some of the 'escaped' or 'fugitive' craftsmen in the Mari documents and Hittite treaties may be foreigners who had sold themselves into slavery to finance their migration to relatively high-wage areas. Babylonia's Hurrians, typically adult males originating in Syria and Assyria, included scribes, leather-workers, weavers, fisherman, and farmers. Hurrian fugitives are noted in the texts, and in the two documented instances in which Hurrians moved into or within Babylonia they were, Brinkman reports, purchased by merchants. As noted above, the *NAM.RA* people were not natives of Hatti. There are texts showing 'seized people' receiving the wherewithal to establish small farms. In Iran, the *kurtaš*, a group including craftsmen of various national origins, who originally received rations sufficient to live on, were later on, according to Dandamayev (1975, p. 78):

> paid not only in kind but also in silver. And now the wage rates became much higher . . . viz, from 1 to 8 shekels per month. The highest percentage of the *kurtaš* received 3 or 4 shekels per month, that is three or four times as much as the wage of a freeborn hired laborer in Babylonia, where in the sixth and fifth century B.C. an adult hired man as a rule was paid 1 shekel of silver per month. At the same time prices of most products in Persia and Babylon were approximately the same.

During this more affluent period the term *kurtaš* apparently came to signify 'worker', not 'slave'.[18]

Assertion 6

The concept of the economy was born with the French Physiocrats simultaneously with the emergence of the market as a supply-demand-price mechanism . . . This was, in the course of time, followed by the revolutionary innovation of markets with fluctuating prices for the factors of production, labor and land. (Polanyi 1981, pp. 6-7)

Land Market

In fact, with the exception of the Ur III Dynasty (2112-2004) and

Middle Babylonian period (1595-1155), sales and leases of privately owned (nonpalace and nontemple) fields are common in all periods of Mesopotamian history from the middle of the third millennium to the sixth century. They are especially common in the earlier centuries of the second millennium. Moreover, beginning in the second half of the twenty-fourth century there is ample and clear evidence of the sale for silver of both large estates and comparatively small parcels of land by individual vendors. The obelisk of Sargon's son Manishtushu (2269-2255), according to Bottéro (1967, p. 114), 'lists the lands he has acquired for sums adding up to something like 650 pounds of silver; there are about 650-odd acres of arable land in four large lots, each made up of parcels bought from individual proprietors (ninety-eight in all) and handed out by him to forty-nine new occupants'.[19] In a large number of early second-millennium texts recording the sale of small parcels of privately owned arable land in southern Babylonia the vendors *appear* to be groups (not individuals) in only 30 per cent of the cases. Although the eminent Soviet Assyriologist Diakonoff (1974a, note 13, p. 49) would like to identify these 'groups' as 'family communes', he admits that the 'kinship relations of the individual vendors between themselves is in such cases not always indicated. . . .' (The question of communal land is dealt with in detail in the next section.) He adds, with respect to the sale of date plantations and gardens, that in both the north and south the percentage of group vendors is insignificant. Skaist (1975, pp. 244-5), in seeking to relate inheritance laws to 'underlying economic and social structures', concludes that: 'The sale of land by more than one person, e.g. partners, is rare in comparison with the sale of land by one individual. Moreover, the sale of land by a single individual is made without reference to any permission that may have been granted by the members of the family that one would expect if we were dealing with joint property.' In attempting to counter this hard evidence, Skaist offers only the thought that perhaps the sellers acted as 'trustees'.

The security of land transactions was enhanced by the inclusion in deeds of conveyance of defension clauses in which the seller promised to 'stand up (in court)' and 'clean (clear)' the property from claims raised by third parties. Survey maps of fields incised on clay tablets are well attested in the later third and second millennia and were sometimes cited in litigations. At the same time, opportunism in the rental market was curbed by contractual provisions demanding briefly that the orchard be 'returned in good condition to its owner' or stating in technical terms the cultivation practices the lessee was expected to follow: 'He shall spade the orchard; of the blossoms he shall take care; for any damage to the grove he will be held responsible.' Quite possibly the damages mentioned in this early second-millennium Babylonian lease were to be assessed by a group of witnesses: 'Any deterioration of the orchard they will estimate and he shall refund' (Pruessner 1930, pp. 219, 232). In the middle of the first millennium, the lessee of a palm orchard was required to redig its ditches, dredge its canals, break up its fallow ground, and take care of the offshoots and fronds. A seventh-century Assyrian lease appears to call for the lessee to put funds in escrow from which the damages to capital goods might be deducted. (Similar provisions, it may be added, are found in rental contracts for ships: 'The well-preserved ship and its fittings he will [retu]rn to its owner in the harbor of Ur intact (?)' (Oppenheim 1954, note 16, p. 10; see also Pardee 1975).) Sixth-century Babylonian contracts, reflecting a long legal tradition, provide that the animals are 'deathless' — i.e. the lessee must replace any losses in stock. A clear appreciation of opportunity costs is manifested in a provision calling for the renter to pay the owner of the ox a sum equal to the value of the services or income foregone (*á-bi*). In Pharaonic Egypt oxen are mentioned under the rubric 'its hoof is money'.

A provision of the Lipit-Ishtar lawcode shows that as early as the twentieth century Babylonian governments were prepared to enforce contractual agreements, transforming, in the economist's terminology, externalities into internalities. (An externality occurs when the production or consumption decisions of one economic actor affect the consumption or production opportunities of another economic actor directly — that is, not through changes in market prices.)

> If adjacent to the house of a man the bare ground of (another) man has been neglected and the owner of the house has said to the owner of the bare ground, 'Because your ground has been neglected someone may break into my house; strengthen your house; (and) this agreement has been confirmed by him, the owner of the bare ground shall restore to the owner of the house any of his property that is lost (Kramer 1969b, p. 160).[20]

Important data testifying to a land market in the early second-millennium are also available in Akkadian documents from Susa, a city in Iran on Mesopotamia's border. Numerous purchase deeds testify to the individual nature of land tenure. Children, having inherited their father's wealth, might divide it among themselves by casting lots and selling their property individually (see further the next section). In fourteenth-century Assyria heirs to a landed estate might sell claims on the inheritance prior to the announcement of the details: the buyer received the option to 'choose and take' from among the portions of the inheritance (termed *'Gattungskauf'*, or nonspecific sale). More generally, individuals were able to sell land called *zittu* (inherited) as easily as land termed *ši>amātu* (purchased). Deeds of landed estates were deposited with creditors to secure loans (see also the discussion of Assertion 5 p. 88). Sales of privately owned agricultural land, including that of defaulting debtors, are also recorded in Syria in the early and later second millennium at Alalakh and Ugarit. Women appear in texts from the latter state as purchasers and sellers not only of land but of farmhouses, olive trees, and vineyards. For instance, Bat-rabi and her son Shubammu sold land to Talaya daughter of . . . Note also the patriarch Abraham's purchase of land for silver in Genesis 23:12-18. Similarly, in Pharaonic Egypt, according to Baer (1962, pp. 25-6): 'It is well known that private individuals could own farm land at all periods of ancient Egyptian history. Documents attesting the conveyance of land are quite common. In most cases they record a donation of some sort, either to a temple or towards the endowment of a mortuary cult, but the acquisition of fields for private purposes is also mentioned from the earliest periods, though not so frequently.' Baer explains that the term *nmhw-n<* means 'privately owned' and adds that documents quoting prices for a field are relatively rare. When, however, the available price data pertaining to different historical periods are compared, they display wide fluctuations. Relatively low prices are observed for well-water-irrigated and 'tired' land. Sixth-century Egyptian rental contracts call for the landlord to receive one-third of the grain crop while the tenant is to take 'two-thirds in the name of oxen, seed-grain, and men' (G.R. Hughes 1952, pp. 18, 75). The lessor has the right to restitution for damage to his land.[21]

Fragmentary land price data are available for Babylonia in the earlier second millennium. For one northern Babylonian city (Sippar) Harris provides land rents (classified by irrigation area and reign) of considerable variation. The field prices assembled by Stone for a city in central Babylonia (Nippur) likewise vary substantially over time. Texts from Nuzi show steep variations in field prices even when account is taken of whether the field was irrigated or adjoined a watercourse. Mention also should be made of a later second-millennium letter fragment found at Aphek whose hypothetical but expert restoration by Hallo conveys the idea that articles (houses and fields?) in short supply sold at high prices. Admittedly, the sources of the observed price variability would be difficult to isolate and quantify. On the other hand, it is fair to say that the evidence provides little comfort to those who, like Polanyi, would deny the existence of a land market and role for supply and demand in determining land values. The evidence presented above also discredits Diakonoff's (1974a, p. 51) claim that 'private property in land in the modern sense was not known in any of the ancient societies'.[22]

Individual versus Communal Land Ownership

It is in order at this point to devote additional attention to the question of communal versus individual land ownership in Near Eastern antiquity. The first point is that the 'groups' cited above by Diakonoff may actually consist of witnesses, not vendors. The need for long lists of witnesses to validate land sales would diminish whenever the state itself played a more active role in registering land sales. For example, forty documents from the royal archives of Ugarit effecting the transfer of private property, mostly land and houses, bear the imprint of the dynastic seal rather than a lengthy list of witnesses. (Apparently these documents take the form of fictitious land grants.) On the other hand, the land sales recorded in rather difficult-to-interpret southern Mesopotamian contracts of the twenty-seventh through twenty-sixth centuries were made, according to Edzard (1967a, p. 75), 'for the most part, not by individuals but by families or clans', and the tablets have been found 'individually and not in archives, as they are private and not public records.' Early second-millennium private sale contracts from Mari show that the šapiṭum, 'judge or provincial governor' received a payment, probably a registration fee. More directly, a tablet from Ugarit records that a certain Abdiya gave the ruler gold and silver when, in the ruler's presence, he transferred his home, fields, and other property to his grandson. Genesis 21:25-30, involving Abraham and Abimelech, king of Gerar, not only illustrates this point but seems to argue the advantages of fees for state registration.

> Then Abraham reproached Abimelech for the well of water which his servants ['subjects' is probably a more accurate rendering[23]] had seized. But Abimelech said, 'I do not know who did this, you did not tell me, nor have I heard of it until today.' Abraham took

sheep and gave them to Abimelech; and they two made a covenant. And Abraham set aside seven ewe-lambs of the flock. And Abimelech said to Abraham: 'What mean these seven ewes which you have set apart?' He replied: 'You are to take these seven ewe-lambs from my hand, that it may be a witness that I dug this well.

It should be noted parenthetically that inscriptions of the earlier first millennium reveal that privately owned wells existed side by side with those belonging to the pharaoh. Also, Tablet B of the twelfth-century Assyrian laws recognises private ownership of wells and of irrigation canals in paragraphs 17 and 18.

The witnesses to land sales are especially likely to be confused with vendors. It is quite reasonable for neighbours of the vendor to serve as witnesses. (Note the legal formula in which eye-witnesses are termed 'men of the place and of the word'.) The problem is that kin are likely to be among the vendor's neighbours. Thus the presence of the vendor's kin in a sale contract does not necessarily mean 'communal ownership' or an 'extended family group'.[24]

Another point is that land sale contracts might include the approval of those relatives of the vendor granted an annual income from the property in question by the parent(s) of the vendor. This practice has been noted by Jelínkova in Egyptian contracts until very late times. The statement 'there is no claim (against the property transferred)' followed by a list including anyone descended from the seller's parents, as, for example, in the Karnak Stela of the Seventeenth Dynasty (mid-seventeenth to mid-sixteenth century) provided buyers with blanket protection against legal challenges in an economical form. Communal property is beside the point. Note also in this connection the application of the legal term *ul imutta*, 'they will not die' to animal stock given by an eighteenth-century Babylonian to his daughter. We are dealing here, of course, with an annuity. Oppenheim's (1955, p. 90) reasonable interpretation is that the stock 'continue to pasture with the head of the family; their yield in lambs, wool, cheese, and hides is to constitute the income of the daughter.' Surely, the daughter would then have to grant permission for the sale of the stock and, perhaps, of the pasture as well.

The Hungarian Assyriologist Komoróczy (1978, p. 9) disagrees with Diakonoff's views on the importance of communally owned land in the first half of the second millennium: 'The "land community" (in the original sources *uru* or *ālum*, both meaning "city") . . . is in my opinion nothing more than an organization of civil rights. It has no economic role, it has nothing to do with proprietorship, and the alienation of landed property takes place outside its authority; the lands are in private ownership.' There is evidence, however, from the ancient Near East that communal ownership or control over agricultural land is not, as is often supposed (e.g. by Leemans 1983, p. 58), an original or pristine form of organisation. In Mesopotamia, according to Diakonoff (1974b, p. 535), 'the nuclear families which had begun to play the major role under Hammurabi again yielded place to the household communes of the Kassite period.' Komoróczy (1978, p. 12) adds that 'on the former irrigable lands in the south (hardly or not irrigable by now) tribal landed property appears.' This, he adds perceptively, 'is not the remainder of archaic conditions, but the phenomenon of re-archaizing well-known in ethnography.' But why did this 're-archaizing' occur? Unfortunately, little seems to be known about Kassite economic and administrative policies beyond the famous *kudurru*'s they used, beginning in about 1400, to make land grants and give tax exemptions (see Chapter 1 p. 20).[25]

The much more ample European evidence raises the strong possibility that communes arise as an adaption to the state's imposition of joint responsibility for taxation. One's neighbours and, now, tax-partners would understandably be on their guard against shirking and tax-shifting behaviour. De Vries has called attention to the fact that even the growing of novel crops might be frowned upon as an attempt to evade one's tax obligations. At the very least, the 'commune' would demand veto power over the entry of new tax-partners via land sales. Toumanoff's (1981, p. 183) findings on the evolution of the Russian commune justify quotation.

> During the two centuries between 1600 and 1800 the existing organization of independent peasant householders sharing forests, pasture lands, and streams, gradually evolved into the serf commune, consisting of from 5 to 150 households. The serf commune was responsible for payment of obligations to the lord, distribution of land among its members, decisions regarding the choice and tilling of crops in the open fields and so on. Two types of commune evolved: repartitional and hereditary. The difference between the two types lay in the practice of periodically repartitioning the scattered strips according to varying criteria of household size. Households in the hereditary commune held their scattered strips in hereditary tenure, and *had the right to sell their*

strips subject to approval by the commune officials [italics added].

In the case of England the origins of the commune are even hazier, but with respect to the Midland belt we are informed by Donkin (1973, p. 83) that 'the level of cooperation implied by the existence of two or three great "fields" may be no older than the eleventh or twelfth centuries.' Only at this point in time is community-regulated cropping observed. Interestingly, the history of joint responsibility for taxation seems to go back to the geld and hidage system of the last decade of the tenth century.

The Mari documents of the early second millennium appear to provide evidence for collectively owned agricultural land in northern Syria. One text, for instance, has a 'clan' (the text says 'house' and lists thirteen 'sons' of Awin assigns a field as a 'hereditary portion' (*nahālum*) to an individual made into a 'brother' by a legal fiction (compare the discussion of sale-adoptions at Nuzi on p. 140). There is, however, some evidence that the royal administration of Mari followed a policy of settling its migratory steppe-dwellers for purposes of military security and income (rent and taxes). As T.L. Thompson (1978, p. 9) points out, the economy of these 'tribal' groups must be understood in the light of their 'subordination to the state bureaucracy and military'. There is, moreover, a Mari text recording sheep-taxes (*miksu*) levied on various *hibrum* — meaning 'clan' or 'commune'.[26]

Summarising recent research, Batto has suggested that the primary reference of the terms *nahālum* and *nihlatum* (the root *nhl*) is the perpetual royal grant rather than tribal patrimony. (The biblical counterpart is the term *naḥ^{a}la(h)*.) When the income from a publicly granted landed estate (or territory) serves to compensate the recipient individual or family or tribe for the performance of a public function, however, inalienability and even indivisibility are understandable. The public functions may be of military, sacerdotal, artisanal, or commercial nature.

Real estate is well suited to this objective since, generally speaking, it is more difficult to dissipate a field than other capital goods. Thus, in the event of unsatisfactory performance the public might without undue losses repossess and transfer the estate. In medieval Europe under the contractual arrangement best named 'lordship', the vassal's obligation was to provide military service in the form of a self-equipped, highly trained mounted knight.[27] Originally, the vassal was not permitted to subdivide, diminish the value ('abridge'), or alienate the fief (landed estate) provided to support him. Tenure might be for life, or the heirs of the vassal might have the right of investiture. In the event that the vassal failed to fulfill his obligations ('felony') the lord had the right to confiscate the fief (*commissum*).

Ancient Near Eastern contracts spelling out in detail the mutual obligations of lordship are, apparently, unavailable. However, paragraphs 36 through 38 of Hammurabi's Code prohibit a 'bearer of dues' from selling his 'field, orchard, or house' or deeding them to his wife, daughter, or creditor. No doubt the fiefs (*eqil kurummati*, 'fields of maintenance') held by 'chariot warriors' in second-millennium Syria (the *mariyannu*), Hittite Anatolia, and Egypt were indivisible and inalienable (see also the discussion of Assertion 12, p. 137). While Hittite practices are not well understood, it appears that the vassal did not have the right to sell his fief, and, with the exception of inheritance by a son, new fiefholders had to be selected or approved by the king. We do know that in Ugarit and Assyria royal service-men classified as *nayyālu*, 'the man who did not perform his obligations' might have their fiefs (Ugaritic *ubdy*, Akkadian *pilku*) confiscated and transferred to new servicemen or sold. Heltzer (1976b, pp. 53-4) presents a text from Ugarit in which the king transfers a fief from the *nayyālu*, to his niece; specifies that the fief may in the future be transferred only to 'a certain Nurishtu, the sons of Yarimilku, or the *sākinu* (*skn*) of her household (majordomo)'; and calls for the performance or payment of *unuššu*. (The Hebrew cognate *mwš*, 'land tax', is found in Isaiah 33:8 and 1 Kings 10:14.) *Nayyālu* is derived from *nālu*, 'to recline,' suggests Speiser, who goes on to provide a lengthy discussion of *našû-nadānu*, 'take (away) and give', the standard legal formula for the transfer of real estate. Labaschagne finds the biblical Hebrew equivalent in *lqh-ntn*: 'And he (the king) will take your fields, and your vineyards, and your olive yards, even the best of them, and give them to his servants' (1 Samuel 8:14). In another text from Ugarit translated by Heltzer (1982, p. 20) the house and fields of the *nayyālu* are taken and given to an individual who is 'freed from the leatherworker and put . . . to the bronze-caster.' Paragraph 46 (Tablet 1) of the Hittite laws of the middle of the second half of the second millennium provides that if a craftsman does not perform the service due from his fief, the fields will be reclaimed by the palace.

The Mycenaean texts point to the presence of craftsmen required to perform labour service but not paying production taxes on their land.

These craftsmen may well correspond to the 'public workers' (*demioergoi*) of the *Odyssey* (see also 'Contractual Slavery' under Assertion 5, p. 91). Also in early Greece, according to Mireaux, the land (*chrema* or *temenos*) allocated by the community authorities to a family (*genos*) so that it might carry out certain avocations had to remain within the family. Similarly, the priestly Levites were not permitted to sell the fields granted to them surrounding the forty-eight Levitical cities 'in the midst of the possession of the children of Israel' (Leviticus 25:34, Numbers 35:1-8, Joshua 21:1-42). Mettinger sees the fields of the high priests Abiathar (1 Kings 2:26) and Amaziah (Amos 7:17) as sacerdotal fiefs. Legal texts from Ugarit show priests and a 'family of priests' holding royal fiefs. Ugaritic literary texts use the term $nah^{a}la(h)$ for landed property held by a deity and, in the earlier second millennium, the god Adad writes from Aleppo to the king at Mari requesting a *niḥlatum*. Documents of third-millennium Egypt employ the term *ḥt* to denote land held by priests in return for sacerdotal services. Finally, the creation of commercial fiefs is found as early as the middle of the third-millennium at Lagash. At Ugarit the king provides Abdihagag with a fief and calls for him to provide merchant service. (See further the discussion of Assertion 11, p. 132.)[28]

Another point about communal land is that, especially in pre-industrial societies, a preference, statistically speaking, for intrafamily land sales is quite understandable even in the absence of laws or customs frowning upon alienation. Sales within the confines of the family may merely reflect residential proximity or, more important, the process by which joint ownership previously created by inheritance or marriage is dissolved and transformed into exclusive ownership. This aspect of the dynamics of family trading patterns has been dealt with statistically in a recent study by Marcus of the real estate market in Aleppo in Syria in the mid-eighteenth century CE. While no comparable study exists for the ancient Near East, T.L. Thompson has brought together several division-of-inheritance contracts from the first half of the second millennium. A text from Nuzi, for example, records an agreement between two brothers in which one gives the other title to three sheep he had inherited and in return receives exclusive title to an inherited field. An early second-millennium text from Nippur shows a son giving silver for the inheritance share of his paternal uncle. Transactions of this sort are explicitly sanctioned in paragraph 38 of the Laws of Eshnunna: 'If one of several brothers wants to sell his share (in a property common to them) and his brother wants to buy it, he shall pay . . .' (Goetze 1969, p. 185). Paragraph 1 (Tablet B) of the twelfth-century Assyrian laws also regulates joint inheritance, but division is by birth order, not by purchase. A text from Ugarit discussed by Heltzer shows three brothers buying out the share of the fourth in the family property. Esau, of course, sold his 'birthright' to Jacob (Genesis 25:29-34). Proximity and joint ownership, however, do not offer a full explanation of why intrafamily land sales (and other transactions, including loans) occur at a higher than random frequency, giving the illusion of 'communal' ownership of land. The addition of altruistic motives improves but does not complete the picture. Account must also be taken of the fact, implicit in Marcus's study, that trading with members of one's own family (or friends or co-religionists) serves to reduce, perhaps quite significantly, transaction costs (see the discussion of family firms in Chapter 2, p. 39).[29]

Slave Market

The ancient Near Eastern world, of course, knew an active, legally recognised market for slave labour. This is documented from the middle of the third-millennium in Mesopotamia and from the sixteenth century in Egypt. A slave-sale contract from an Assyrian trading station in Anatolia states that the document was written before an official, 'the chief of the market'. Officially witnessed slave sales are also found among the Nuzi texts. In early second-millennium Sippar, sale prices of slaves classified by sex and reign display pronounced variations. A rental market for slaves and, once again, familiarity with opportunity cost is evidenced in the Laws of Eshnunna (paragraph 22): 'If a man has no claim against a(nother) man, but nevertheless distrains the other man's slave-girl, the owner of the slave-girl shall [decla]re under oath: "Thou has no claim against me" and he shall weigh out silver as much as the hire of the slave woman (Yaron 1959, p. 169). An Egyptian document (Papyrus Berlin 9784, line 22) includes the instruction: 'Buy for yourself two days of the slave Henut' (Peet 1932, p. 169). Babylonian documents revealing a willingness to invest in slaves by apprenticing them to learn trades (including potter, dyer, and weaver) are available from the time of Hammurabi and also from the time of Cyrus (sixth century).

As in the case of the land market, the market for slaves was made more efficient by contractual warranties making the seller responsible for claims by third parties. An Egyptian woman swore 'as (the god) Amon lives and as Pharaoh lives' that the slave she offered for sale did not belong to 'anyone in the whole land who will be able to claim(?) him tomorrow or after tomorrow', and she added, 'As to him who shall speak (object?) let not his utterance be heard in any bureau of writing' (Bakir 1952, p. 29). (The term hrw, 'voice', is a technical term for written pleadings which are found as early as the third millennium; compare Section 1 of Chapter 2.) In addition, Assyrian sale contracts of the eighth century include risk clauses in which the seller guarantees against flight and certain illnesses. Similar rights to initiate a legal action against the seller were provided to purchasers of slaves by paragraphs 278 and 279 of Hammurabi's Code. If the slave exhibited symptoms of 'epilepsy' within a month from the date of purchase, the seller had to return the purchase price. Contractual and mandatory warranties of this kind are quite understandable in the case of a relatively expensive, durable good whose 'defects' might be well known to the seller by experience but would not be apparent to a potential buyer by inspection. It is probable that trial rentals were also employed. After calling in line 22 for the purchase of 'two days of the female slave Henut' (see above), Papyrus Berlin 9784 continues in lines 25 through 28: 'He said "I am fully and completely paid with the price of (my) slave. As (the god) Amon endures and as the Ruler endures, if the two days are unsuitable ($\check{s}mm$, literally 'hot') which I have given you in the female slave Henut, compensation (a refund?) shall be given piece by piece (of silver)" — in the presence of many witnesses' (J.A. Wilson 1948, pp. 144-5). Perhaps a trial rental also underlies a clause in a first-millennium Assyrian slave-sale contract calling for the payment 'to be bound to the foot' of a god. This expression may very well be related to clauses in Nuzi documents requiring the so-called 'brideprice' or indirect dowry to be 'bound in the hem' of a daughter — i.e. set aside for her (compare section 6 of Chapter 2, p. 47).

In various ways, therefore, the ancients sought to limit the severity of a problem identified by economists as adverse selection, or the lemon principle. This refers to a process initiated by an inequality of costly information about quality between buyers and sellers in which distinct contingent markets do not exist and, consequently, market transactions come to be restricted to objects of below-average quality. To understand this process, imagine a distribution of all slaves over a quality scale. If consumers know the mean quality but have no additional information about the quality of any individual slave offered for sale, then bids will be based on this expected value. Owners knowing their slaves to be of below average quality will be willing to sell at a price reflecting mean quality, while some owners of above-average slaves will decide to withhold them from the market. It follows that the average quality of slave sold will be below that of the entire slave population. As a result of this adverse selection process, buyers will eventually adjust their bids downward, again lowering the quality of slaves offered for sale and the volume of trading.

An individual seeking to purchase a slave did not, however, have to rely entirely on estimated mean quality, inspection, and legal-contractual warranties. The reputation of the seller might also play an important role. For example, during the early Roman empire, skilled expensive slaves were sold in shops rather than in the temporary facilities erected for periodic auctions of lesser-quality 'merchandise'. The commitment of the supplier to permanent and relatively expensive quarters operated to increase the confidence of buyers in his product. In Rome information about nationality, health status, and tendency to run away was conveyed by means of legally required placards worn by slaves on the platform. Egyptian contracts typically noted the parentage of the slave. Beyond this, the avilability of quality signals is well illustrated by an Egyptian letter (Papyrus Bologna 1086) of the late thirteenth century: 'I have made inquiry in (the case of) the Syrian of the temple of Thoth about whom you have written me . . . For your information, his Syrian name is Neqdi, son of Sereretj; his mother is Qedi from the land of Arwad; slave from the ship-transport for this temple in the boat of Captain Kener' (Jozef Janssen 1955-56, p. 64). Papyrus Brooklyn (see Chapter 2, section 6, p. 45) includes biographical data for the slaves owned by a woman who lived in the eighteenth century. Information of this kind was presumably available to Babylonians from the slave registry hinted in paragraph 18 of Hammurabi's Code. (A register of hundreds of names was found at Sippar and a text from Kish has been termed a 'birth certificate'.)[30]

The rather limited nature of the warranty, which protected the buyer only against flight and specific illnesses, served to lessen the deterrent effect of market insurance on the self-protection measures of the slave purchaser. Consequently, the impact of a problem called moral hazard in the insurance literature was mitigated, and the ability of the slave market to allocate risk-bearing was not seriously impaired.

Market for Free Labour

Several older scholars, including Struve and Fish (but see also

Diakonoff), saw free agricultural wage workers in 'considerable numbers' as early as the middle of the second half of the third millennium. (The texts of this era include a list of priced worker days.) Gelb, on the other hand, argues strongly in favour of drawing this line in the late third millennium. It is generally agreed that agricultural wage-workers are common in Babylonian tablets of the earlier second millennium. The legal texts regard the seller of his labour-power as being hired 'of himself'. Harris (1975) informs us that at Sippar harvesters received a wage (Akkadian *idum*) of one-third to two shekels per month. The wages of hired workers other than harvesters vary markedly even when account is taken of whether the worker was an adult or child, duration of employment contract (daily, monthly, or yearly), and whether the wage was paid in silver or in barley (a factor that might, for example, reflect differences in measurement, transport or storage costs or liquidity). Several texts indicate that workers might choose among alternative payment modes.

Late third-millennium texts from Umma show women (*gemé*) receiving grain designated as wages (Sumerian *á*) for tasks in connection with agriculture, irrigation, building, and oil pressing. Note that *gemé* does not mean slave-woman in these texts. (Fish translates one text as registering a grand total of 93,781 full-time-equivalent workers per day!) Note also texts from Umma and other cities specifying the daily wage paid to men for various tasks (e.g. digging irrigation ditches, transporting grain, towing ships, ploughing and sowing). This era also knew firms employing specialist craftsmen, including smiths, carpenters, sculptors, goldsmiths, and stonecutters. Similarly, texts from the earlier second millennium refer to artisans (for example, bricklayers, grinders, brewers, and carpenters), boat-towers, sailors, oxen-drivers, irrigation-canal-diggers, and even individuals hired 'to do business' who worked for wages. A nineteenth century contractor was instructed to hire 1,800 workers to do emergency work on a canal for which he was to pay no more then ten minas of silver. The latter stipulation seems to indicate that wage rates were not known in advance and, therefore, might be subject to market forces. Less ambiguous, albeit much later, evidence of supply/demand-determined wage rates is provided in Babylonian letters of the seventh through sixth centuries showing that hired labour was commonly employed for regular canal work and, more importantly, as Dubberstein (1938, p. 39) point out, 'at times it was even difficult to hire as much free labour as was needed. This is corroborated by the statement that the labourers were hired for five shekels a month, an unusually high scale of wages, even in comparison with the rising prices of the period.'

The letter of an Egyptian farmer dating from about 2000 specifies the barley-wage to be paid to a hired labourer (see the discussion of Assertion 13, p. 138). In the early second millennium, according to Giveon, the Egyptians employed in the turquoise mines of Serabit el Khadim, a topographically complex area over a mile in extent located in the southern Sinai, were remunerated on a piecework basis for stone deliveries beyond the required output quota. Giveon's conclusion is supported by a distinction in the texts, noted by Mueller, between '*qw*, denoting 'base wage', and *fq*, meaning 'bonus'. This payment scheme is quite rational, given the widely dispersed and, consequently, costly-to-supervise mines at Serabit el Khadim. One is hardly encouraged by this evidence to accept Jacob J. Janssen's (1975a, p. 139) claim that 'labor (in other words: time) possessed only a vague value' to the Egyptians. In the caption of a scene from the second half of the third millennium showing workers uprooting and bundling flax, the worker who urges his fellows to work hard so that 'the gang may be permitted to eat bread' may well have had piece wages in mind (Badawy 1983, p. 662). C.J. Eyre in a forthcoming volume on labour in the ancient Near East provides evidence about payments in kind to Egyptian craftsmen in the second half of the second millennium. A tablet dated on palaeographic grounds to the period from the late eighth to the sixth century records the payment of wages in silver. Egyptian artisans received 'favours' as incentive payments. Perhaps an echo of this practice can be detected in Exodus 3:21-22 wherein the Israelites who found 'favour in the sight of the Egyptians' ask for and receive silver, gold, and clothes.[31]

Conclusion

The evidence summarised above especially the Egyptian, is fragmentary and sporadic with respect to time and place, but it scarcely supports Polanyi's view that land and labour markets are innovations of nineteenth-century Western Europe. Moses Finley's (1973, p. 65) unsubstantiated claim that: 'Historically speaking, the institution of wage-labor is a sophisticated latecomer' does not fit the facts. Given, however, the availability of a legal market for slaves and, more basically, the prevalence of family firms in the ancient economy due to high transaction costs, it is predictable that the importance of an impersonal market for wage-labour would be much less than in the modern West (see Chapter 2, section 4, p. 39, and section 7, p. 48)

But this is not to say that transaction costs were large enough to make the wage-labour market inactive or even thin.

Assertion 7

Polanyi (1981, p. 135) suggested that 'a supply-demand-price system implies fluctuating prices that control supply, if not production itself.' But he did not in so many words deny the existence of a supply response in Near Eastern antiquity. This position, however, has been explicitly put forward by Humphreys (7a) and Diakonoff (7b):

Assertion 7a

The major distinction between the modern economy (capitalist or socialist) and that of earlier or less developed societies is that exchange prices in the latter, whether fixed of bargained have little connection with production decisions. (Humphreys 1978, p. 49)

Assertion 7b

Commodity circulation did exist [in the ancient Near East], but commodity production as such did not — i.e. there was no system having as its object the creation of profit by the production of commodities specifically for the market. Hence no accumulation of capital took place. (Diakonoff 1974b, p. 523)

The Supply Response

The evidence points in the opposite direction. Discussing the early second-millennium Assyrian trade with Cappadocia, J. Lewy (1958a, p. 91) notes that: 'If informed that the demand for these commodities [garments and tin] was particularly heavy the merchants in Assur who had them for sale helped their customers by assembling goods, donkeys, and drivers in advance so that the next caravan could leave immediately.' The merchant Puzur Assur wrote to Waqartum in Assur informing her in technical detail about the type of textiles she should produce for the Anatolian market. Another letter, presumably to a refiner, requests the making of good copper so that the writer's customers will buy it. Based on available documentation Larsen estimates that Assur shipped by donkey about eighty tons of tin over some fifty years. At a copper:tin ratio of 9:1, this amount of tin would have been combined with 720 tons of copper to produce 800 tons of bronze. Again, one text from a southern Babylonian city of about 1800 refers to eighteen tons of copper received at Tilmun. Another text from Mari lists some 11,000 pounds of tin deposited in the palace storehouse. It is difficult to imagine that tin and copper in these quantities would have been mined in the absence of a market orientation. Copper-smelting facilities have recently been excavated in the Oman Peninsula, probably the Magan of the international-trade-oriented Babylonian texts of the later third millennium. Note also during the period from 1500 to 1100 the distribution from Sicily to Israel, and even northern Babylonia, of copper ingots produced for export in a standard shape (the 'ox-hide' or 'double-axe') suitable for carrying and 'walking' and, perhaps, of a standard weight. Indeed, a shipment of these ingots was found off Cape Gelidonya (southwestern Turkey) in the wreck of a sunken freighter which had probably been sailing west from Cyprus, where evidence of copper production has been found. A thirteenth-century Egyptian inscription describes Alashiya (probably Cyprus) as producing copper 'in millions, in endless masses, in hundreds of thousands' (Holmes 1975, p. 91). A Babylonian metal inventory of the eighteenth century includes 'refined copper of Alashiya'; Millard (1973, p. 212) noting that this *erû misû* was transported in blocks suggests that 'we may, perhaps, envisage the ox-hide shaped ingots or their ancestors here.' The importance of the supply response is also attested to by a tablet from Ugarit calling for the fitting out of a fleet of 150 ships.[32]

Comparative Advantage and Textile Exports

In the middle of the third millennium Ebla exported fabrics to Anatolia, Mesopotamia, and Syria-Israel as well as to Byblos and other Lebanese coastal cities. An Ebalite text shows the import of 17,000 sheep from various cities. By the end of the third millennium, however, Babylonia was the leading exporter of woollen textiles. A number of its cities possessed large workshops employing hundreds of women in spinning and weaving. For example, a late third-millennium text from Eshnunna lists 585 female and 105 male employees in a weaving house. Interestingly, the excavations at this site uncovered a sizeable building dating from this period with an elaborate water system, perhaps a 'women's house' in which large numbers of women lived and produced textiles. One of the excavators, P. Delougaz, considers it more likely that the building houses a tannery; leather-making consumes large quantities of water. Note in passing that in the early second millennium the Isin region in southern Mesopotamia exported leather products to Syria and Iran.

Oppenheim (1970, pp. 131-2) suggests that: 'The popularity of the Babylonian production has to be accounted for by certain specific qualities which we have no means of establishing in spite of the elaborate Sumerian and Akkadian terminology describing such cloth and specific items of clothing.' Attempts at imitation of Babylonian textiles are, perhaps, reflected in Assyrian texts describing garments as being *ša Akkedê*, 'after the fashion of the Akkadians'. An alternative explanation for this 'popularity', may be that Babylonia had a cost advantage in the production of woollen textiles generally or, more probably, in certain branches of the industry. Specialisation in textiles can be understood in terms of comparative advantage — that is, Babylonia had relatively low marginal costs of producing textiles in terms of the various goods it (ultimately) imported.[33]

Investment in Capital Goods

Eshnunna's tannery or textile-producing facility was noted above. Excavations at a southern Mesopotamian city (Girsu) uncovered not only a text testifying to the export of fish to another city in the region but drains, large tanks, complete and stacked fish skeletons, and other evidence suggestive of a fish industry, all dating from about the middle of the third millennium. Elsewhere in Girsu, excavations revealed a ceramic-making installation with a minimum of fourteen potter's kilns.

The effort of covering the landscape of southern Mesopotamia with large groves of sucker-propagaged female date palms artificially pollinated to increase yields (male flowers were tied down on the female) is difficult to understand except as a response to emerging market opportunities. The easily preserved calorie-rich fruit is well suited for export. (No wild-growing species of date palm have been discovered.) Sumerian texts of the early second millennium include a large variety of terms for different kinds of palms and their parts. The date palm does not bear fruit until the age of five years and requires skilled care in transplanting, pollination, and fruit treatment. Paragraphs 60 to 65 of the Code of Hammurabi and business documents deal with owners giving out their grain fields to 'gardeners' to convert into date orchards or with owners having their date groves pollinated. Fragmentary data presented by Pruessner indicate that in the eighteenth century the selling price of an orchard (expressed per unit of land) was double that of a grain field. That a roughly similar ratio of values held in mid-first-millennium Babylonia is indicated by Dubberstein's handful of price quotations (see also Stolper).

It may be assumed that market possibilities justified the construction of Mari's elaborate irrigation system in the late nineteenth century. The texts show us the extensive manufacture of small boats and rafts and their use in transporting grain and livestock from one shore of the Euphrates to the other. Similarly, the laborious construction of agricultural terraces for vineyards in the hills behind Ugarit and around Jerusalem can be understood only in terms of the lucrative markets provided by the neighbouring urban centres. Note in this connection a Ugaritic literary text: 'I will put into his fields vineyards, into the fields of his zeal a tunnel (or channel) I will set up' (Baldacci 1981, p. 366). Heltzer provides data indicating that land prices in terms of silver were higher at Ugarit than at other ancient Near Eastern sites.

Market opportunities can be detected behind the industrial installation excavated at Ugarit and Israelite Debir and Gibeon. Very significant olive-oil producing facilities were excavated at Ugarit. At Tell Beit Mirsim (possibly the Biblical Debir), southwest of Hebron on the main road linking Egypt with the Judaean hills, large numbers of loom weights as well as dyeing vats (or possibly olive presses), each weighing about a ton, were found.[34] At Gibeon, northwest of Jerusalem, no less than 63 underground wine vats and cellars were discovered, some seven feet deep, capable of storing 25,000 gallons of wine. Note also the discovery of a late Babylonian 'factory' producing oil jars and hints of industrial installations in seventh- to fifth-century Babylonian references to the 'city of the metal workers' 'city of tanners', and so on, and in biblical references to the 'valley of the craftsmen' (1 Chronicles 4:14; Nehemiah 11:35).

The trade objective explains the massive stone quays and copper-smelting facility founded no later than the middle of the third millennium at Buhen just below the Second Cataract of the Nile in Sudanese (or Lower) Nubia. A seal with the inscription 'supervisor of copper workers' has been recovered at Mergissa (recall the discussion of ports of trade under Assertion 1, p. 76). This point is underlined by a Sixth Dynasty tomb inscription at Aswan in which Harkuf, an 'overseer of dragomans' (see p. 64), boasts that the pharaoh had sent him to Yam (Nubia) 'in order to *wb3* (the) road to this country. I did it within seven months (and) I brought back the beautiful and exotic products therefrom.' Kadish (1966, pp. 23-4) explains that the phrase 'to *wb3* a road' (used also in Hatshepsut's account of her expedition to Punt: see below) means to open or keep open the trade routes. Also in the third millennium, a channel cut through the rocks of the First Cataract permitted boats to penetrate the region. A larger channel was cut under Sesostris III in the nineteenth century and widened in the fifteenth by Thutmose III (see further Chapter 1, section 1, p. 14 and the discussion of Assertion 1, p. 76). There is, moreover, little reason to doubt W.S. Smith's suggestion that a faience-manufacturing facility at Kerma, dating from the first half of the second millennium, close to the Third Cataract in the Sudan (Upper Nubia or Kush), served the interests of trade.[35] The evidence for manufacturing at this site consists of raw materials and discarded imperfect pieces. Over 500 seal impressions were found, many of which had been affixed to pots, baskets, sacks (for grain?), and wooden containers (for linen?) from Egypt. Gold and incense are generally believed to have been the main Egyptian imports from Nubia.

Also in this period an inscription relates that in order to facilitate trade with the God's Land, a Pharaoh Mentuhotpe 'bored for water in these mountains which had before been impassable'; the officer Seanch adds a description of an elaborate well-station (after Erman 1971, p. 506; see pp. 63-4 above). Well-digging in connection with trade and mining is also found in the thirteenth century. Although the great tombs built for the pharaohs were obviously consumer goods intended to keep them happy for eternity, their vast expenditures beginning in the second millennium or earlier to cut a 'canal of the two seas' between the Nile and the Red Sea were motivated primarily by trade objectives. Indeed, Hatshepsut's boasts concerning the extraordinary character of her expedition to Punt in the fifteenth century may rest, as is hinted in her inscription at Deir el-Bahri, on the use of such a waterway instead of crossing the desert (compare Amon's oracle, p. 24, and Chapter 4, section 1, p. 63). The reliefs appear to show the same ships departing and arriving and omit a cargo-transfer scene. Note should also be taken here of an ambitious reclamation project completed in the reign of Amunemhet III (1842-1797) opening an estimated 17,000 acres in the Fayum depression to agriculture. During the second half of the second millennium there were 'glass factories' at Thebes, Gurob, and Amarna. A later second-millennium reference (Hieratic Ostraca 88.6) to the '*d3d3iw* of Coptos' may, according to Jacob J. Janssen (1975, note 143, p. 159), indicate a geographically concentrated pottery industry on the east bank of the Nile at the origin of the desert route in the heart of Upper Egypt. Vessels of the mid-third-millennium with the same pot-marks have been found at various Egyptian locations. A stela of the earlier second millennium discovered at a port on the shore of the Red Sea refers to 'ships of the dockyards of Coptos' (Sayed 1978, p. 71).[36]

Many of the above capital construction projects might be seen in terms of an investment model. This evidence, taken together with the material in 'Credit and Investment Market' under Assertion 5, p. 85), casts doubt on W.F. Leeman's (1977, p. 5) claim that 'capital invested in commercial enterprises was small.'

Investment in Human Capital

Why, moreover, would presumably self-contained individuals or households have been willing to invest in human capital — that is, to sacrifice current consumption to make the investment required to learn one of the skilled crafts above mentioned or one of the many others recorded in Near Eastern texts beginning in the earlier third millennium unless they perceived a remunerative market for the services? The importance of this factor is underlined in paragraph 189 of Hammurabi's Code by the provision that an artisan who failed to teach an adopted child a trade faced the loss of his apprentice to his biological family. Tablets from Pylos in southwestern Greece of the second half of the second millennium mention a large number of crafts and refer to people training for an occupation. The Hittite Laws, paragraph 200B, set the price a father must pay to have his son trained as carpenter, smith, potter, leatherworker, or fuller.[37]

Conclusion

The evidence presented above (and in Chapter 7, on land consolidation) demolishes Assertions 7a and 7b. In closing this discussion, it is of interest to note that a hint of the operation of the law of demand can be found in Babylonian texts from around and after the time of Hammurabi, pointing to increased use of gold for emblems, statues, thrones, and the like when its price in terms of silver had declined precipitously (see Farber 1978, pp. 4-7).

Notes

1. Sources on treaties, royal commercial correspondence, and commercial participation: Georgiou (1979, pp. 93, 96-8), Gyles (1959, pp. 35-6, 71), Heltzer (1978a, pp. 139-42), Kalluveettil (1982, p. 5), Larsen (1974, pp. 474-5), Liverani (1979a), Mendelsohn (1955, pp. 68-70), Orlin (1970, pp. 180-1), Pettinato (1981, pp. 103-5), Reiner (1969), Sasson (1966a, pp. 137-8), and Yaron (1969a, pp. 71-2, 75).

2. Sources on price formation in international markets; Heltzer (1978a, Chapter 2), Kienast (1960, p. 47), Leemans (1960a, pp. 85-8), Stieglitz (1979, p. 19), Veenhof (1972, pp. 376-7, 399-400), and Zaccagnini (1977, p. 187).

3. Sources on 'ports of trade' as tax collection centres: Boardman (1980, p. 117), Elat (1978, pp. 26-7), Finkelstein (1969a, p. 67), Gyles (1959, p. 93), Jacobsen (1960, pp. 184-5), Kadish (1966, pp. 28-32), R. Lattimore (1951, pp. 180-1), Lichtheim (1973, I, p. 118; 1980, III, pp. 86-9), Liverani (1979, p. 26), Lorton (1974, note 4, p. 114; pp. 139-44, 163), Montet (1968, p. 144), Muhly (1973, p. 223), de Selincourt (1972, p. 200), H.S. Smith and A. Smith (1976, pp. 59, 62), and Vanstiphout (1970, pp. 17-20). The possibility that ports of trade served to collect taxes has been suggested by Merrillees (1972, pp. 286-8); see also Glotz's (1925, pp. 207-9) perceptive remarks.

4. Sources on variations in grain prices: Engnell (1967, p. 43), Grayson (1972, note 64, p. 20), Kramer (1981, p. 266), H. Lewy (1956, p. 204), Postgate (1979, p. 215), Saggs (1962, p. 58), Snell (1982, p. 183), and Veenhof (1972, note 510, p. 383).

5. Sources on changes in supply and grain prices: Ahmed (1968, p. 148), Černý (1933, pp. 176-7), Kramer (1969a, pp. 649-50), Montet (1981, pp. 74-5, 266-7), and Sweet (1958, pp. 112-13).

6. Sources on seasonal variation in grain prices: Baer (1962, p. 28), Dubberstein (1938, pp. 26-7), Jacob J. Janssen (1975b, pp. 117-19, 125-7), Leemans (1950b, pp. 28-9; 1954, pp. 32-3), McCloskey and Nash (1984, p. 182), and M. Müller (1981, p. 451).

7. Alternatively, these transactions are examples of '*verhüllter Fruchtwucher*' ('secret usury in grain' — Edzard 1970, pp. 30-4) — involving an attempt to disguise an interest-bearing loan as an advance payment for grain (or 'prenumerando-purchase') in order to evade maximum interest rate regulations or the force of periodic royal edicts such as that of Babylonia's Ammisaduqa (1646-1626), which cancelled debts but left advances for purchases untouched (see Finkelstein 1968a, pp. 50, 59-60, and Veenhof 1978, pp. 282-5). For additional examples of Near Eastern business subterfuges to circumvent government regulations, see the discussion of Assertion 14, p. 140.

8. Sources on middlemen in the grain market: Batto (1974, p. 61), Bogaert (1966, p. 58), Casson (1980, pp. 26-9), Curtis and Hallo (1959, p. 108), Edzard (1970, p. 49), Fine (1952-53, note 8, p. 230), Foster (1977, pp. 32-3, 36, 38), Heltzer (1978a, pp. 153-4), Hoffner (1974, pp. 116-18), Hopkins (1978, p. 309), Jankowska (1970, p. 155; 1982, p. 139), Leemans (1954, p. 33; 1960, pp. 90-2), H. Lewy (1956, p. 203), Lutz (1931, pp. 6, 19, 27, 47), Meek (1969a, p. 217), Oppenheim (1970, note 53, p. 145), Oppenheim and Reiner (1977, note 13, p. 385), Sasson (1966, p. 132), Strange (1980, p. 102), and Veenhof (1978, p. 283).

9. 'Prophecy', a well-known literary genre in the ancient Near East, involves the employment of pretended predictions and warnings for propagandistic-political ends.

10. Sources on Egyptian middlemen in the grain market: Baer (1963, pp. 3, 9-12), Blackman and Peet (1925, pp. 289-90), Jacob J. Janssen (1961, p. 103; 1975a, p. 162), Lichtheim (1973, I, p. 158; 1976, II, p. 170), Lorton (1974, p. 12; note 3, p. 43), and J.A. Wilson (1969).

11. Sources on private, temple, and palace grain loans: Fish (1938, p. 162),

Gardiner (1948, pp. 206-7), Harris (1960, p. 130; 1963, pp. 121-2; 1968, p. 732; 1975, pp. 46-9), Leemans (1950b, pp. 12-13), Oelsner (1976, p. 262), Silver (1983a, pp. 65-7), and Stone (1982, pp. 57-8).

The preponderance of the *nadītu*'s in Sippar's economic transactions may be due to the concentration of the excavations in the 'cloister' area. According to Stone (1982, pp. 50-1), their role was more modest at Nippur, where the pattern of excavation was more random. Priestess-businesswomen were also prominent in Elam (Hinz, 1973b, p. 63). In an archive discovered in two adjacent rooms of the Sin temple at Khafajah (Tutub) in the Diyala region, the creditor in barley loans was usually the *enum*-priest or, somewhat later, the god Sin. The interest rates were the same for the loans of Sin as for those of *enum*-priests (Harris 1955, pp. 37-8).

12. Sources on business loans: Ahmed (1968, pp. 144-5), Bauer (1975), Butz (1979, note 312, p. 368), Finkelstein (1968, pp. 59-60), Garelli (1963, p. 262), Harris (1955, p. 63; 1960, pp. 130-1), Larsen (1977b, p. 96), Leemans (1950a, pp. 3, 11, 46-7), Oppenheim (1947, note 13, p. 119; 1948, p. 153; 1954, p. 9; 1974, p. 232), Owen (1969, pp. 43-4), Parker (1954, p. 31), Saggs (1962, p. 126), Wiseman (1953, p. 42), and Zaccagnini (1977, pp. 185-6).

13. In fourth-century-BCE Athens a lender for a maritime venture required the prior lenders to subordinate their claims to his (W.E. Thompson 1979, p. 235). The economics of limited liability and opportunistic behaviour by highly leveraged owner-managers are discussed with great insight and clarity by Jensen and Meckling (1976, especially pp. 330-43); see also Ekelund and Tollison (1981, pp. 133-45), Levmore (1982), Mackaay (1982, Chapter 8), and Watts and Zimmerman (1983).

14. Sources on call loans: Harris (1960, p. 130) and Stol (1982, p. 148). An early second-millennium tablet in which the Shamash temple lends a husband and wife five shekels requires, according to the translation of Price (1915-16, pp. 254-5), 'When they see the notice on the wall they shall weigh out to the bearer of the document the silver and the interest thereon. In the month Elul, in the year of (the building of) the great wall of Shamash.' I am assured by an expert, however, that this translation is antiquated; instead of 'When they see the notice on the wall', it reads: 'Should they be seen in the harbour'.

15. Sources on banking, credit, negotiable instruments, and investment: Alster (1974, p. 15), Astour (1972, p. 24; 1981b, pp. 22, 25), Bauer (1975, p. 205), Bogaert (1970, pp. 244-6), Butz (1979, p. 365), Dougherty (1930), Einzig (1962, pp. 15-16), Farber (1978, p. 10), Fine (1952-53, p. 253), Finkelstein (1956, pp. 141-2), Foster (1977, p. 32), Gadd (1975, p. 38), Heltzer (1978a, p. 149), Hillers (1971, p. 259), Larsen (1974, p. 470; 1977b), Leemans (1960a, pp. 30-1, 36-7), Lichtheim (1976, II, pp. 135, 138), Morgan (1927, pp. 153-8), Na'aman (1981, pp. 176-7), Olmstead (1948, pp. 82-5), Oppenheim (1954; 1969a, note 2, p. 199; 1974, pp. 231-2), Orlin (1970, note 91, p. 60), Postgate (1976, p. 293), Pruessner (1927), Rainey (1967), Röllig (1976, p. 293), Sasson (1966, p. 135), Tsevat (1958, p. 113), Udovitch (1979, p. 268), Veenhof (1978, p. 292; 1982, note 13, p. 157), and Zaccagnini (1977, pp. 181-2; 1978, p. 235).

16. Sources on contractual slavery: Artzi and Malamat (1971, p. 80), Astour (1970, pp. 116-19), Bakir (1952, pp. 119-20), Balkan (1974, notes 2, 13, p. 30), Gelb (1973, pp. 77, 92), Giorgadze (1982, pp. 110-12), Harris (1955, p. 99), Hinz (1973b, p. 21), Hoffner (1968, pp. 36, 39; 1974, p. 117), Klengel (1975, pp. 193-6), Leemans (1950a, p. 17), Lipiński (1982, p. 176), McNeil (1970, pp. 64-8), Meek (1969a, p. 220; 1969a, pp. 170-1), Mendelsohn (1949, pp. 14-19), Oppenheim (1967a, p. 91), Postgate (1976, p. 48), Siegel (1947, p. 23), H. Thompson (1941, p. 75), Veenhof (1978, pp. 289-91) and Yaron (1969, p. 72).

Distraint for debt is also assumed in paragraphs 22-4 of the Eshnunna Code (Goetze 1969a, p. 162) and in paragraph 44 (Tablet B) of the twelfth-century Assyrian laws (Meek 1969c, p. 184).

17. Sources on the economics of slavery: Barzel (1977), Fogel and Engerman (1970, p. 145), Gelb (1965, pp. 230-1); 1980, p. 35), Graves *et al.* (1983, pp. 156-7), and Shlomovitz (1979, p. 572).

18. Sources on migration of craftsmen: Brinkman (1981, pp. 33-6); Bubenik (1974); Dandamayev (1975, especially p. 78), Giorgadze (1982, pp. 113-14), Sasson (1968, pp. 51-4), H.S. Smith (1976, p. 186), Uchitel (1984, p. 275), and Zaccagnini (1983a, pp. 258-64).

19. Conceivably, Manishtushu's land purchase and those by Sumerian and Egyptian officials in the third millennium (see Chapter 7) might be cases of 'eminent domain' or even disguised confiscation, but there is no evidence that we are dealing with anything but an ordinary sale.

20. Sources on the Babylonian land market: Ahmed (1968, pp. 145-7), K.T.M. Atkinson (1972, pp. 45, 57-9, 73-4), Bottéro (1967, p. 114), Clay (1938), Diakonoff (1974, pp. 47-52), Gelb (1971; 1979, pp. 47-52), Hallo (1964, pp. 57, 61), Harris (1975, pp. 213-14), Kramer (1963, p. 75; 1969b, p. 160), Krecher (1976), Leemans (1975, pp. 137-8; 1983, pp. 53-4, 61-2, 72-3), Oates (1978, p. 477), Oppenheim 1954, note 16, p. 10; 1955), Pruessner (1930, pp. 219, 232), Rabinowitz (1961, pp. 59-61, 71-3), Roth (1980, pp. 131-3, 139-40), Skaist (1975, pp. 244-5), Spar (1972, pp. 83-4), Struve (1969, pp. 34, 41), and Yaron (1958).

The oldest records of land transactions are pictographs from the twenty-seventh century. In the Ur III Dynasty there are no clear cases of field sales, but there are two contracts that may refer to private land sales. There are references to privately owned land, rental contracts, and sales of privately owned orchards (Gelb 1979, pp. 69-70), Leemans (1983, pp. 91-2). In the Middle Babylonian period there are sales of extensive grain fields and land purchases by the ruler (Leemans 1983, pp. 73, 97).

21. Sources on land markets outside Babylonia: Baer (1962, pp. 25-6), Gadd (1975, p. 38), Helck (1975, pp. 280-1), Heltzer (1976a, pp. 92-5), Hinz (1973, p. 285), G.R. Hughes (1952, pp. 18, 75), Muffs (1969, p. 20), Postgate (1971, note 62, p. 513), Tucker (1963, p. 82), and Wiseman (1953, pp. 49-50).

22. Sources on Babylonian land prices: Diakonoff (1974, p. 51), Hallo (1981), Harris (1975, p. 277), Stone (1977, p. 272), and Zaccagnini (1979, pp. 5-6).

23. 'Subjects' is also the interpretation of van Selms (1958, p. 198), who notes that in Genesis 26:20 'the herdsmen of Gerar' maintain 'the water is ours', not 'the water belongs to the king'. (See also Kalluveettil's (1982, p. 10) discussion.) This interpretation is also supported by paragraph 129 of Hammurabi's Code: 'If the wife of a seignior has been caught while lying with another man, they shall bind them and throw them into the water. If the husband of the woman wishes to spare the wife, then the king may spare his slave.' Meek (1969b, p. 171) is justified in rendering 'slave' as 'subject'. The Egyptian word *ndt*, sometimes rendered 'serf' or 'slave', had the meaning 'subject, taxpayer' in the fifteenth century (see Lorton 1974, p. 115, note 4, p. 163, and the discussion of 'ports of trade' under Assertion 1, p. 76).

24. Sources on witnesses or joint claimants versus vendors: Edzard (1967a, p. 75), Jelínkova (1957, pp. 50-1), Labuschagne (1974, pp. 176-7), Leemans (1983, pp. 54-9), Marzal (1971, pp. 203-4), Meek (1969c, p. 186), Mendelsohn (1959), Mettinger (1971, p. 106), Oppenheim (1948, p. 141; 1955, p. 90), H. Thompson (1941, pp. 74-5), and Yaron (1960a, pp. 387-91).

The procedure for identifying cases in which vendors are large groups seems suspect: 'Under sellers, we include all individuals who received gifts in return for their sold property, that is, both primary sellers (who received the price and gifts) and secondary sellers or primary witnesses (who received only gifts)' (Gelb 1979, p. 69). Why should those who received 'gifts' for undertaking to validate the sale against future legal challenges be classified among the sellers?

J. Lewy (1961, p. 39) has noted the prevalence of relatives as witnesses to the transactions of the Assyrian merchants involved in the Cappadocian trade.

25. Sources on the antiquity of Near Eastern communes: Diakonoff (1974b, p. 535), Komoróczy (1978, pp. 9, 12), and Leemans (1983, pp. 74-5). J.A. Brinkman (personal correspondence) informs me that the household communes of the Kassite period are attested only for the periphery of Mesopotamia, not for Babylonia proper. Numerous new population centres emerged in the sixteenth to fifteenth centuries (see Leemans 1983, pp. 72-6). A recent study of I.S. Sventskaya (1976, p. 63), accessible to me only in an English summary, concludes: 'In the Homeric poems the territorial village finds no reflection . . . On the contrary, . . . the epos seem to reflect communities where all the land was divided into individual holdings (*kleroi; temene*) which were transmitted by inheritance to male descendants of the holders.'

26. Sources on the evolution of the commune: *Russia* — Toumanoff (1981, p. 183), see also D. Atkinson (1983, pp. 7-11), Blum (1971, pp. 162-3), Hellie (1971, p. 121), Kovalevsky (1891, pp. 95-6), and Sumner (1943, pp. 133, 140-6). *England* —Denman (1958, pp. 57-8, 88), Donkin (1973, p. 83), Finn (1973, pp. 25-9), and Vinogradoff (1904, pp. 196, 275-6, 319); see also Hoffman (1975, pp. 31, 44, 49) and Thirsk (1964, p. 7). *General* — de Vries (1976, p. 41). *Near East* — Heltzer (1978b, pp. 7, 10), Leemans (1983, pp. 74-5, 97), Malamat (1962, pp. 145-9), and T.L. Thompson (1978, p. 9).

According to Heltzer (1976b, pp. 23, 25), 'it is definitely clear' that in Ugarit 'the village as a whole had the collective responsibility for performing obligatory labor' and paying royal tithes. I have as yet been unable to locate concrete evidence of agricultural communes at Ugarit. Heltzer (1969, p. 37) does, however, cite a text mentioning the *sbr* in six villages, a term that may refer to local communal assemblies. On the other hand, it appears that Mycenaean Greece knew the agricultural commune under the term *damos*. The *damos* is encountered as owner and leaser of land, and, in one text, it determines that land held by a priestess is subject to taxation (see Mylonas 1966, pp. 266-7). It is of interest in this connection that the Ma tablets fix tax assessments by town (Shelmerdine 1973).

27. The term 'feudalism' is best reserved for a decentralised political system involving franchises: see Auster and Silver (1979, pp. 38-9).

28. Sources on public land grants: Batto (1980, pp. 227-9), Fabricus (1929), Ganshof (1964, part III, chapters 1, 2), Goedicke (1971-72, p. 74), Goetze (1969b, p. 191), Gurney (1966, pp. 102-3), Heltzer (1976b, pp. 53-4; 1982, pp. 20-37, 98), Hillers (1971), Hoffner (1973, p. 209), Killen (1979), Labuschagne (1974, pp. 179-80), Leemans (1950a, note 118, pp. 41, 43), J. MacDonald (1980, pp. 54-9), Malamat (1962, p. 149), Meek (1969b, pp. 167-8), Mireaux (1959, pp. 52-4, 107-9, 149, 155), Mettinger (1971, p. 81), Postgate (1971, pp. 508-12), Saggs (1962, pp. 166, 237-8), and Speiser (1955, pp. 157-62, 164).

29. Sources on intrafamily land sales: Goetze (1969a, p. 163), Heltzer (1976a, p. 90), Marcus (1983), Meek (1969c, p. 185), and T.L. Thompson (1974, pp. 281-4).

R. Wilson (1983, p. 8) observes that in today's Middle East:

Customers frequently go to a moneychanger who is a member of the same family, tribe, or religious sect, as is the case with other souk business . . . Customers from other towns and cities often knew by the names of the establishments who belonged to what religion, and their sect or tribal grouping . . . There is little sign that such affiliations are breaking down, indeed, in many parts of the Middle East they seem to be growing stronger.

30. Sources on the slave market: Bakir (1952, pp. 29, 91), Boese (1973, pp. 148-50), Edzard (1967a, pp. 76-9), Farber (1978, pp. 12-14), Harris (1972, p. 104; 1975, pp. 342-4), Hayes (1955, pp. 128-30), Jozef Janssen (1955, p. 64), H. Lewy (1964b, pp. 184-5), Meek (1969b, pp. 167, 177), Mendelsohn (1949, pp. 34-42, 106, 113-15), Mercer (1914, p. 205), Paradise (1980, pp. 205-7), Peet (1932, p. 123), Postgate (1976, p. 26), Struve (1969, p. 54), H. Thompson (1934,

p. xvi), Veenhof (1978, p. 26), J.A. Wilson (1948, pp. 144-5), and Yaron (1959, p. 169; 1969b, pp. 31, 183-5).

An Egyptian lawsuit (Papyrus Cairo 65739) of the second half of the second-millennium raises the possibility that merchants travelled from house to house (residential? commercial?) offering slaves for sale (see Gardiner 1935, pp. 141-2, 145).

Sources on the problems of adverse selection and moral hazard: Akerlof (1970), Arrow (1974, pp. 35-6), Ehrlich and Becker (1972), Greenwald and Glasspiegel (1983), and Silver (1981, pp. 113-14).

31. Sources on wage labour: Badawy (1983, p. 669), Černý (1932), Diakonoff (1974a, p. 50), Dubberstein (1938, p. 39), Farber (1974, pp. 58-9), Finley (1973, p. 65), Fish (1953), Gelb (1965, pp. 242-3), Giveon (1978, p. 54), Goetze (1962), Grayson (1972, note 64, p. 20), Harris (1975, pp. 245-6), Jones and Snyder (1961, p. 255), Klengel (1971b, pp. 42, 47-8), Leemans (1960b, pp. 90-2, 103, 108), Mueller (1975, note 25, p. 255), Snell (1982, p. 12), Steinkeller (1981a, p. 124), Struve (1969, pp. 41, 50), and Walters (1970, p. 35).

32. Sources on the supply response: Fensham (1967, p. 221), Forbes (1964, IX, p. 93), Holmes (1975, p. 91), Howard-Carter (1981, pp. 222-3), Larsen (1976, p. 89), J. Lewy (1958a, p. 91), Malamat (1971, p. 31), Millard (1973), Muhly (1980, pp. 42-4, note 40, p. 58), Oppenheim (1954, p. 10), Roaf (1982), Veenhof (1972, pp. 103-9), and Wheeler *et al.* (1979).

33. Sources on comparative advantage and textile exports: H.E.W. Crawford (1973, p. 236), Delougaz (1967, pp. 196-8), Gelb (1972, pp. 3-4), Leemans (1960, pp. 98-9, 140; 1968, p. 179), Oppenheim (1970, pp. 131-2), Pettinato (1981, pp. 202-6), Veenhof (1977, pp. 114-15). Note that the export success of Yorkshire in the sixteenth to seventeenth centuries was based on its production of cheap woollen cloth of excellent value.

34. The identification of Tell Beit Mirsim with biblical Debir has been challenged by Kochavi (1974), who prefers Khirbet Rabûd.

35. Originally (c. 4000), faience was made by heating shaped pieces of soapstone covered with one of the ores of copper so that the surface of the object became a blue-coloured glass. Later, in Predynastic times, the soapstone was replaced by a synthetic material made by heating quartz, sand, and soda until the sand particles fused (Hodges 1977, pp. 62-4). Aldred (1978, pp. 17, 30) suggests that the search 'for a dark blue substance which imitated the expensive imported lapis lazuli .. was pursued with all the diligence that European chemists in the eighteenth century AD exercised in their endeavors to imitate Chinese porcelain.'

36. Sources on investment in captial goods: Aldred (1978, pp. 17, 30), Badawy (1967, pp. 103, 107), Baldacci (1981), Burke (1964, p. 71), H.E.W. Crawford (1973, pp. 234-5), Dubberstein (1938, pp. 36-7), Edelstein and Gibson (1982), Emery (1961, p. 203; 1967, p. 174), Erman (1971, p. 506), Fairservis (1962, pp. 81-2, 115), Foster (1977, note 93, p. 38), Har-El (1977, p. 77), Heltzer (1978a, p. 118), Kadish (1966, pp. 23-5), Kemp (1983, pp. 131, 135-6), Klengel (1980), Kramer (1963, p. 109), Leemans (1960c, p. 234), Lichtheim (1976, II, p. 25), McCown (1943), Montet (1981, pp. 182, 184, 189), Oppenheim (1970, note 46, p. 144), Oppenheim and Reiner (1977, pp. 84, 312), Petrie (1923, pp. 160, 185-7), Pirenne (1961, I, p. 269), Pritchard (1962), Pruessner (1930), Sasson (1966b, note 6, p. 172), Säve-Söderbergh (1946, pp. 13-18), Sayed (1978, p. 71), H.S. Smith (1976, pp. 181-6), W.S. Smith (1965, pp. 39-40), Stager (1982, p. 118), Stolper (1974, I, pp. 191-3), Trigger (1976, pp. 46, 85-6), and Vercoutter (1967b, pp. 378-9).

37. Sources on investment in human capital: Charvát (1979, p. 16), C.J. Eyre (in press), Goetze (1969b, p. 197), Meek (1969b, p. 175), and Samuel (1966, p. 84).

6 THE CREDIBILITY OF MARKETS

Assertion 8

Not Babylon but rather Athens may have . . . to be credited with
the possession of the first important city market . . . [Second
millennium] Babylon . . . possessed no markets . . . [Note also]
the coexistence of the Mediterranean emporium of Tyre with
its Palestinian hinterland, whose towns, as a rule, contained no
marketplaces . . . And it was not backward Attica, but in Asia
Minor that we first meet, as late as the seventh century B.C. . . .
the retailing of food in the local market of Salamis. (Polanyi
1981, pp. xl, 78-9, 146)

Polanyi (1981, p. 124) explains his preoccupation with the absence of
marketplaces as follows: 'Obviously, the market as a *place* preceded
any competitive mechanism of the supply-demand type.' It should be
noted first that although markets require mechanisms enabling traders
to communicate, they do not require face-to-face gatherings of all
traders. Nevertheless, Polanyi's assertion is rather surprising because
marketplaces — that is, the geographic concentration of transactions
— are a predictable adaptation to high costs of information and
transportation. There is, however, ample evidence of marketplaces in
the ancient Near East.

Textual Evidence for Marketplaces

Oppenheim (1970) provides evidence from third millennium Sumer
for food pedlars who sold imports such as salt and wine, as well as
domestic beer, roasted grain, pots, and alkali (used for soap). The
Leningrad Larsa project concluded that in the early second-
millennium city dwellers purchased food with silver (see also the
discussion of Assertion 9 below). 'Bought bread' is referred to in a
Babylonian letter (see p. 82). Of course, we lack reliable evidence on
the relative importance of such purchases. A royal inscription from
early second-millennium Assyria refers to the prices of barley, wool,
and oil in Assur. At roughly the same time, a ruler erected in the
city of Susa a stela stating the appropriate prices for various
merchandise. In the Bible, Nehemiah 13:16 (dating to the fifth

century) tells of the 'men of Tyre . . . who brought in fish, and all manner of ware, and sold on the sabbath unto the children of Judah, and in Jerusalem.'

The larger of the Assyrian commercial stations in Cappadocia were called *kārum*, a word whose original meaning appears to be 'embankment, quay'. A text from southern Babylonia records the ownership of land in the *kārum*, and another concerns the sale of a house in the 'fish *kārum*'; various documents refer to the sale of grain, wool, and slaves at the *kārum*. Note also the Egyptian word *mryt*, meaning 'quay' or 'marketplace'. An unsuccessful attempt to sell some cloth on the 'bank' is reported in an early twelfth-century Egyptian text (Ostraca University College, 19614, Setnakht).

The term for 'streets' (Akkadian *sūqu*), often found in the documents, also connotes a marketplace. Sumerian texts of the second half of the third millennium speak of goods being 'on the street', and tablets of the first half of the second millennium refer to the *suq šimātim* or 'commercial street'. The *sāhirum* or 'retailer' sold goods on the 'street'. A text from Sippar mentions rows of contiguous shops of goldsmiths (or moneychangers — see the discussion of Assertion 9, p. 125). Fifteenth-century Nuzi had a 'street of fowlers'. Similarly, Jeremiah 37:21 refers to a 'baker's street' in Jerusalem. The Bible also notes streets in commercial contexts in 1 Kings 20:34 and, probably, Ezekiel 26:11-12. 'Gates', actually the areas around them, also served as marketplaces. Wool, perhaps royally owned, is 'placed at the gate' in a late third-millennium text. A will from Nuzi includes a clause that the inherited property 'to anyone at the gate she [the wife] may not sell' (Beich 1963, pp. 44-5). Note also the evidence of grain sales at Samaria's gate in the ninth century (2 Kings 7:1). Babylonian and Assyrian texts of the first millennium speak of the 'gate of buying'. Several of the gates of Jerusalem appear to have specialised in particular kinds of merchandise: the 'Fish Gate' (Zephaniah 1:10; 2 Chronicles 33:14; Nehemiah 3:3), the 'Sheep Gate' (Nehemiah 3:1, 32; 12:39), and the 'Pottery Gate' (Jeremiah 19:2). A suggestion of pronounced geographic specialisation is found at Athens (as Polanyi suggested) in the inclination of Athenian writers to identify places in the Agora with the goods sold there (wine, olive oil, pots, garlic, fish, perfume, clothes). Early empire Rome had a number of markets specialising in different types of slaves. The clustering of similar economic activities is, of course, a feature of today's Middle Eastern souk.

Economic Importance of the Geographic Concentration of Similar Trades

In a world without daily newspapers and the like, the location of similar trades in a compact area served to reduce the cost to consumers of acquiring information about prices and product characteristics. The resulting increase in the amounts of search (including more frequent shopping trips) and information reduces price dispersion and helps traders interpret market signals accurately. (There is little variation in charges amongst different moneychangers in the same souk.) The gains from reducing travel time between shops would, of course, be greatest for highly standardised goods and for 'search goods' whose quality is easily ascertained by inspection. For irregular and 'experience goods' whose quality is evaluated after purchase during the process of consumption, the extensive margin of search — that is, obtaining additional price quotations — decreases in importance relative to the intensive margin of search — obtaining more information about each offer.

It is well to note, however, that advertising was not unknown in antiquity. Information was conveyed by tablets posted on the gate and by public criers in the commercial streets. The echo of the marketplace is heard in the Second Isaiah's (Isaiah 55:1) call to 'come and buy wine and milk without money and without price.' The twelfth-century Assyrian laws call for the herald to make several announcements before the sale of land is finalised and registered. Early second-millennium Babylonian texts show us the *mušaddinu*, 'collection officer' (literally, 'one who causes to give') who 'calls' (*šasû*) for the performance of compulsory labor and the payment of debt. Also, the loss of a Sumerian merchant's seal was announced in the streets by a horn-blowing herald '(so that) no one may have any claim against him' (Ali 1964).

Additional Textual Evidence for Marketplaces

There are many references to the *bābtum*, a term arguably derived from *bābum*, 'gate' (also 'city quarter'). Second-millennium texts record that the copper of several individuals lies at Assur in the *bābtum* and show merchants using silver from the *bābtum*. Edward Lipiński (personal correspondence) has called my attention to the *bāb abulli*, an expression designating the gate as the place where business is transacted. Another term, *maḥīru*, often has an abstract meaning (for example, 'market value') but Röllig, who has studied this term, explains that it also describes a concrete location for the 'receiving' (*maḥāru*) of goods. An 'omen text' predicts that 'the people will bring their possessions to the market', and another early Babylonian text explicitly links such sales with famine. A letter includes the instruction to buy two bags 'at the market'. Loans were repaid 'at the market'. A Nuzi tablet describes itself as being written 'at the market'. Captured Arab camels are sold at 'market gates' in the seventh century. In each instance, Röllig points out, the term *maḥīru* is used.

An Assyrian contract of the first half of the second millennium deals with the sale of some real estate near the '(city) square' (*ri-be-tim*). Genesis 10:11 refers, according to Speiser (1964, p. 68) to 'Assur' building, in the thirteenth to twelfth century (?), 'public squares' (*rᵉḥōbōt iŕ*); ninth-century Assyrian sources mention city squares (e.g. *rebīt* Nineveh). Babylonian texts reveal that cities such as Sippar possessed a 'place' (*ribītu*) in which were located shops (*bīt maḥirim*) and taverns. The Gilgamesh Epic mentions Uruk-*rebītu*. Dahood (1981, pp. 301, 307) even suggests that in the mid-third millennium the city marketplaces of Ebla were identified by the element *mar-*, for example, 'the exchange (or shopping center)' of Canaanite Taanach or Aphek.[1] He adds that the name of the city Carchemish means the 'trading center of the god Chemish'. Also of interest in this connection is the etymological link between the Hittite words for market (*ḥappar* or *ḥappir*) and city (*ḥappira*).[2]

Archaeological Evidence for Marketplaces

Buildings thought to have incorporated shops have been excavated not only at ports such as Ugarit but at inland sites, including first-millennium Hazor in northern Israel, mid-second-millennium Jericho, in the early second-millennium strata at Kanesh — the main Assyrian commercial station in Anatolia — where a small open square was also excavated, and in third-millennium Eshnunna. The four ovens believed to be capable of baking leavened bread found in one Eshnunna structure suggest a bakery. Several Jericho shops contained rows of jars full of grain, and one structure housed a grain-milling establishment. The excavators of Assur found near the 'Gate of the Coppersmiths' houses whose rooms had wide openings onto the street. Rooms entirely open at the front, suggesting a 'showroom', were also excavated at early second-millennium Ur. Excavation in a Hittite city of the second millennium uncovered the remains of a grain shop or food store, including a 'bar' of mudbrick. Catering facilities have also been found at Kanesh and Tory.[3]

Assertion 9

Even in highly stratified archaic societies such as Sumeria, Babylonia, Assyria, the Hittites or Egypt, storage economies prevailed; and, in spite of large-scale use of money as a standard, its use for indirect exchange was negligible. This may, incidentally, explain the complete absence of coins in the great civilizations of Babylonia and Egypt . . . [In] Asia Minor . . . we first meet, as late as the seventh century B.C. the use of coined money. (Polanyi 1981, pp. 119-20)

Economic Significance of Money

From the perspective of standard economic analysis the main advantage of an exchange money system over a barter system is that it lowers trading costs by reducing both the average number of transactions a trader must participate in and the number of prices he must know. Money reduces the required number of two-way market channels and makes circuitous trade patterns viable. The disadvantage is that it requires a society to make a significant investment of scarce resources in increasing its stock of the money commodity and in creating a new capital good, a general agreement or convention to use some specific commodity (or commodities) for this function. It will not pay a society to make the investment until economic development has increased the division of labour and the number and variety of goods traded, and, consequently, has elevated search costs beyond some level. At this point, however, the introduction of exchange money contributes to economic development by lowering transaction costs and thereby facilitating further increases in the number and variety of goods, the number of transactors, the extent of economic specialisation, including professional middlemen and specialised traders, and the diversity of the credit market. Armen Alchian (1977, p. 139) has put forward an alternative approach tracing the origin of money to the costliness of information about attributes of the goods available for exchange.

> If costs for some goods are low and generally low across members of society, the good will become a medium through which information costs can be reduced and exchange made more economical. But it will rise only with the rise of chains of experts in various goods and commodities, who know the goods cheaply,

whose reputation for reliable evaluation is high, and who, because of that knowledge and low cost of assuring buyers, become specialist middlemen and buying and selling agents.

Thus Alchian's theory, like the standard version, suggests that money will be introduced only when economic development has carried specialisation to a certain point. Barter exchange, of course, would tend to persist in commerce with moneyless communities, with those having different money commodities, and where the number of traded commodities was small. Brunner and Meltzer add the observation that the magnitude of money's net social productivity increases with the rapidity of economic development — that is, the rate of introduction of new products, methods, and markets. Polanyi qualifies his argument to the point of incoherence, but his thrust is unmistakable: exchange money appears as an adjunct of market exchange, so the absence of exchange money implies the absence or at least the unimportance of market exchange.[4]

The Use of Money in Near Eastern Antiquity

In fact, the ancient Near East knew money very well in the generic sense of a common medium of exchange. Mesopotamian texts of the middle of the second half of the third millennium already show us street vendors, and, according to Foster (1977, notes 47 and 48, pp. 35-6), the use of silver to pay rents and purchase dates, oil, barley, animals, slaves, and real estate; in addition, 'Silver was widely used in personal loans and was often in possession of private citizens and officials. A businessman might have silver on deposit at various places.' (It would not be surprising if the combination of relatively high communication costs, gaps in markets for income-earning assets, and the vulnerability of the ancient economy to shocks operated to increase the demand of business enterprises for cash balances.) Documents from late in the third-millennium make reference to 'silver of deliveries' (for paying for deliveries) and silver for buying cassia, salt, and tin (Hallo 1963, pp. 138-9). M. Lambert, who studied sale contracts, loan documents, and tax receipts, found that silver was used by many levels of society, not just by merchants. Silver also served as a medium of exchange during the earlier second millennium. In Babylonia the price of silver in terms of barley was some 7.5 times greater than in Cappadocia, where silver, being the main export good, was presumably in abundant supply. Much or even most of this silver may have served to augment the money stock of the importing region.

Silver was employed to make small payments at this time, for instance, paying a courier to deliver a letter or to purchase some fish for a meal. It was also used to pay for slaves, temple offices, house rentals, fields, and a large consignment of paint. Indeed, in the law codes dating from the era (Hammurabi's Code, Laws of Eshnunna) the tort law sometimes calls for restitution in kind but usually requires payment in silver. The monetary restitution feature is also found in the laws of Ur-Nammu (late twenty-second century), the Lipit-Ishtar Code (twentieth century), the Hittite Laws (third quarter of the second millennium), and even in the supposedly 'tribal' Covenant Code in Exodus 21:33-34: 'And if a man shall dig a pit . . . and an ox or an ass fall therein, the owner of the pit shall make it good; he shall give silver to the owner of them . . . And if one man's ox hurts another's so that it dies; then they shall sell the live ox, and divide the price of it.' In fifteenth-century Alalakh copper was employed as a means of payment. During the New Kingdom in the second half of the second millennium Egypt knew the payment of taxes and the sale of land, slaves, oxen, cloth, barley, meat, cakes, wine, and honey for gold and silver and, in addition, interest-bearing loans of gold. A much earlier inscription of the twenty-fourth century mentions that craftsmen were paid copper (see also the next section, on evidence for coinage).[5]

The evidence is mounting that in Mesopotamia coils (Sumerian *ḫar*; Akkadian *šewirum*) of metal — mainly silver but also gold, bronze, lead, tin, and copper — served monetary purposes in the late third millennium and earlier second millennium. They were manufactured in standard sizes corresponding (roughly at least) to multiples of the shekel and could be used for exchange by placing entire coils or pieces on a balance and weighing them. (Visual evidence possibly reflecting a similar practice is provided by a scene from an Egyptian tomb of the second half of the second millennium where an individual is weighing out coils of metal.) 'Ring money' is mentioned in the Mari texts and is common in Babylonian texts of the early second millennium. Note also Genesis 24:22 wherein Abraham's agent gives Rebecca 'a golden ring of half a shekel weight, and two bracelets of ten shekels weight of gold' (see also Job 42:11). Nippur texts of the late third millennium refer to silver that is 'broken' or in 'pieces'. From roughly the twenty-third to the fifth century Mesopotamian texts call a type of silver used in payments *šibirtu*. Several scholars understand the term to mean a block or lump of silver. Powell, however, argues for interpreting *šibirtu* as scrap silver or fragments. The Assyrian documents from Cappadoca demonstrate that small payments were settled in tin, the *annak qatim*, literally 'tin of hand'. Slightly later Babylonian texts cited by Stol refer to 'loose' silver (*pit-rum*). 'Beaten copper' or 'copper in beaten state' was used by Egyptian traders to make up differences in the values of the goods they exchanged in the middle of the second half of the second millennium (Černý 1954, p. 907).

Mesopotamian sale documents of as early as the second half of the third millennium refer to weighing of silver paid out by the 'smith' (compare the discussion of Assertion 8, p. 119). In Ur the metals disbursed by Lú-^{d}Enki 'the smith', possibly an official of Ibbi-Sin (2028-2004), often take the form of rings of various weights. Hoards of precious metals found at various Near Eastern sites dating from as early as the middle of the third millennium are often referred to as *Hacksilber* ('cut-silver'). Balmuth (1975, p. 296) suggests that: 'Although many of these have been called silversmith's hoards the practicability of exchange by weight suggests that *Hacksilber* could simultaneously be both material for a jeweller and material for exchange.' Loewe (1955, pp. 146-7) reflects on 2 Kings 12, which records that in the ninth century

> a collection-box for a repairs fund was set up in the Temple with a hole bored . . . (v. 10) in its lid for the reception of (presumably) small fragments of silver (*Hacksilber*). When some quantity had been collected, the officers concerned *tied it up* (v. 11, *warrāsūrū*) and counted it out (. . . v. 12, *hakkeseph ham^{e}thukkān*).

In Genesis 42:25 and 44:1 we find that Jacob's sons, travelling to Egypt to purchase grain, carried 'money sacks' (or, perhaps, 'tied pieces of money'). The money sack or bundle (*seror kesep*) is also found in Proverbs 7:19-20 wherein a woman seeks to entice her lover by telling him: 'For my husband is not at home, he is gone on a long journey; he has taken the bag of money with him.' The hymn to the god Shamash recorded on Assyrian tablets dating from the seventh century refers to the merchant as 'he who bears the bag (*nāš kīsi*)'. The *naruqqum* and, somewhat later, the *kīsum* in which merchants carried their money assumed the meaning 'business capital'. A text of the earlier second millennium includes the request: 'Open my money bag and [. . .] a ring of sufficient weight'. Interestingly, Egyptian market scenes of the middle of the third millennium show traders with small linen sacks tied behind their shoulders. The linen sacks appear considerably smaller than the sacks for carrying wares to the market, and thus may be for money (see Hodjash and Berlev 1980, p. 45).

The Cappadocian texts refer to several kinds of money (for example, 'fine'), probably identifying differences in metal quality, as Garelli points out. References to the quality of gold are also found in Egyptian texts of the later second millennium. All of this evidence, of course, testifies to a considerable sophistication of metalworking techniques.[6]

Evidence for Coinage

The evidence regarding the origins of coinage and its presumed absence in the ancient Near East is not nearly so plain as Polanyi suggests. To begin with, references to 'tied pieces of money' recall the earlier second millennium's sealed bags of silver (*kaspum kankum*) mentioned in the discussion of banking under Assertion 5, pp. 87-8). (Sealed silver is also noted in the texts of the late third millennium.) It is quite interesting that in eleventh-century-CE Egypt and North Africa and earlier in Rome and Carthage, and in Talmudic times (see Tobias 1:14; 4:1, 20; 5:3; 9:5), various coins (and metal fragments?) were kept in purses labelled on the outside with the number of coins and sealed by governments or private merchants. In addition to keeping the coins 'fresh' — that is, preserving their full weight — Udovitch (1979, p. 267) who studied medieval Islam explains that

> These packaged and labelled purses made settlement of accounts much more convenient . . . by obviating the need to weigh, array, and evaluate coins for every individual transaction. Significantly, most payments and transfers of funds were executed by the actual physical transfer of the purses.

In short, the sealed purses were large-denomination coins. That the *kaspum kankum* played the same part is suggested by eighteenth-century contracts from Larsa requiring merchants to pay for palace-owned goods with 'sealed silver'. In one tablet the source of 'sealed silver' is a certain Sin-uselli, possibly the person whose seal inscription identifies him as 'Assayer of the House of Truth (*bīt kittim*) of Ur' and 'Servant of (King) Samsuiluna' (Stol 1982, pp. 150-1). Heichelheim (1958, I, p. 110) refers rather tersely in this connection to 'pots and leather bags which we have found officially sealed . . . in Bronze Age Egypt.'⁷

Although they are in the minority, some Egyptologists believe that Egypt knew a silver coin in the later second millennium. The foundation of their belief is the expression of prices in terms of the 'piece' — that is, a weight, the word for which, *shaty* (or *seniu*), is always written ideographically. It is significant that this term denotes the seal of a signet ring in a magical text. Note in this connection that *sēma*, the Greek word for mark or token, has been found on seventh- and sixth-century coins from the temple of Artemis at Ephesus: 'This is the mark of Phanes.' Balmuth (1971, p. 3), after summarising the evidence, concludes that 'the Ephesus coin [is] . . . the equivalent of a sealed piece of pre-weighed metal.' Visual evidence of the *shaty* in use may, perhaps, be provided in a scene from a thirteenth-century tomb at Thebes. As described by Glanville (1935, p. 36), the scene

> shows a woman in a booth . . . In front of the woman is a basket, behind her a stand with a wine jar and a beer jar on it. A man is taking away a skin, presumably containing beer or wine, in exchange for two white circular objects. These have been taken to be bread, but it seems more likely that they are enlarged representations of the *shaty*.

There is even an Egyptian inscription (on the Giza monument) of the middle of the third millennium in which the price of a house is quoted in this uncertain monetary unit. A market scene of the mid-Fifth Dynasty at Saggara shows two traders offering to exchange a roll of cloth for six *shat*. Ankhtyfy in a late third-millennium inscription cited in Chapter 4, section 1, p. 62, claimed that he paid for a 'house' (a tomb?) 'with my own copper' (Fischer 1961b, p. 62). A mysterious monetary unit is also found in Genesis 33:19, where Jacob purchases a parcel of land at Shechem 'for a hundred *kesitahs*' (see also Job 42:11). More directly relevant to the Egyptian data is the fact that the documents from Cappadocia refer to payments of metal 'of (or under) my seal', or 'of your seal', or 'of the seal' of a third party. Carlo Zaccagnini (personal correspondence) suggests that these references may be to 'intact parcels'. According to S. Smith (1922, p. 183) the 'mina of the *bīt karim*' is an official coin of the Assyrian trading colony (see also the discussion of Assertion 12, p. 137). There are also references in the earlier second millennium to silver 'of the seal of Babylon' and other cities.

Genesis 23:16, in which Abraham 'weighs' for Ephron's field the sum of 400 shekels of silver 'current money of the merchant' raises two important issues. First, how is 'weighing' to be understood in this context? Balmuth (1975, pp. 295-6) has suggested that words used for amount of money — Sumerian *MA-NA*, Akkadian *manu*, Hebrew *maneh*, and Greek *mna* — all derive from roots meaning 'to count' or 'to weigh' or 'to cut off'. Similarly, *shekel* is derived from *šql*, a root expressing the action of weighing. She adds, however, that the English pound and the Greek *statēr* and *talanton* evolved from weights into coins just as the meaning of Greek *koptein* and Aramaic *prs* changed from 'to cut' to 'to strike (coinage)'. Seen in this evolutionary perspective, the term 'weighed' may have come to mean 'paid'. (By means of a similar linguistic process, according to Loewe, the meaning of *serōr* drifted in meaning from the act of tying a bundle of silver to a purse for coins.) The expression 'current money of the merchant' may refer to a coin guaranteed by a merchant's stamp or seal. The coins from Ephesus mentioned earlier are quite possibly from the mint of a private merchant (or, alternatively, of a god) named 'Phanes'. It is known that fifth-century moneychangers in Israel personally guaranteed Greek and Persian coins by striking them with a countermark.

Ugaritic epics of the second half of the second millennium compare the flow of tears to quarter shekels or pieces-of-four and fifth-shekels or pieces-of-five. In 1 Samuel 9:8 Saul's servant has a quarter-shekel to give to the man of God. A stronger hint of coinage is provided in the annals of Assyria's Sennacherib (704-681): 'I caused a mold of clay to be set up and bronze to be poured into it as in making half a shekel.' The king is explaining how he cast great lions and bulls, using as S. Smith (1922, p. 178) explains, a process that was already known.[8]

Assyrian loan contracts of the eighth to seventh centuries record the advance of 'silver of (the goddess) Ishtar'. However, Lipiński argues cogently against interpreting this to mean temple capital. Such expressions, he points out, refer to metal quality and their inclusion in contracts makes no sense unless the metal is impressed with a stamp of guarantee. This stamp might have taken the form of the goddess's image or symbol. (Some temple loan tablets of the earlier second millennium display the crescent of Shamash or the sun disc of Sin.) Lipiński also points out that two contracts refer to 'loaves' of silver possessing the 'high degree of fineness of Ishtar', which may signify metals of a specified weight. His working hypothesis is that these temple-issued 'loaves' or coins were accepted without the necessity of expending resources in tests of metal quality and weight. Mentions of 'silver of Ishtar' or 'silver of Shamash' are found in cities of northern and southern Babylonia in the second-millennium. The legal documents of Alalakh knew 'silver of Ishtar' in the eighteenth century, and talent or 'loaves' (*kakkaru*; Ugaritic *kkr*, Hebrew *kikkar*, Akkadian *biltu*, Sumerian *GÚ/GÚUN*) appear in the fifteenth. An eighteenth-century letter from Mari about an inheritance and a letter originating in fourteenth-century Cyprus include the term 'silver of the gods' (*kasap ilim*). 'Silver (and) gold of the deity' are carried by the merchants of Ura is an epic-style Hittite text. (In these noncontractual examples, however, the mention of deities might merely signify metal of the highest quality.) Egyptian administrative documents and commercial contracts of the seventh and sixth century mention silver (from the treasuries?) of various gods (e.g. Harsaphes and Ptah). Arguably, they signify metal impressed with a temple's stamp.[9]

More concretely, several bread-shaped ingots inscribed with the name of an eighth-century king preceded by the Aramaic letter *lamed* were found in the palace of a north Syrian state (Zinjirli), located on the only good crossing of the Amanus mountains from east to west. What the possessive *lamed* means is uncertain. One possibility is that it means 'belonging to' in the sense of personal possession. Balmuth (1971, p. 3), however, suggests that it means 'on behalf of' or 'in the name of' (its meaning on later coins) and that the inscription represents a royal guarantee. The excavations at Assur uncovered lead ingots bearing a (now invisible) stamp and lead discs of various sizes stamped with a symbol on one side. S. Smith concedes that the discs might merely be ornaments rather than coins, but he maintains that the ingots are speciments of the 'sealed lead' encountered in the Cappadocian texts (compare the discussion of Assertion 5, p. 87). There is also the so-called 'Elamite coin', a three-quarter-inch square of silver with a fragmentary inscription found in a hoard near Kabul. But is this a coin or, as Grierson believes, a piece of silver with an owner's inscription that was probably cut from a tray or box-top? Unexplained markings have also been observed on the ox-hide copper ingots of the second half of the second millennium (see the section on 'The Supply Response' under Assertion 7, p. 108). An additional bit of archaeological evidence from a seventh-century site in Iran is a fragment of a silver bar with traces of cuneiform writing.[10]

The Question of Token Coinage

Such evidence as we have suggests that in various places and times the ancient Near East had at least partially guaranteed money, stamped by temple or merchant to lower transaction costs and facilitate the widening and intensification of market exchanges. The possibility even of a royally stamped 'token' coinage is indicated by a Babylonian word found in the seventh to sixth centuries, *nuḫḫutu*, and a later word, *ginnu*. (Briefly defined, a token coinage circulates for more than its commodity value.) The former word is found in a phrase often translated to mean 'low quality silver which has one-eighth alloy in each shekel' (Powell 1978, pp. 223-4). The use of a token money would have increased living standards by making the real resources employed in acquiring the medium of exchange — for example, in mining silver or in producing, say, cloth for export — available for alternative productive activities.

A token money would also reduce storage and transport costs.[11] The danger, as in our own times, was that governments seeking to increase their command over national output could have disrupted the economy by 'printing' excessive amounts of the token. In the end, the outcome of the imposition of an 'inflation tax' may have been a return to a strict commodity standard, whether or not the ruler agreed.

Interestingly, the ancient Near East experienced periods of steep price inflation. This happened in Babylonia during the period of Persian rule and much earlier in the late third millennium under Ibbi-Sin, the last ruler of the Ur III Dynasty. A tablet from the Persian period discussed by Levey (1959, p. 180) provides that 'stamped silver is not to be paid. Take pure silver . . .', and another reports: 'The lord sent me 20 shekels of silver . . . only 3 shekels . . . were of fine quality; the remainder was with the *ginnu*-mark.' (Apparently the melting down of silver pieces with the *ginnu*-mark was illegal.) Inflation is also found in Egypt during the later second-millennium in the middle of the Twentieth Dynasty under Rameses VII. Was it merely coincidental that prices ceased to be quoted in 'pieces' (see above) at about that time? The importance of token money would, however, be difficult to isolate because during the later Ramesside era the availability of gold, silver, and copper increased because of looting of temples and tombs.[12]

Assertion 10

Trade over the longest distances generally preceded that over shorter distances, just as the farthest colonies were usually founded first ... [Note] the preponderance of foreign over domestic trade in Hammurabi's Babylonia ... (Polanyi 1981, pp. liii, 78)

The allegation here is that whereas the more important long-distance trade is of an administered nature (compare Assertion 1, p. 73), local trade, with its presumably greater potential for regularised exchange of bulk items, is still in its infancy. In a strange way, Assertion 10 can be interpreted as an unconscious tribute to what Polanyi condescendingly calls 'economistic thinking'. If transport costs are put aside, differences in comparative advantage and, conseqently, in the gains from trade would tend to increase with the distance between trading partners. That is, due to differences in resources or technical knowledge, as the distance between two 'countries' increased, so would the difference between the slopes of their transformation curves for, say, cloth (C) and metal (M), for given C and M.

In fact, the available evidence does not demonstrate the preponderance of long-distance over local trade or the unimportance of local trade. Mesopotamian texts from the later third millennium provide clear evidence of inland navigation and trade in locally available products. Indeed, Snell, who studied texts of silver-balanced accounts from three merchants, composed in one city in the same month of the same year, found that in terms of silver value about 90 per cent of the goods acquired were of local Mesopotamian origin (e.g. fish, grain, leather, wool) and only about 10 percent were of foreign origin (e.g. fruits, spices, metals). Many Babylonian letters of the earlier second millennium refer to domestic trade, mostly by boat (for example, the *má-šě* 'grainboats' of the south). The ports of call were numerous, as were the goods transported: foodstuffs, wool, timber, bricks, metals, and so on. At the docks, ships and captains were available for hire, along with men and oxen to tow them.[13] Large quantities of wine were shipped from within Syria to Mari one shipment, probably from Carchemish, amounted to 1,100 gallons. In the early first-millennium Assyria's capital served traffic on the Tigris with a massive quay some thirty feet in depth constructed of dressed limestone blocks of at least a cubic yard. Rameses II (1290-1224, or 1304-1237) claims in a stela that he had 'brought by water Upper Egypt to Lower and Lower Egypt to Upper, in barley, emmer, wheat, ..., fruit(?), and beans without number' (Gardiner 1947, I, p. 21). Egyptian papyri of the later second-millennium confirm the internal transport by freighter of various goods, including oil, wine, olives, fish, cucumbers, salt, garments, and papyrus. Papyrus Lansing, in extolling the life of the scribe, recounts that: 'The merchants fare downstream and are as busy as copper, carrying wares (from) one town to another, and supplying him that hath not. But the tax-gatherers exact(?) gold, the most precious of all minerals(?)' (Blackman and Peet 1925, p. 288).[14]

Assertion 11

[The] livelihood [of the Mesopotamian trader known as the *tamkārum*] was not dependent on the commercial transaction in hand; it was secured by status revenue, mostly through landed property or at least through the claim to maintenance according to his rank from the royal or temple store ... The so-called 'Cappadocian' trading colony ... practiced a riskless type of business under fixed prices, the trader's profit being made on commission fees ... This is a far cry from the modern merchant who makes a living from the differences between buying and selling prices on the one hand, bad debts on the other. (Polanyi 1981, pp. xlii, 87, 138-9)

The implication is clear enough. It is difficult to conceive of business without risk-bearing businessmen. 'At some time before our era', Polanyi (1981, p. 139) explains, 'the figure of the *tamkārum* was replaced by a figure resembling that of the merchant.' The following response is intended merely to illustrate the independent business role of merchants, not to explore fully the long-debated topic of palace versus 'private' trade (but see Chapter 3) or to trace in detail the evolution of the *tamkārum*'s role and changes in the usage of the term. (For the latter the reader should consult Dandamayev 1971.)

Tamkārum and Dam-gàr

It is quite true that merchants sometimes receive land and appear on 'ration lists' together with other members of the royal household, but the evidence does not demonstrate that trade was monopolised by the ruler. Heltzer's disputed view is that Ugarit knew two categories of merchant; *tamkārū ša šēpi*, who were dependents of the king; and *tamkārū ša mandatti*, who clearly possessed their own trade goods and for whom there is no direct evidence that they traded with royal goods rather than their own. A list from Ugarit provides direct evidence of the private ownership of both heavy ships (*br*) and light ships (*ṯkt*): a tablet from the main palace concerns a merchant's (*mkr*) attempt to purchase ships. Elsewhere the king declared the vessel of Sinaranu the son of Siginu to be 'exempt from duty when it arrived from Kabtur' (Crete) (Strange 1980, p. 102). We also have texts in which private individuals, including merchants (*mkrm*), pay large sums of gold for trading concessions and the right to collect harbour taxes. In requesting payment for a shipment of lumber, the ruler of Cyprus informs Pharaoh that 'the people of my land murmur against me' (Liverani 1979a, note 42, p. 29). Why? Were the 'murmurers', so to say, 'stockholders' in a royal export enterprise? Or were they perhaps independent businesspersons seeking payment for their lumber? Somewhat earlier, *tamkārū* appear on royal ration lists at Nuzi, but individuals also employed them for their own business enterprises. Moreover, one lawsuit record cited by Zaccagnini testifies to the existence of self-employed merchants at least in the slave trade: a merchant who wished to sell a slave for 60 shekels of silver refused to heed the buyer's objection that a royal proclamation had fixed the maximum price at 30 shekels. Other texts show merchants of Nuzi borrowing from private lenders for business ventures.

During the earlier second-millennium there is little evidence connecting *tamkārum* and state (palace). The (*w*)*aklu* or *wakil tamkari* has been called a 'palace overseer'. Perhaps this is accurate. In the Cairo Geniza documents of the eleventh to twelfth centuries CE the *wākil* is the legal representative and agent of foreign merchants and not, at least not obviously, a government employee. In Babylonian texts of the eighteenth century BCE the *wakil tamkar* is noted in connection with *asīru*, quite probably foreign traders. Apparently, the *akil kar-ri* played a similar role at Ugarit. During the reign of Hammurabi and his son Samsuiluna over Larsa, the 'Overseer of Five' (*PA nam.5*) and the 'Overseer of Merchants' (*PA dam-gàr*; the *dam-gàr* is apparently the Sumerian counterpart of the Akkadian *tamkārum*) were involved in the collection and sale of tax-goods and the delivery of the proceeds to the palace. Stol (1982, p. 148), however, points out that 'Overseers of Five engaged in *private* commercial activities with the goods entrusted to them . . . This system would have made it possible for Shep-Sin [the Overseer of Merchants] to grant the many private short-terms loans of which we know.' Powell adds that although the balanced account documents of the late third-millennium were prepared by (or for) a central accounting agency, little in the accounts demonstrates that the merchants (*dam-gàr*) were employees of the state. The balance, he notes, might be privately loaned out. To place the asset, expenditure, and balance sections in economic perspective, it should be recalled that independent audits, whether initiated by private trading houses or government bureaus, are standard tools for monitoring the activities of businessmen operating with outside capital (see the discussion of Assertion 5 pp. 86-7).

The *dam-gàr* does not appear on royal ration lists during the middle of the second half of the third-millennium, according to Foster. Quite probably the *dam-gàr* was a private businessman who served various clients, including the palace. The business records of a couple in this period should be noted in this connection. The husband was involved in animal husbandry, while his wife made interest-bearing loans, sold wool, and took part in other transactions. A lengthy Eblaite text records the export of textiles to (or by) the merchants of various cities and the payment of a tax-in-textiles by 'Ishma-ya the merchant (*lú-kar*) of the city Mari'. The translator, Pettinato (1981, p. 114), reports that *lú-kar* ('the man of the commercial center') is employed more frequently at Ebla than *dam-gàr* and, moreover, 'another term *kas₄* or also *lú-kas₄* literally "messenger" . . . appears to be a merchant of the state while *lú-kar* refers to private businessmen.' (On the role of 'messengers' and 'commissioners' in the royal gift trade, see p. 37.)[15]

Veenhof's impression is that the Assyrians trading with Cappadocia were basically private businessmen, not government employees. This point is illustrated by a letter from a great merchant complaining that he was losing much profit because of delays in obtaining a loan needed to finance an enterprise. Merchants sent their goods to Cappadocia without guarantee of prices in advance, and, indeed, losses are often referred to. Merchants sometimes instructed their agents not to sell below a specified price and in other instances authorised sale 'at any price' (*batiq wattur*). A certain Pilahā wrote to Kulumā and Buzazu: 'As to the price of my *šilipka*-garment, your common interest should not be violated. Make as much as you can and send me (the proceeds) whether little or much' (Balkan 1967, p. 400). At roughly the same time the Persian Gulf trade with Tilmun was in the hands of merchants who styled themselves *ālik Tilmun* (best translated as the 'go-getters of Tilmun', according to Mallowan 1965b, p. 6). The *ālik Tilmun*, like those who consigned goods to

Cappadocia, were indeed risk-takers. Apparently, they were financed by private investors entitled to buy the copper they brought back at a contractually specified price but not responsible for any losses (*ibbisû*) of the venture. This arrangement bears some resemblance to the medieval *commenda* which held for the duration of one voyage with no liability of the agent toward the investor or of the investor toward third parties (compare the discussion of Assertion 5, pp. 88-9). One document shows us the sale of a share in a maritime venture. Lines 105-9 of the hymn to the god Shamash, probably of the seventh century, warn, according to the translations of Nakata (1971, p. 101) and Thomas (1958, pp. 108-9):

> As for him who invests money on a (short) term (in a trading mission?) and is lawless, what does he gain? He is disappointed about profit and loses his capital. As for him who invests on a long term (in a distant trading mission?) and multiplies a shekel to t[wo], is it not pleasing to Shamash, and he pro[longs] (his) life.

In line 69 of the hymn we read that Shamash 'saves from the storm the *tamkārum* carrying his capital', and there is a reference to the 'travelling *tamkārum*, the agent who is carrying capital' in line 139 (W.G. Lambert 1960).[16]

Merchants in Egypt

With respect to the claim that trading in Pharaonic Egypt was a virtual state monopoly, Jacob J. Janssen (1975a, p. 163) remarks that: 'At present there is not material to prove that this is what happened, although there is no document proving the contrary . . .' This conclusion is much too cautious. The lines from Papyrus Lansing quoted in the discussion of Assertion 10 show us merchants subject to the tax-collector, which, contrary to Reinecke's views, does not suggest that they were government employees. (Additional evidence on the taxation of Egyptian shipping is included in Chapter 1, pp. 19-21; and in the discussion of 'ports of trade' under Assertion 1, p. 76). Another papyrus dating to this period (1350-1200) refers to 'the itinerant merchant (who) sails downstream to the Delta to get trade for himself' (Wilson 1969c, p. 432). An inscription of Rameses II (1290-1224) reveals that temples turned over imported goods to merchants for marketing within Egypt, after which the merchants settled accounts ('taxes'?) with the temple administration. An earlier text (Papyrus Louvre E 3226) shows that departments of the royal administration regularly gave grain to specialised traders (*bnryw*) who, somewhat later, delivered dates. The terminology employed raises the possibility that the grain was sold and the proceeds used to purchase dates, or perhaps this was a barter transaction. The document does not disclose who produced the dates or where they originated. On the other hand, it is apparent that the date sellers were not government employees. According to Campbell (1970, p. 59) a papyrus of the fourteenth century from Kahun published in 1906 lists three business transactions involving private persons. (Unfortunately, I have been unable to obtain a translation of this text.)

That a private individual might own a cargo-boat is hinted in the late third-millennium tomb inscription of Qedes of Gebelein (see p. 44) and proven by the Edict of Haremhab dating from the second half of the fourteenth century. Papyrus Anastasi IV further demonstrates that even a seagoing vessel was not beyond the means of a rich man: a rich man is mentioned as using his ship to bring goods to Egypt from Syria. Also, as in Ugarit and Babylonia, there are references to 'the ship of Personal Name' (Säve-Soderbergh 1946, p. 61). Moreover, two other papyri concerned with merchants suggest that private commercial firms(*pr nb*; compare the discussion in section 4 of Chapter 2, p. 39) operated in Egypt as elsewhere in the Near East. Papyrus Lansing states that: 'The ship's crews of every "house" (firm) they take up their freights. They depart to Syria' (Blackman and Peet 1925, p. 288). The account of Wenamon provides strong hints that Syrian trading firms operated in late eleventh-century Egypt (compare the discussion of Assertion 1, pp. 73-4). Wenamon, who travelled to Lebanon to purchase lumber for the bark of the god Amon, was there informed by the king of Byblos: 'As for . . . Sidon . . . surely there are . . . fifty freighters there which are in commerce with Warkatara, for it is to his "house" that they haul' (Wente 1972, pp. 147-8, but compare Goedicke). Warkatar was probably a merchant operating from Tanis in the northeast portion of the Nile Delta.[17]

Assertion 12

Antiquity knows of no figure of a trader other than those who belonged either to the upper or to the lower class. The first is connected with rulership and government, the other depends

for his livelihood on manual labor. . . . The commercial middle
class of the nineteenth century is a late product of Western
development. (Polanyi 1981, p. 86)

We have seen that in the ancient Near East there were numerous
merchants who were not merely employees of the state. That merchant
firms varied in size and wealth is also evident from the documents. In
the Assyrian trade with Cappadocia the largest firms belonged to the
kārum. Note also that some Babylonian trading firms used agents of
varying degrees of independence. In Ugarit one merchant refers to the
'merchants under my authority' and another to 'my merchants'
(Rainey 1964, p. 319). The relative importance of 'middle-class'
merchants (a vague term) cannot be neatly determined from the
evidence. It is nevertheless of some interest that a text from Ugarit
seems to provide a hint of a commercial middle class. In a lengthy list
of taxpayers the highest social group is that of *mrynm* ('charioteers').
This group included the large landowners and merchants who
provided chariots at their own expense and served as the elite corps of
the armed forces. But Astour (1972, p. 26) argues that 'merchants of
lesser importance fulfilled their duty toward the defense of the
kingdom by serving with their own weapons in the ranks of *mžrġlm*'
('guards'). Furthermore, as noted earlier, the Assyrian trade of the
early second millennium was conducted not only by large merchants
belonging to the commercial establishment, but also by smaller
entrepreneurs who functioned as transporters and junior agents.
Veenhof cites several instances in which these 'middle-class'
businessmen succeeded in rising to become members of the *kārum*.
The evidence also suggests that Egypt had wholesalers of meat,
cakes, and wine (Papyrus Boulaq 11) and 'purveyors of precious
stones' (Hood Papyrus).[18]

Assertion 13

Economic solipsism, as it might well be called, was indeed an
outstanding feature of the market mentality. Economic action,
it was deemed, was 'natural' to men and was, therefore, self-
explanatory. Men would barter unless they were prohibited to
do so, and markets would thus come into being unless
something was done [by government] to prevent it. (Polanyi
1981, pp. 14-15)

Ancient Economic Man

Polanyi's main thrust anticipates scholars such as Moses Finley (1973) who maintain that, unlike modern economic man, ancient man was motivated primarily by considerations of status and communal solidarity.[19] The postulate of wealth-maximising used by modern economists is said to be utterly inappropriate to the 'irrational' (that is, nonutilitarian) ancients. These allegations have rarely been confronted by competent economists. Indeed, the dogmatic and unimaginative contribution of economist Daniel B. Fussfeld in a volume edited by Polanyi in 1957 served only to mislead its readers regarding the nature of economic analysis.

It is not easy to find historical evidence casting light directly on motives, whether of status or profit. But the letters from an Egyptian farmer named Hekanakht to his family in about 2000 are revealing. (The translation is that of Baer 1963.)

> *Letter I*
>
> Be energetic in cultivating! Take care! My seed must be preserved . . . You should send Heti's son Nakht and Sinebnut down to Perhae to cultivate [for us] *x arouras* of rented land. They shall take its rent from the *mn*-cloth woven there where you are. But if they have sold the emmer which is in Perhaa, they shall pay it (the rent) out of it (the payment for the grain) also, so that you will not have to concern yourself with the *mn*-cloth of which I said, 'Weave it, and they shall take it to be sold in Nebesit, and they shall rent land for its price.' . . . Now as for everything which Heti's son Nakht will do for (me) in Perhaa, I have allotted him a ration (for) not more than one month, amounting to a *h3r* of northern barley, and I have allotted a second (ration) amounting to 5 *hk3t* of northern barley to his dependents at the first of the month. If you overstep this (limit), I will treat it as a misappropriation on your part.

> *Letter II*
>
> You shall only give this food to my people as long as they are working. Take care! Hoe all my fields, sieve (the seed grain?) with the sieve and hack with your noses in the work. If they are energetic, you will be thanked, so that I will not have to scold you . . . Be energetic! You are eating my food . . . Now I have caused 24 *deben* of copper for the rent of land to be brought to you by Sithathor. Now have 20 (?) *arouras* of land cultivated for us in

Perhaa beside Hau the Younger by (paying) the rent with copper, clothes, northern barley or any[thing], but only after you have sold the oil and everything else there.

Obviously, Hekanakht did not possess the antimarket mentality of fourth-century BCE Greek philosophers. Indeed, he possessed the 'marketing mind', said by Polanyi (1981, p. 5) to be 'peculiar to conditions of life under the type of economy the nineteenth century created throughout all industrial societies.' Nor was pride in material achievement completely lacking in antiquity. On a stela dated to the second half of the third-millennium, an Egyptian records: 'I was a commoner of repute, who lived on his (own) property, plowed with (his own) span of oxen, and sailed in his (own) ship, and not through that which I had found in the possession of my father, the honored Uha' (Wilson 1969d, p. 326). Another third-millennium text records a man's claim that during the period in which he was in charge of his brother's 'possessions' the 'property increased more in his *pr* ("estate") than (in) the *pr* of any other noble' (Spencer 1984, p. 15; on *pr*, 'house', see p. 39).[20]

Economic Models of Antiquity

This is not to suggest that our ancient Egyptians spent every moment 'accumulating capital'. Marx's capitalist and the modern economic theorist's profit-maximising entrepreneur are, after all, caricatures or models, not realistic representations of businesspersons. Finley's (1973, pp. 23, 144) assertion that antiquity's 'prevailing mentality was acquisitive but not productive' is entirely without merit; his claim that 'no modern investment model is applicable to the preferences of the men who dominated ancient society', simply misunderstands the nature of economic models. Finley might just as well have pronounced that mathematical models of investment are not applicable to the preferences of the men who 'dominate' modern society. Economic theories are not tested by evaluating the 'realism' of the underlying assumptions or the 'mentality' of economic actors.

Assertion 14

In Nuzi society of the fifteenth century B.C. one of the chief transactions, designated as *ditennutu*, may be described as the free exchange of the use of land, persons, cattle, money, or other goods . . . Clearly the uses comprised in *ditennutu* would, in modern terms, be described as usufruct, tenancy, renting, labor service, or profit. But these distinctions are here ignored. The one vital condition of validity is the absence of gain made at another's expense. (Polanyi 1981, pp. 70-1)

Polanyi wishes here to emphasise the importance in ancient societies of communal solidarity as opposed to economic motivations, but, inadvertently, he has accomplished the opposite result. The *tidennūtu* contracts Polanyi describes were in all likelihood ingenious subterfuges designed to overcome legal obstacles to 'exploitive transactions'. More specifically, there is reason to believe that they represented an attempt to disguise illegal or illegally high interest charges as land or labour services.[21] Another legal subterfuge for which Nuzi is justly famous is the *mārūtu* contract. It would appear that at this time land, or some categories of land, could be legally transferred only to a relative of the landowner (compare the discussion of joint taxation under Assertion 6, pp. 98-9). Alternatively, land sales were unenforceable in the courts or were highly taxed. In order to circumvent the restriction, the landlord, in return for a 'gift' (*qīštu*) equal to the estimated value of the land, legally adopted the buyer. According to T.L. Thompson (1974, pp. 208-11), however:

The purpose of the various types of 'adoption' contracts at Nuzi is not to 'circumvent' an objectionable law or custom; these practices are rather the ordinary means (generally common to the Near East) of maintaining the basic structural order and the responsibilities involved in family relationships and the transference of property, and at the same time allowing considerable freedom to extend these structures beyond the ordinary limits given by custom . . . The basic concept involved in these Near Eastern contracts is the extension of familial relationships by legal means.

But the objective of these adoptions was obviously to alienate land for a price, not to widen the circle of familial love. Note that adoptees were not required to perform filial duties such as mortuary offerings (see Chapter 2, section 7, pp. 49-50). If Thompson means that adoption (as opposed to sale) was the standard Near Eastern vehicle for the transfer of land, he is mistaken (see the discussion of Assertion 6, pp. 92-6). Interestingly, mentions in Nuzi lawsuits of land sale and price may well be references to adoption and gift. In a text cited by

Weeks (1971, pp. 299-300; see also Greengus 1984, p. 366). 'The defendant complains that he did not receive the price due for the fields. The transaction being referred to is an adoption tablet.' A recently published adoption tablet (IM 70764) actually refers to the transfer of land as a 'sale' (*šīmu*). The publisher of this text, Fadhil, suggests that it is among the oldest found in Nuzi.[22]

Assertions encountered in the literature that only the lender profited from a *tidennūtu* contract and discussions about whether the adopter or adoptee instigated a *mārūtu* transaction are economically naive. An uncoerced exchange benefits both parties. Unless each of the contractors views his post-exchange position to be superior to his pre-exchange position, exchange will not take place. Trade is a positive-sum game. This fundamental point is not understood by Finley. After mentioning the operation of the supply-demand mechanism in 'Adam Smith's world', Finley (1965, pp. 65-6) goes on to claim that: 'Behind the market lies the profit motive, and if there was one thing that was taboo in Homeric exchanges it was gain in the exchange. Whether in trade or in any other mutual relationship, the abiding principle was equality and mutual benefit'!

The warning not to 'impose' modern economic structures on ancient societies should not be used as a crutch or as an excuse for failure to employ the best available tools of analysis. I would venture to add that Polanyi's and Finley's 'anachronistic' and Marx's 'simple abstraction' are terms that deserve a lengthy period of benign neglect. A main lesson of the *tidennūtu* and *mārūtu* transactions is that when ancient Near Eastern governments sought to stamp out economic exploitation, ancient men and women sought to find legal expedients by which they might continue to exploit or be exploited. The legal fictions became as convoluted as those of today.[23]

Notes

1. Dahood connects Eblaite *mar* with Hebrew *mûr*, 'to change', but Shea (1983, pp. 594-6) prefers to translate *mar* as 'new'.
2. Sources on marketplaces: *Economic theory*: Clower (1969, pp. 11-12), Nelson (1970, pp. 323-5) and Rees (1966) *Ancient texts*: Ali (1964), Beich (1963, pp. 44-5), Boese (1973, pp. 149-50), Dahood (1981, pp. 301, 307), Edzard (1967b, p. 196), Elat (1979, note 66, p. 543), Finkelstein (1968a, pp. 48-9), Foster (1977, note 63, p. 36, p. 40), Grayson (1972, p. 20), Harris (1975, pp. 17, 20), Hoffner (1973, pp. 206-7; 1974, p. 113), Israelit-Groll (1982, p. 45), Jacobsen (1970, p. 217; note 7, p. 422), Jankowska (1970, p. 155), Leemans (1960a, pp. 101-2), Machinist (1983, note 2, p. 720), Meek (1969c, p. 185), Oppenheim (1970, note 54, p. 145), Oppenheim and Reiner (1977, p. 129, note 13a, p. 351), Röllig (1976), Saggs (1962, p. 287), Speiser

(1964, p. 68), Veenhof (1972, pp. 354-6), Weinfeld (1982a, note 36, p. 36), and Wycherly (1978, pp. 93-6).

3. Sources on archaeological evidence for marketplaces: Davies and Faulkner (1947), Eyre (in press), Gelb and Sollberger (1957, p. 175), Hill (1967, pp. 148, 170, 179), Hodjash and Berlev (1980), Kenyon (1960, p. 197), Macqueen (1975, p. 69), Mellink (1969, p. 206), Özgüg (1969, p. 253), Röllig (1976, p. 287), and Wooley and Moorey (1982, pp. 151-4).

4. Sources on economics of money: Alchian (1977, p. 139), Brunner and Meltzer (1971, p. 800), Hirshleifer (1980, pp. 249-50), Melitz (1970, pp. 1030-2; 1974, pp. 57-67), and Polanyi (1981, pp. lii, 141).

The magnitude of the investment required to produce a common medium should not be exaggerated. Robert A. Jones (1976) has shown that once the costs of finding a trading partner have increased beyond some point, a very common good will emerge as a commodity money through the concerted market behaviour of traders. That is, all will settle on the same good without centralised decisions or arrangements. As Jones points out, however, this result follows only under several restrictive assumptions. Strangely, research by economists on this fundamental issue is still in its infancy.

5. Sources on money in the ancient Near East: Curtis and Hallo (1959, p. 105), Finkelstein (1969, pp. 68-70), Foster (1977, notes 47 and 48, pp. 35-6), Gardiner (1951, p. 115), Goetze (1969a; 1969b, pp. 189-90), Hallo (1963, pp. 138-9), Jacob J. Janssen (1961, p. 103), Kramer (1969b, p. 160), M. Lambert (1963, p. 80), Leemans (1960a, pp. 130-1, 185-6), H. Lewy (1964, note 1, p. 182), Meek (1969a, pp. 218-19; 1969b), Milgrom (1976), Montet (1981, pp. 75, 167, 266-7), Stone (1977, pp. 272-3), and Sweet (1958, pp. 175-6).

6. Sources on coils, weighing, and money bags: Artzi and Malamat (1971, note 11, p. 78), Balmuth (1975, p. 296), Butz (1979, p. 379), Černý (1954, p. 907), Dayton (1974, p. 41), Fish (1938, p. 169), Garelli (1963, pp. 26-7), Harris (1955, pp. 98-9), Hodjash and Berlev (1980, p. 45), Leemans (1950b, p. 31), Lipiński (1979, note 13, p. 567), Loding (1974, pp. 152-3), Loewe (1955, pp. 146-7), Powell (1978a), Stol (1982, p. 151), Veenhof (1972, p. 37), and R. Wilson (1983, pp. 6-7).

7. Sources on sealed bags of coins: Goitein (1967, pp. 231-4), Heichelheim (1958, I, p. 110), Oppenheim (1948, p. 159), Stol (1982, pp. 150-1), Sweet (1958, pp. 211-13), and Udovitch (1979, p. 267).

8. Sources on stamped metal and other textual references suggesting coinage: Balmuth (1971, p. 3; 1975, pp. 295-6), Boardman (1980, p. 101), Černý (1954, p. 910), Einzig (1949, p. 212), Fischer (1961b, pp. 61-4), Glanville (1935, Plate III, p. 36), Helck (1975, pp. 270-1), James (1984, pp. 256-61), Jacob J. Janssen (1975b, p. 105), Levey (1959, p. 180), Lipiński (1979a, II, p. 568), Loewe (1955, pp. 143, 149), Montet (1981, p. 166), Powell (1978a, p. 224), and S. Smith (1922, pp. 178, 182-4). I am informed by J.A. Brinkman (personal correspondence) that my earlier reference (1983c, p. 819) to an 'inspector of silver' (*ba⟩tānu kaspi*) is derived from a mistaken reading.

9. Sources on temple-issued coins: Artzi and Malamat (1971, pp. 83-4), Bakir (1952, pp. 91-2), Harris (1960, note 8, p. 127), Helck (1975, p. 281), Hoffner (1968, pp. 41-2), Lévy (1967, pp. 17-18), Lipiński (1979a, note 21, p. 569; pp. 571-5, 578), Olmstead (1923, pp. 321, 537; 1930, p. 226), and Wiseman (1953, pp. 14, 60).

10. Sources on archaeological evidence for coinage: Balmuth (1971, p. 3), Bivar (1971, p. 102), Grierson (1977, pp. 8, 17, 32; note 8, p. 36), Hemming (1956), and S. Smith (1922, pp. 180-2). Grierson holds that the weight (about 500g) of the inscribed discs from Zinjirli makes it unlikely that they served a monetary purpose. The objection is not altogether convincing; Grierson himself cites the example of the sale of a Syrian slave girl for a price amounting to 373g of silver (Gardiner 1935, pp. 145-6).

11. Silver was Anatolia's main export to Assur. It is possible to speculate that the

introduction of token coinage in Mesopotamia contributed to the apparent demise of this vigorous trade by decreasing the demand for silver. Of course, it is also possible that with the passage of time this commerce became so routinised and familiar that the Assyrian enclave was replaced by a system of relay trade.

12. Sources on token coinage and inflation: Brunner and Meltzer (1971, p. 801), Burns (1927, chapter 12), Černý (1954, pp. 911, 921), Curtis and Hallo (1959, note 35, p. 109), Dubberstein (1938, p. 43), Friedman (1959, pp. 4-9), Jacob J. Janssen (1975b, pp. 551-2), Levey (1959, p. 180), Montet (1981, p. 167), and Powell (1978a, pp. 223-4).

13. The interests of merchants and shipowners were protected by legal stipulations requiring boatmen to make restitution for ships and cargoes lost due to negligence (*eqùm*): see paragraph 5 of the Eshnunna Code (Goetze 1969a, p. 161) and paragraph 237 of Hammurabi's Code (Meek 1969b, p. 176).

14. Sources on internal trade: Blackman and Peet (1925, p. 288), Foster (1977, p. 37), Gardiner (1947, I, p. 21), Graham (1971), Jacob J. Janssen (1961, pp. 71, 82-3, 98), Leemans (1950a, p. 3; 1960a, note 2, p. 117; 1960b, pp. 90-2), Lichtheim (1976, II, p. 170), Oppenheim (1954, note 8, p. 8), Saggs (1962, p. 181), Sasson (1966b, pp. 171-2), and Snell (1982, p. 49).

Graham (1971) points out that Pithecusae (Ischia), Greece's earliest colony in the West, was also its most distant. The archaeological evidence suggests that this hilly volcanic island little suited to grain cultivation, basing itself on Tuscan metals, was the centre of a metallurgical industry which exported its products to the eastern and western Mediterranean (Klein 1972).

15. Sources on merchants: Astour (1970), Dandamayev (1971), Foster (1977, pp. 33-4, 37; 1982, p. 78), Garelli (1963, p. 233), Gledhill and Larsen (198?, p. 213), Goitein (1967), Heltzer (1978a, pp. 128-30), Knapp (1983), Larsen (1974, p. 469), Leemans (1950a, pp. 81-95, 113; 1961, p. 64), Liverani (1979a, pp. 28-9), M. Müller (1971, pp. 55-6), Oppenheim and Reiner (1977, pp. 24-7, pp. 79-80), Pettinato (1981, pp. 203-25), Powell (1977, pp. 24-7), Rainey (1964, pp. 314, 319), Snell (1982, pp. 48, 56-7, 99-103, 114), Stol (1982, p. 148), Strange (1980, p. 102), and Zaccagnini (1977, pp. 173-5).

16. Sources on merchants and risk: Balkan (1967, p. 400), W.G. Lambert (1960, pp. 121-38), Lopez (1971, p. 76), Mallowan (1965b, p. 6), Nakata (1971, p. 101), Oppenheim (1954, pp. 8-11), Thomas (1958, pp. 108-9), and Veenhof (1972, pp. 87-8, 356).

I have found no evidence of formal market insurance in the ancient Near East. Conceivably, given information costs, it was not feasible to gather enough customers with the same underlying probability distribution of payoffs to employ the law of large numbers to convert uncertainty for the individual policyholder into certainty for the insured population as a whole. By alternative explanation, if potential customers had much more information about their own risks than an insurance company, the emergence of a market might be prevented by the adverse selection problem (see the discussion of this problem with reference to the 'slave market', pp. 103-4).

In fourth-century Greece, merchants did not have to repay maritime loans if their cargoes were lost due to shipwreck or piracy. As might be expected, lender-insurers reduced the severity of the moral-hazard problem by requiring coinsurance: 'There are indications in the sources that the value of the security in a maritime loan had to be twice the size of the sum borrowed. This meant that an *emporos* [merchant] would have to bear the cost of half the cargo, and the insurance coverage would only be partial' (Millett 1983, p. 44). In addition, the lender had first claim on the proceeds from the sale of the cargo (W.E. Thompson 1979, p. 234). The Rhodian Sea Law, and quite probably the Athenian, provided that any loss for which no specific person might be held responsible must be shared by all the traders on board (Isager and Hansen 1975, p. 80). In the sixteenth century CE Near Eastern merchants participating in caravans or convoys formed syndicates to share losses resulting from shipwreck, piracy, and so on (Goitein 1967, p. 348). It seems reasonable to assume that similar techniques were employed by ancient Near Eastern merchants.

17. Sources on Egyptian merchants: Blackman and Peet (1925, p. 288), Campbell (1970, p. 59), Erman (1971, note 1, p. 516), Goedicke (1975a, pp. 66-72), Jacob J. Janssen (1961, pp. 99-104; 1975a, p. 163), Lichtheim (1976, II, p. 170), Megally (1977, pp. 254-7), Pflüger (1946, p. 261), Reineke (1979, p. 11), Säve-Söderbergh (1946, p. 61), Theódoridès (1958), Wente (1972, pp. 147-8), J.A. Wilson (1969c, pp. 432-4), and Zaccagnini (1976, pp. 162).

18. Sources on middle-class traders: Aldred (1978, pp. 17, 20), Astour (1972, pp. 12, 26), Jacob J. Janssen (1975a, p. 162), Leemans (1950a, chapter 3), Rainey (1964, p. 319), and Veenhof (1978, pp. 117-18).

19. For an effective refutation of Finley's views based on Pompeii's market-oriented wool industry, see Moeller (1976, pp. 56, 72, 105-10).

20. Sources on 'economic man' in the ancient Near East: Baer (1963), Spencer (1984, p. 15), and Wilson (1969d, p. 326). Another example is a letter from an important Ugarit merchant to an associate informing him of lucrative trade opportunities in Hittite Anatolia (see Astour 1981b, p. 22).

21. See Silver (1983a, chapter 18). There are no data on Nuzi lawcodes. There is, however, the evidence of proclamations and records of law courts that dealt with economic matters (see, for example, Zaccagnini 1975, pp. 202-5).

22. Sources on the *marūtu* contract: Cross (1937, p. 5), Fadhill (1981), Greengus (1984, p. 366), Paradise (1980, pp. 189-207), T.L. Thompson (1974, pp. 208-11), and Weeks (1971, pp. 299-300). In some cases debt settlements rather than outright sales lie behind the adoption transactions (Maidman 1976, p. 96). Hinz (1973a, pp. 101-2) cites a sixteenth century case report from Elam involving a dispute over a plot of land that had been transferred by adoption; the adoptee's son, a certain Bêli, won his case by stating that his possession of the land was: 'In accordance with the paths of justice established by the god Inshushinak and goddess Ishmekarab, which affirm that adoption of a brother is to be considered as brotherhood and adoption as a son to be considered as filiation'. Note also in this connection a group of rather suspicious Ur III and earlier second millennium rental contracts in which the lessee grants a loan to the lessor (see Maekawa 1977, note 25, p. 31; Steinkeller 1981, note 13, p. 115; and Waetzoldt 1978).

According to Pestman (1969, p. 62): 'In the [Egyptian] Middle and New Kingdoms the *ỉmy.t pr*, a written document in which a fictitious lawsuit is recorded . . . is generally used when one wishes to transfer property rights to another person, not only in the case of a bequest of property to an heir but also in the case of property to a buyer'. It is possible to surmise that the object was to evade transfer taxes.

23. A striking feature of business life in Communist countries which discriminate against private business activity by means of steep taxation is the emergence of the 'semiprivate' enterprise — that is, private firms wearing various 'socialist disguises' (see Rupp 1983).

PART THREE

THE RESPONSE TO CHANGES IN ECONOMIC
INCENTIVES AND PUBLIC POLICY

7 NEW MARKETS AND LAND CONSOLIDATION

Historically, the introduction of new agricultural products for new markets has often resulted in the consolidation of land ownership (see Silver 1983a, chapter 6). The land consolidator is typically an individual who has acquired some familiarity with the needs and circumstances of relatively distant markets and has access to the capital needed to implement his insights. For the reasons given in Chapter 3, ancient land-consolidating entrepreneurs would be drawn largely from the ranks of merchants and officials of temple or palace. Sometimes, as we will see, the resulting changes in local economic organisation might be profound. According to W.F. Leemans (1977, pp. 5-6):

> the cases known and the quantities of . . . trade are so small, that it cannot be concluded that there is evidence that the trade of the Babylonians, and earlier of the Sumerians, was really very important.

But the economic transformations described below supplement Leeman's evidence and attest indirectly to the importance of long-distance trade.

1. Sumer

This pattern of transformation becomes evident in Sumer in the middle of the third millennium. The rulers of Lagash ('Storehouse') are known to have purchased large estates and small fields during an era of flourishing intercity and long-distance trade involving southwestern Iran (Elam) and the Persian Gulf. (A hint of the latter commerce is provided by several texts of the twenty-first century that refer to a Meluhha village located in the old Lagash territory.) A tablet appears to show a priest purchasing fields from a number of sellers, including King Enhegal (circa 2570). Documentary and archaeological evidence indicates that grain, flour, and woollen textiles were exported in return for lumber, cattle (see Chapter 2, section 6, pp. 41-2), stone, and metals. The imported metals were employed not only for works of

147

art but it is safe to assume, to manufacture various industrial and agricultural tools (see the discussion in note 1). Texts from a town (Girsu) in the Lagash area record individual grain shipments of about ten tons and substantial amounts of copper. Analysis of plant remains demonstrates that wheat, as a better quality cereal suitable for bearing the costs of export, was cultivated during this era, possibly representing seventeen percent of the crop. Something of the nature of this trade is reflected in the epic poem 'Enmerkar and the Lord of Aratta', wherein the ruler of a Sumerian city exported grain in return for semiprecious stones (see p. 62). It does not follow that Sumer had 'surplus' grain or that Iran's agricultural productivity was necessarily low. The explanation lies in international cost differences and efficient allocation of scarce resources. Iran, compared to Sumer, was a high-marginal-cost producer of wheat in terms of the worth of the stone and metal it could have produced instead. This means, of course, that Iran, compared to Sumer, was the low-marginal-cost producer of stone and metals in terms of the worth of wheat production foregone.

Land consolidation may have involved the extension of the existing natural watering to high lands requiring artificial irrigation. Barton's (1929, p. 81) venerable translation of one of King Urukagina'a inscriptions refers to the digging of wells on the 'highest parts of . . . [the royal] elevated field'. Kramer (1963, p. 318) translates: 'If the king's retainer dug a well in the highest part of the field . . .' 'Enki and Ninmah', a Sumerian epic portraying the gods as digging canals in order to obtain their sustenance, should be dated in this era, suggests Komoróczy. Note that irrigation devices and weirs are already mentioned in tablets of the first half of the third millennium from Ur, according to Charvát. A simple type of machine for raising water, the shādūf, is actually pictured on a cylinder seal from the middle of the second half of the third millennium. In the earlier second-millennium, Mari's ruler boasted that he had opened canals and thereby 'made the lever-and-bucket (*Schöpfeimer, dālum*) disappear from my land' (Klengel 1980, p. 79). In the Lagash area the technical terms for irrigation facilities and their management appear in about the middle of the third millennium. Adams (1981, p. 144) suggests that the newly emerging technical vocabulary denotes 'a transition from localized, ad hoc, generally small-scale irrigation concentrated along the backslopes of particular natural levees to extensive, increasingly artificial, intercommunity systems.' That the baked bricks for two weirs were laid in more than 500,000 quarts of bitumen (*kar*) provides a hint of the magnitude of Lagash's undertaking.

In any event, the process of land consolidation evidently transformed a significant fraction of the class of commoners into clients. According to Barton's translation of Urukagina's disputed text, the freemen who dwelt on the elevated royal fields became 'serfs' when the fields were irrigated. More precisely, the formerly independent farmers assumed the status of *šub-lugal* (originally 'king's man' or 'subject'?), meaning that in return for labour services they received allotments of 'nourishment land' and, or instead of, wages in kind. A second, equally obscure, labour category involved in this text, the *igi-nu-dug$_8$*, may be either slaves or wage workers. The explanation of the emergence of a large body of dependent workers as an adjustment in economic organisation to take advantage of the opening of new trade opportunities that ordinary working farmers were unable to exploit is consistent with the data. It appears to provide a solution to a problem that has concerned ancient historians, for, as Oppenheim and Reiner (1977, p. 96) point out: 'To speak here of conquered and subjugated population strata offers a much too obvious answer, which moreover has no base in the known history of the region.'[1]

Actually, there is no reason to assume that small farmers sold their land because they were forced to or because they were impoverished or that their living standards deteriorated as dependent workers. Just the opposite was probably the case.

2. Old Kingdom Egypt

Egypt provides another example. In the twenty-fourth century one Metjen, a late Third and early Fourth Dynasty official who served, for example, as 'supervisor of the king's flax', purchased land from numerous *nswtjw* (originally 'those of the king'?). These *nswjtw*, Baer believes, were small freeholders, and the area they sold amounted to about 1/1000 of Egypt's arable area at the time. (The *meret*, an obscure labour category found on large estates of the third millennium, have been compared to Sumer *šub-lugal*s.) The Fourth Dynasty was an age of great affluence: pyramid building flourished during the period. Besides a trading station in Lower Nubia (see the discussion of Assertion 7, p. 110), Egypt possessed a fair-sized commercial station at Byblos. The first ruler of the Dynasty, Snefru, is known from the Palermo stone to have sent fleets of as many as forty ships to Lebanon for timber ('s-wood). The name 'Byblos' occurs in a Fourth Dynasty tomb at the Giza necropolis on the Nile opposite Cairo and on a Sixth Dynasty bas-relief from Byblos. More concretely, a voyage to Byblos by a 'Treasurer of the God' (or expedition leader) is commemorated in a Sixth Dynasty tomb inscription at Aswan. Also a hieroglyph-engraved axe-head of Khufu or Sahure (Fourth or Fifth Dynasty) found in Syria gives the name of a lumberjack gang or ship's crew. Small tablets of two early First Dynasty kings record the delivery of 'cedar' and fir, no doubt from Byblos, but the series of Egyptian 'dedications' in the temple precinct of Byblos begins with the last king of the Second Dynasty. His name, like that of rulers and other Egyptians of the Third through the Sixth Dynasties, appears on a stone vessel. Helck (1979, p. 363) adds that 'we do not hear anything about the Byblos trade from the kings of the second half of the First Dynasty and the Second Dynasty.' (Apparently, the wood found in Egyptian tombs dating from before the Third Dynasty is of local Egyptian origin.) Archaeological evidence indicates that in addition to wood the Syrian olive oil was also imported in quantity. We may note in passing a Pyramid Text (2350-2175) referring to the gods eating a Syrian type of bread. (Thirteenth- to twelfth-century literary texts cited by Erman list 'much oil of harbor', 'various breads', and wine among Egypt's imports from Syria; the eighteenth-century Second Stela of Kamose attests to the continuing import of wood from the Levant.) The scarcity of Egyptian artifacts in Lebanon is consistent with 'invisible exports', which would fit in nicely with land consolidation in Egypt.

'Invisible exports' are also consistent with the myth of Osiris, a mortuary god as well as a god of fertility and, according to classical sources, a patron of the agricultural arts. The idea of rebirth, no doubt, is the link between the funerary and vegetative dimensions of the god's personality. Note in this connection the Osiris-shaped boxes that were lined with linen, filled with earth, planted with grain, and deposited in tombs of the second millennium. Representations of Osiris are not known from the third millennium, but those of later times are quite suggestive: Osiris is usually shown carrying implements which have been identified as the shepherd's crook and the flail used to thresh grain, and he is always pictured in mummified form. (Not very long after the Third Dynasty the normal hieroglyph for 'god' changed from a staff with streamers(?) to a staff(?) wound with cloth.) Osiris is identified with barley in the Dramatic Ramesseum Papyrus (late third or early second millennium) and, quite possibly, in the earlier Pyramid Texts. His links with flax, linen, and, ultimately, Byblos are reinforced by the Pyramid Texts. For example, Osiris is addressed as 'He who is in the chest, He who is in the shrine, He who is in the sack' (Griffiths 1970, p. 311). In another Pyramid Text the god Horus (the son of Osiris identified with the living king) equips his king (the dead king identified with Osiris) 'with woven linen(?) which came from him' (Griffiths 1980, p. 69). A textual link between mummification and Byblos occurs in the thirteenth-century papyrus 'The Admonitions of Ipuwer': 'None indeed shall sail north to Byblos today. What shall we do for pine trees for our mummies' (Lichtheim 1973, I, p. 152). Foreign jars containing fragrant resin from a coniferous tree have been found in tombs of the Fourth through Sixth Dynasties, according to W.S. Smith. 'First quality oil of the ʿš-tree' and 'resin' (ṣfṯ-oil), also a product of the ʿš-tree (*ash*), are mentioned frequently in tombs subsequent to the Fifth Dynasty. In the Osiris legend, as recounted by Plutarch, the chest into which Osiris had been shut and cast into the Nile by his brother Seth was sought for and found by the innovative goddess Isis incorporated in the trunk of a tree at Byblos. The goddess cut down the tree, wrapped it in a linen cloth and presented it to the people of Byblos. Later, the sacred tree containing the body of Osiris was returned to Egypt by Isis.

By the Third Dynasty, Egypt was growing both flax and wheat (*swt*). Indeed, granaries filled with wheat are mentioned in the Third Dynasty and in the Fourth under the builder of the Great Pyramid, Khufu, Snefru's successor. The sign of the bag or sack was used in writing the words for 'linen' and 'grain'. Thus the 'sack' in the Pyramid Text quoted above may well be a reference to linen sacks filled with wheat. Scenes of flax workers are accompanied by captions listing bundles of 20,000, 62,000, and over 73,000. Another scene described by Erman (1971, p. 440) shows 'treasury officials [expedition personnel] packing linen into low wooden boxes, which are long enough for the pieces not to be folded. Each box contains but one sort of woven material.' The boxes or chests of linen were next taken to the 'house of silver'. Labels are written above each of the four chests depicted in the Sixth Dynasty tomb of Ankhmahor: 'royal linen', 'ššrw-linen', 'i3-fabric(?)', and 'good Upper Egyptian cloth' (Gardiner 1930, p. 175). Linen chests are painted on several tombs including Sahure's, a ruler of the Fifth Dynasty. Stelae inscribed with linen lists run from the Second to the Sixth Dynasty and are especially common in the Fourth; these lists specify such features as colour, fineness, width, and presence of fringes. Very fine linen was being produced in the First Dynasty; the selvedge fringe was an innovation apparently dating from the Third Dynasty. The Osiris myth is consistent with the hypothesis that in return for lumber and oil from Byblos, Egypt exported agricultural products, probably wheat and linen. (For evidence of Egyptian exports of wheat and linen in later periods, see section 3 of Chapter 2, p. 37; section 2 of Chapter 4, p. 65; Isaiah 19:9; 23:3, and Ezekiel 27:7.)

The main problem with this line of interpretation is that while Osiris is mentioned in the Pyramid Texts, there are no conclusive references to the story of the chest in this era. There are, however, many strong hints, including the reference to Osiris being in the 'chest' and the 'sack'. Several Pyramid texts tell of Seth throwing Osiris 'on the ground' or 'on his side', probably meaning that he killed him. Pyramid Text 972, for instance, states: 'You have come in search of your brother Osiris, when his brother Seth had thrown him on his side on that side of the land Gehesti' (Velde 1977, p. 84). Other Pyramid Texts show Osiris being worshipped as a tree and reveal that he drowned. For this a Coffin Text (late third to early second-millennium) blames Seth: 'He (Seth) let him (Osiris) be drowned' (Velde 1977, p. 85). The Pyramid Texts also mention a 'water ritual' in which Osiris is carried by his brother Seth, who swims or floats beneath him. In discussing this, Griffiths (1980, p. 75) takes note of a passage in the Dramatic Ramesseum Papyrus which 'throws light on the "water ritual", for Seth is represented by a ship, and it is said that "Osiris is he who is placed on Seth's back", an expression echoing Pyramid Text 651c, "he has placed thee on his back".' (An Egyptian papyrus of the thirteenth century enumerates the 'bark of Baal' among the gods in the harbour of Memphis; see further below.) Velde cites additional utterances from the Pyramid Texts indicating that the ship of Osiris was decorated with the head of a sacrificial bull representing Seth, who, it should be noted, has power over water. Apparently, the Egyptians very early identified Seth with the routes to Asia and, quite probably, with the Syro-Canaanite god Baal who, among other functions, controlled the sea and who was worshipped in Byblos (see the discussion of syncretism in Chapter 1, p. 13). A relevant point here is that a Second Dynasty pharaoh (Sekehemib) whose epithet is 'conqueror of Asia' took a Seth-name (Peribsen). Several scholars, in addition, believe they have found allusions and word-play associations between Byblos and Osiris in the Pyramid Texts. His probable origin in the eastern Delta lends credence to Syrian affinities for Osiris.

Another significant hint is found in a Coffin Text in which Hathor, the Lady of Byblos, makes the 'steering-oar' for the dead.

Taken as a whole, the evidence lends support to the hypothesis that the Egyptians paid for the lumber and oil they imported in the third millennium with linen and wheat. It appears also that the 'water ritual' is a metaphorical reference to the carriage of Egypt's exports to Asia in 'Byblos-ships' (*kbn*-ships) belonging to or constructed by Asiatics. ('Byblos-ships' appear for the first time in a Sixth Dynasty inscription.) A variation on this theme is that the Byblos ships were constructed by Syrians resident in Egypt, probably at the dockyard of Perunefer, the port of Memphis, where, in the middle of the second-millennium, Syrian workers worshipped the gods Baal and Astarte. Reliefs carved on the tomb of the Fifth Dynasty ruler Sahure show boatloads of Syrians, not prisoners apparently, paying homage as they arrive in Egypt led by the gods Seth and Soped (see W.S. Smith 1965, figure 6, p. 7). Above some of the men, Egyptians if we can rely on their wigs and clean-shaven faces, is the label 'dragoman' ('expedition leader'). The Sixth Dynasty ruler Pepi II sent a delegation to recover the body of an Egyptian who had been killed by Asiatics of the *Hrjw-šʿ* 'when he was building a *kbn*-ship there for Punt' (Säve-Söderbergh 1946, pp. 10-11). Säve-Söderbergh places the dead shipbuilder in the neighbourhood of Suez, but Montet prefers Byblos. Perhaps the simplest interpretation of the 'water ritual' metaphor is that it refers to the use of Syrian wood to construct the ships. Note in this connection two early second-millennium texts, one recording a military action in which twenty ships of *š*-wood participated and the other mentioning the use of *š*-wood for the mast of a Byblos ship. More importantly, a Fourth Dynasty text records the use of coniferous woods to construct three ships measuring 170 feet in length.[2]

Much of the evidence for imports of Syrian wood and oil comes from the tombs of the wealthy. But W.A. Ward's (1963, p. 54) claim that 'little, if any, of this bounty filtered down below the highest strata of society' exceeds both the evidence and the requirements of economic theory. At the very least, many small landowners profited from the increased demand for their land. Moreover, it seems quite possible that the 'higher strata' had to offer higher real wages in order to attract labour into the production of wheat or flax, both of which are relatively labour-intensive crops — more labour-intensive, surely, than the domestic substitutes for olive oil, including animal fat (*ʿd*) and ben-oil (*b3k*), the oil of the moringa tree. There is, in fact, evidence relating to this era of organised migration into under-populated districts and the founding of 'new villages' whose administrative centre is 'the house of agriculture', *pr šn*ⁱ, literally 'house of the plow' (Badawy 1967, p. 104).[3]

3. Babylonia

In the southern Babylonian, city of Larsa during the reign of Rim-Sin (1822-1763) there is evidence of a resurgence in the export of southern Babylonian woollen garments to Tilmun in exchange for copper and of a flourishing trade with Eshnunna in northern Babylonia. (Rim-Sin's immediate predecessor, Warad-Sin, built a 'Tilmun' temple to the god Innin at Ur.) Businessmen such as Balmunamhe and other *tamkārū* (merchants) from the city of Larsa purchased many fields and had villages named after them. Balmunamhe raised sheep on a large scale, as did the king, Rim-Sin, and Iltani, a princess and priestess, and the Nanna and Ningal temples in Ur. A similar trend toward land consolidation took place at Nippur beginning about 1900, according to the documents studied by Stone. This evidence is consistent with the flow of capital into more profitable opportunities.

Palaeobotanical and textual evidence strongly suggests that by the end of the third millennium southern Babylonian agriculture had experienced a drastic reorientation, away from the cultivation of wheat and into that of barley. (Wheat declined to two percent of the crop and then disappeared in the first half of the second millennium.) This has been interpreted as a reaction to soil salinisation due to widespread irrigation agriculture, barley being much more salt-tolerant than wheat. On the other hand, although agricultural documents from this period are abundant, they do not, in contrast to those of the third millennium, refer to soil salinity. Morever, as Adams points out, agriculturalists would, in any event, have cultivated more barley to provide fodder for their enlarged herds of sheep. (Texts from the late third millennium frequently mention barley-fed sheep.) This leaves open the possibility that specialisation in stockbreeding and land consolidation may have been triggered by increased external demand for wool and textiles, combined with an increased demand for meat in response to higher incomes. A variety of qualitative indicators and quantitative data on real wages (in terms of silver and barley) suggest that in the earlier second millennium

Babylonia enjoyed significant prosperity, if not, as some believe, a 'golden age'. Indirect evidence of increased meat consumption is provided by Oppenheim's (1967, pp. 44-5) observation that 'references to fishing and the role of fish as a staple diet begin to become rare in the second half of the rule of the Hammurabi Dynasty', raising the possibility that another 'protein-rich source of food came newly within reach.' A nineteenth-century text from Larsa shows 'fat-tailed sheep' being consumed, possibly as part of the remuneration of canal-diggers. An economic change explanation of the shift from wheat to barley is also strengthened by the fact that salinisation is not inevitable. It can, as Adams explains, be controlled by appropriate land use and irrigation practices. That this was understood at the time is hinted by the recommendation of a fallow system and elementary forms of drainage in a Sumerian 'agricultural manual' (Georgica), actually a literary text inscribed in about 1700. Indeed, texts from Girsu in Lagash show us as early as the twenty-fourth century the effort to combat soil salinity by means of a weed fallow system to dry the soil deep down. Thus the decision by agriculturalists to channel scarce investment resources into building up flocks instead of investing them in anti-salinisation projects (weed fallows, application of irrigation water in excess of immediate crop needs, intensive drainage systems) was quite possibly a rational (in cost-benefit terms) response to newly emerging market opportunities. Note also that the rising trend in stockbreeding, a relatively land intensive production activity, may well have contributed to a decreasing trend in the population in the former heartland of southern Mesopotamia.[4]

Notes

1. Sources on new markets and land consolidation in Sumer: Adams (1981, p. 144), Barton (1929, p. 81), Charvát (1979, p. 16), H.E.W. Crawford (1973, p. 233), Diakonoff (1969b, p. 178), During-Caspers (1979, pp. 122-3), Forbes (1964, II, pp. 17, 34), Gadd (1971, pp. 131-3), Jacobsen (1960, p. 182; 1979, note 48, p. 12; 1982, p. 62), Klengel (1980, p. 79), Komoróczy (1976, pp. 28-30), Kramer (1963, p. 318), Laessoe (1951, p. 32), Leemans (1950a, pp. 40-1; 1983, p. 56), Mallowan (1965, pp. 19-20), Oppenheim and Reiner (1977, p. 96), Parpola *et al.* (1977, pp. 151-3), Potts (1982, pp. 46-9), Semenov (1974, pp. 581-4), Struve (1969, p. 35), and Vanstiphout (1970, pp. 18-19).

With respect to the uses of the copper imported by Sumer, the archaeological evidence is dominated by statues, vessel-stands, and fine daggers and axeheads, although producer goods, including tools (saws, goads, awls) and agricultural implements (mostly sickles; rarely, picks, hoes, spades, and ploughshares also appear). Clearly, however, this represents a biased sample because it is drawn primarily from graves, temples, and palaces. The metal usage pattern is also distorted by the understandable Mesopotamian practice, also known for wood, of recycling the scarce metals of aging or damaged tools while passing on works of art from generation to generation as heirlooms (see Kramer 1963, p. 103; Moorey 1982). Thus, for example, all metallic tools and products had been removed from an early second-millennium coppersmith's shop excavated at Uzar-Lullu near Baghdad, leaving behind only objects of clay: pot-bellows, crucibles, pipes, and the like (al-Gailani 1964, pp. 37-8). Note also in this connection the Sumerian word *ba-zi-ir* meaning, according to Finkelstein (1970, p. 248), 'metal implements to be scrapped or already formed into scrap.' One text of the late third millennium records the issue for agricultural work of 6 copper axes, 21 copper hoes, 18 copper sickles, and 12 copper trowels, and another lists 270 copper hoes and 540 copper sickles (Hallo 1958, pp. 91-2; see also Finkelstein 1970, note 25, p. 248). Contracts for the manufacture of copper tools are also available (Forbes 1964, VIII, p. 87). Literary evidence comes from a composition with the modern title 'The Copper-Silver Debate' which mentions the 'stubble-loosening copper mattock', the 'plough fashioning copper adz', the 'firewood cutting copper axe', and the 'grain-cutting copper sickle' (Kramer 1963, p. 265).

The shādūf or sweep utilises the lever-and-bucket method: a pole mounted on a fulcrum operates like a seesaw, with a bucket at one end and counterweight on the other to facilitate lifting when the bucket is full of water. There is evidence that waterwheels were also employed in Mesopotamia. A relief of King Sennacherib of Assyria (c. 700) has him replacing simple instruments with heavier ones, perhaps, therefore, substituting animal for human power (see Davies 1933, pp. 36, 70-2).

Archaeological excavations reveal that the production of stone vases became common at a site in the highlands of southeastern Iran in the early third millennium. Samples of this production have been found at various places in Sumer (Kohl 1978, p. 468).

2. Sources on new markets and land consolidation in Egypt. *Concentration of land ownership*: Badawy (1967, p. 104), Baer (1963, p. 13), Forbes (1964, V, pp. 31, 228), Kaplony (1962), Semenov (1974, pp. 588-90), and Wenig (1962). *Linen, wheat and trade*: Badawy (1983, p. 669), Ben-Tor (1982, pp. 11-13), Dixon (1969, pp. 138-9), Erman (1971, pp. 188, 448-9, 516), Fakhry (1938), Fischer (1964, pp. 29, 34), Frankfort (1959, p. 85), Gardiner (1930, pp. 170-5, 179; 1947, I, p. 8), Helck (1979, p. 363), Horn (1963, pp. 52-3), Kadish (1966), Kemp (1983, p. 147), Lichtheim (1973, I, p. 152), MacDonald (1972, p. 76), Newberry (1938, p. 182), Pirenne (1961, I, Chapter 10), Smith and Smith (1976, pp. 60, 70), W.S. Smith (1935, pp. 134-6, 148-9; 1969), Vercoutter (1967a, pp. 287-8), Wainwright (1938, p. 12), W.A. Ward (1965, p. 169; 1971, pp. 65-7), and J.A. Wilson (1951, pp. 88, 101; 1969b, p. 227). *Osiris myth*: Boylan (1922, p. 15), Brunner (1975), Griffiths (1970, pp. 33-9, 52-5, 311, 321-3; 1980, pp. 5, 28-34, 41-4, 58-9, 69, 74-5, 108, 163-70); Hornung (1982, p. 34), Kaster (1968, p. 74), Van Seters (1966, pp. 99-100, 174-7), and Velde (1977, pp. 84-5, 97-8, 110-11, 122-4, 129). *Construction of Byblos ships*: Helck (1970, p. 35), Montet (1968, p. 42), Sasson (1966a, note 4, p. 127, note 13, p. 128), Säve-Söderbergh (1946, pp. 10-11, 32, 37, 53-4), and W.S. Smith (1965, figure 6, p. 7).

It should be noted that Baer's *aroura*, the basic unit of land measurement in Egypt, is much larger than that proposed by other Egyptologists.

A literary text about social anarchy and reversal of fortune mentions the *nswtjw* as eating beef and otherwise living well. Papyrus Leiden 344, Recto, whose modern title is 'The Admonitions of Ipuwer' is of the thirteenth century, but it may describe events at the end of the Sixth Dynasty (see Lichtheim 1973, I, pp. 149-63, especially note 21). The survival of this population stratum into the Sixth Dynasty is attested by a cylinder seal probably belonging to a tax official with the inscription 'counter among the *nswtjw*' (Wenig 1962).

The view put forward, for example, by Emery (1961, pp. 182-204) that the wood found in Egyptian tombs of Archaic times (c. 3100-2700) was imported from Lebanon has been called into question by the evidence in Lucas and Harris (1962, pp. 429-48). Trigger (1983, pp. 29-30) suggests that pine, cedar, and other woods found at still earlier Predynastic (Badarian) sites may not have come from Syria: 'Since . . . the climate of North Africa was moister then than it is today, the wood may have been indigenous to the Red Sea Hills and better climatic conditions would have made the exploitation of that area easier than it is at present.' Ben-Tor (1982) finds evidence of the intensive importation of Syrian oil in the fact that the Egyptian hieroglyphic determinative sign for oil takes the form of the Syro-Canaanite jar in which this commodity was probably transported. Also, large numbers of Syrian-type jars have been found in tombs from the Third Dynasty onwards.

3. Sources on income distribution and substitutes for olive oil: Badawy (1967, pp. 103-5), Brothwell and Brothwell (1969, p. 153), Darby *et al.* (1977, pp. 757, 778-84), and W.A. Ward (1963, p. 54).

4. Sources on new markets and land consolidation in southern Babylonia in the nineteenth and eighteenth centuries. *Concentration of land ownership, trade and sheep herds*: Adams (1981, pp. 149-50), Hallo (1965), Leemans (1950a, pp. 65-6; 1960a, pp. 18-22; 1960b, pp. 13, 36, 54, 117; 1968, pp. 178-9; 1975, pp. 139-40; 1983, pp. 93-4, Potts (1983, p. 128), and Stone (1977, p. 284). *Barley and salinisation*: Adams (1981, pp. 149-52), Hallo (1958, p. 93), Jacobsen (1982, pp. 9-11, 16, 57-60, 67), Kohl (1978, note 11, p. 470), Kramer (1981, pp. 65-9), and Lloyd (1978, p. 18). Adams (1981, pp. 151-2) and Jacobsen (1982, p. 39) present data indicating that grain yields declined from c. 2400 to c. 2100 and, perhaps, to c. 1700. But, aside from the obvious measurement problems, such changes need not be due to deterioration in the intrinsic quality of land — for example, less frequent fallow periods would lower yields (see Pettinato and Waetzoldt 1975, and Silver 1983b). *Prosperity*: Champdor (1958, p. 45), Farber (1978, pp. 38-40), Gadd (1973, p. 212), Leemans (1950a, p. 113), Macqueen (1964, p. 42), and Wellard (1972, p. 116). *Consumption of meat*: H.E.W. Crawford (1973, pp. 232-4), Gelb (1973, pp. 82-3), Limet (1979, p. 238), Oppenheim (1967a, pp. 44-5), and Walters (1970, p. 23). Sumer also possessed large flocks of sheep in the late third millennium. A number of texts from this period attest to the consumption of meat (sheep, cattle and equids) by women weavers and other workers. Powell (1978a, pp. 173-4) suggests that land consolidation took place in Ur III, but he attributes this to salinisation, not to changes in market opportunities. On population trends in southern Mesopotamia, see Brinkman (1984, pp. 172-4).

8 CHANGES IN ECONOMIC POLICY AND ORGANISATION

While Polanyi quite properly criticised ahistorical 'stage theories' with their 'predilection for continuity', his own view of economic development is similarly flawed. Ancient economic institutions, according to Polanyi, 'evolved everywhere from the embedded economies of the tribal stage, and this development was never unrelated to the transcendent requirements of social solidarity.' Social solidarity was accomplished through the declaration of 'equivalencies' by the state — that is, by pervasive controls over prices, wages, rent, and interest. With the partial exception of 'small city states such as Athens and (partly) Israel, of the peasant type' this pattern of government control over exchange persisted for millennia (Polanyi 1981, pp. lii, 61-2, 68). The market economy emerged in the eighteenth to nineteenth century as a 'new phenomenon, never witnessed before'. The proper task of the economic historian is to seek the source of this 'inherent discontinuity of development'; the problem is to explain 'the origin of fluctuating prices, not of fixed prices' (Polanyi 1981, pp. liii, 6). But the record shows that the oldest of recorded civilisations experienced lengthy periods of unfettered market activity interspersed with periods of pervasive economic regulation by the state. Egyptologists, for example, have pointed to the increased documentation of private commercial activity during 'intermediate periods' when the monolithic power of the Pharaonic state was shattered or weakened (see Helck 1975, p. 138). In the later second millennium, according to the evidence of Kruchten (1979, p. 523), Egyptian temples increasingly turned from the direct management of their estates by means of agents ($r\underline{w}dw$) to renting out fields to individuals. To employ Polanyi's terminology, the location of ancient Near Eastern economies along a scale of 'disembeddedness' – 'embeddedness' with respect to the political sphere is variable, not constant. While the underlying arguments of North and Thomas (1973, p. 1) in their admirable book *The Rise of the Western World* are, of course, quite different from Polanyi's, their claim that 'the affluence of Western man is a new and unique phenomenon' is likewise ahistorical. It should be added that Near Eastern antiquity also experienced 'Dark Ages' in which household economy greatly increased in importance relative to both markets and hierarchies. (It appears that ancient Mesopotamian social-religious thought was inclined to attribute these disasters to over population.)

As is the case with other facets of ancient societies, the evidence concerning *changes* in economic policy and organisation is fragmentary. The widely discussed but philogically obscure reforms in 2351 to 2342 of King Urukagina in Lagash challenged tradition and established a new economic order in which (it seems) creditors might not seize property or persons for debt and the gods were 'instated' as masters over fields that, apparently, had belonged to the city ruler in earlier times. (Does this perhaps refer to the 'high fields' discussed under Sumer in Chapter 7?)[1]

An inscription in Assur of very early in the period of the Assyrian trade with Cappadocia (about 1940 to 1800) states that the king 'established' the *andurārum* of silver, gold, copper, tin, grain, wool, and other goods. J. Lewy interprets *andurārum* in this disputed passage as referring to 'free movement' or 'free trade'. Earlier, the father of this king had 'established the *andurārum* of the Akkadians', which probably means that he implemented policies to attract traders from Babylonia to the market in Assur. He records in a difficult building inscription: 'I freed the Akkadians and their sons (from forced labor) and cleared (literally "washed") them of their (obligation to pay) copper (as tax)' (Balkan 1974, note 25, p. 33). (In the Cappadocian texts 'washing' occurs in metallurgical contexts with the meaning of purification or refining. 'Pure' has the meaning 'exempt, clean' at Mari and in Akkadian texts from Ugarit.) Steinkeller (1981b, pp. 165-6), taking note of the places mentioned in the inscription (e.g. Der located on the main route from northern Babylonia to Elam), suggests that the mention of 'washing' might 'be explained as an allusion to a trade agreement by which Ilushima [the Assyrian ruler] opened the trans-Tigridian trade routes to the Babylonian merchants and permitted the exportation of copper to Babylonia.'[2]

Some suggestive evidence is also available for Nuzi. Nuzi, as noted in the discussion of Assertion 14 (p. 140), is famous for its *mārūtu* contract, which disguised land sales as adoptions of the purchaser by the landowner. One of the earliest Nuzi tablets (JEN 552) tells of a *witnessed* — that is, legal — *land sale*.[3] Another early adoption tablet refers to a land sale (see p. 141). This evidence raises the possibility that the *mārūtu* or sale-adoption contract arose in response to an intervening royal edict banning land sales. In connection with this hypothesis, note that government intervention in the economic sphere is reflected by the inclusion in many Nuzi contracts, among them sale-adoptions, of a *šūdūtu* clause: 'This tablet was written in Nuzi after the proclamation.' As noted in the discussion of Assertion 11, a royal decree fixed the maximum price of slaves. Another more directly relevant proclamation issued in the 'holy festival month' in the 'city of the gods' had the effect of cancelling a transfer of land. Unfortunately, the document does not make clear the nature of the voided transfer. The *šūdūtu* clause itself appears in the contracts only after a certain point in time. Furthermore, several texts make reference to 'the new proclamation'. In one legal text an individual is accused of having violated the *šūdūtu*. A recently published trial document hints vaguely at local government controls over grain prices (or interest rates). The dispute involves the advance of a shekel of gold, to be repaid, it appears, after the harvest in barley at the going market price. But in his defence the borrower successfully refers to a statement by the 'elders(?)' of Tupshani(ni) that the lender must take barley 'according to our price' (after M. Müller 1981, p. 446; but compare Greengus 1984, p. 365).[4]

The data on major changes in economic policy is most plentiful in the Old Babylonian period (1900-1600), whose most famous representative is Hammurabi (1792-1750). According to Oppenheim and Reiner (1977, p. 102): 'After the fall of Ur III [2112-2004] when legal and economic texts come to light, private property and trade appear to have reached a high state of development.' It would seem that there was a pronounced change in economic policy during the affluent reigns of Rim-Sin in Larsa and of Hammurabi in Babylon. The nature of the economic reforms they introduced is not entirely clear, but they probably involved government intervention in the sale and rent of houses and fields; minimum wages; maximum prices of barley, wine, bricks, and other goods; and maximum interest rates. (According to M. Müller similar reforms were undertaken at Isin, Eshnunna, Mari, Hana, and Alalakh.) A business letter dating to the reign of Hammurabi's son makes reference to 'the wage of a hired laborer . . . written on the stele', possibly Hammurabi's (Sweet 1958, p. 109). An ordinance or decree of Rim-Sin is mentioned in a legal tablet; apparently he permitted an (adopted) son to reclaim an orchard sold for silver by his father to a third party. (A steep increase in redemption texts as a proportion of total land sales is noted at Nippur in the second half of the eighteenth century.) Then Rim-Sin's Larsa was conquered by Hammurabi. During the following years in which Hammurabi and his son Samsuiluna ruled Larsa we find 'mysterious' texts in which fish, dates, garlic and wool were 'sold at one-third of their price'. These texts may tentatively be reconstructed as follows. The goods that were sold at one-third the price (including state property) by members of the *kārum* to independent merchants (e.g. Pirshum) were for *future* delivery. Thus, assuming constancy of prices, the 'sale' was actually a loan at a rate of 66⅔ per cent with interest deducted in advance by the 'buyer'. The aim of this procedure was no doubt to evade maximum interest rate regulation — 20 per cent for silver and 33⅓ per cent for grain in Hammurabi's Code.[5] About twenty years after Hammurabi's conquest attacks by the Kassites, a mountain people, coincidentally with local revolts, severed Larsa and the southern area as a whole from Babylon's rule. The conquest in 1600 by the Hittites of Babylon itself, by this time a small principality, begins the 'Dark Age' (1600-1347). During this era urban life and legal documents relating to private commercial activities decline steeply. Leemans (1950a, p. 122) concludes: 'There is not much evidence of trade and consequently of prosperity.' The Dark Age is also characterised by the 'disappearance .. of all vestiges of social reforms — or experiments — of the Hammurabi era' (Oppenheim and Reiner 1977, p. 159).[6]

Notes

1. Sources on Urukagina: Cardellini (1981, pp. 5-11), Edzard (1974, pp. 145-9), Foster (1981), Hruška (1974), Maekawa (1973-74) and Stephens (1955, pp. 134-5).

2. Sources on Assyrian free trade policy: Balkan (1974, note 25, p. 33). Fisher (1958, note 5, p. 113), Larsen (1976, pp. 70, 75), Lemche (1979, pp. 16-17), J. Lewy (1958b, p. 23), Steinkeller (1981b, pp. 165-6), and Veenhof (1972, pp. 47-8).

Perhaps Ur-Nammu (2112-2095), the first ruler of the Ur III Dynasty, also followed a free trade policy. His laws state that: 'By granting immunity in Akkad to the maritime trade from the seafarers' overseer, to the herdsman from the "oxen-taker", ... he established the freedom (*šu.bar*, literally "to open the hand") of Sumer and Akkad.' On the other hand, the wording resembles Urukagina's (see Finkelstein 1969a, pp. 281, 301-2).

3. Weeks (1971, pp. 281, 301-2). The buyer Puhishenni 'gave' gold for the land. The land was acquired not by *šīmu* (Akkadian 'sale') but by its Kassite equivalent, *irana*, according to Fadhil (1981).

4. Sources on the *šudūtu* clause: Breneman (1971, p. 27), Eichler (1973, pp. 32-3), Greengus (1984, p. 365), Hayden (1962, p. 189), M. Müller (1971, pp. 56-8), Weinfeld (1982b, p. 496), and Zaccagnini (1975, pp. 197, 200). See also note 7, p. 113, on *verhüllter Fruchtwucher*.

5. Sources on reforms of Hammurabi and Rim-Sin: Heichelheim (1958, I, p. 185),

Leemans (1950a, pp. 113, 117, 122), M. Müller (1971, p. 59), Oppenheim and Reiner (1977, p. 102), Saggs (1962, pp. 220-1), Stone (1977, p. 281), Sweet (1958, pp. 103-11), Tyumenev (1969, pp. 86-7), and Yoffee (1977, pp. 145-7).

6. Sources on Babylonia's economic retrogression: Adams and Nissen (1972, pp. 37-41), Leemans (1950a, p. 122), and Oppenheim and Reiner (1977, p. 159). For a brief discussion of the Edict of Ammisaduqa, see note 7 on '*verhüllter Fructwucher*', p. 113, and the section on Credit and the Investment Market', p. 86, see also Silver (1983a, pp. 233-6).

9 CONCLUDING REMARKS

Analysis of transaction costs provides numerous insights into the structure of the ancient economy. The role of temples as centres of commerce, inculcation of professional standards by gods, elevation of technology to the status of divine gift, religious syncretism and the composition of elaborate mythologies, and many more seemingly exotic, even bizarre, practices are comprehended as elements in a strategy to cope with high transaction costs and limit opportunism by increasing the stock of trust capital. Similar considerations lie behind the ubiquity of diversified, multinational family firms or houses, the relatively important entrepreneurial role of highborn women, the concentration of similar trades in compact areas, and the holding of 'excess' stocks of staples and cash balances. The prominence within the contractual process of publicly performed conventional gestures and recitations, the stress placed on names, the intrusion of gifts, friendship, and ethical codes into exchange relationships, and other manifestations of personal economics fall into place as techniques for economising on the resources used up in the process of transferring ownership rights.

Evidence is abundant of the accumulation of human and material capital, including circulating capital not directly involved in the production process — warehouses, specialised pack animals, navigational channels, and large, purpose-built cargo vessels — and fixed capital — tools of artisans and agriculturalists, machines for lifting water, irrigation channels, metallurgical facilities, industrial installations for wine, oil, cloth, and ceramics, terracing and other forms of land improvement and reclamation, specialised animal stock, and signficant investments in tree and vine stock.

We know, moreover, that the ancient Near East was able to support towns and great urban centres (on the average from 10 to 20 percent of the total population?) without evident difficulties. For example, in third-millennium Sumer the built-up area of Ur occupied 100 acres, and Uruk's walls enclosed 1,280 acres; by the second half of the second millennium the built-up area of Thebes, Egypt's largest city, covered 3,200 acres. Also in the second millennium, the Hittite capital Hattusas spread over 400 acres. First-millennium Babylon occupied 2,500 acres and Nineveh over 1,850 as compared to classical Athens' 550. (Bietak 1979, p. 125; Hammond 1972, p. 38; Macqueen 1975, p. 77; Oppenheim 1969b, p. 15.) Assur, on the edge of the rainfall zone and without a sizeable agricultural hinterland, could not produce its own food. With respect to the underlying agricultural productivity, the findings of Maekawa's (1974, p. 42) quantitative study of third-millennium Sumerian grain production deserve quotation.

> The Sumerians used the plow to which the drill for sowing was attached. A large volume of seed grain can be saved by the use of such a seed drill, compared to the scattering of seed ... Employment of wide furrows was the pattern in Sumer. This is deduced from the fact that three men followed two oxen with the seeder plow ... By using the drill and making wide furrows for lessening the seed volume, the Sumerians could expect maximum growth of cereals. This coupled with proper irrigation, produced 76:1-fold of the seed amount in pre-Sargnoic Lagash, which need not be attributed to fantasy.

Less systematic data pertaining to this era indicate quite respectable wool yields and dairy productivity (Waetzoldt 1972, pp. 5-6; Gomi 1980, pp. 1-3).

This evidence relating to productivity raises the more general question of technical sophistication in the ancient Near East. It is often assumed that technological knowledge depends on the application of prior scientific knowledge, of which there was little in antiquity. But Nathan Rosenberg (1982, pp. 143-4), a leading scholar of technology, offers a more realistic perspective.

> [Technology] is a knowledge of techniques, methods, and designs that work, and that work in certain ways with certain consequences, even when one cannot explain exactly why. It is therefore ... not a fundamental kind of knowledge, but rather a form of knowledge that has generated a certain rate of economic progress for thousands of years ... Thus, the normal situation in the past, and to a considerable degree also in the present, is that technological knowledge has *preceded* scientific knowledge.

Rosenberg's point is well illustrated for antiquity by artificial pollination of date palms, control over water levels by gates (Akkadian *erretum*; Klengel 1980, pp. 81-3), the speed of sailing vessels, Egypt's discovery of substitutes for lapis lazuli, C.S. Smith's (1970, p. 409) observation that Ur's metalwork in the middle of the third millennium 'reveals knowledge of virtually every type of metallurgical phenomenon except the hardening of steel that was exploited by technologists in the entire period up to the end of the 19th century AD', and the finding that (in the middle of the second millennium) 'the beads at Nuzi reveal that every major form of ancient glass-making technology (including sophisticated uses of glass rods) was known there a thousand years earlier than had previously been supposed' (Gavin 1981, p. 151). Needless to add, the industrial era's increased reliance on scientific knowledge and its increased range and variety of fixed capital goods have steeply accelerated the rate of technical progress. The ancient epoch was, however, quite capable of sustaining lengthy periods of rising labour productivity and per capita income.

The relatively high costs of communicating, contracting, and transporting did not prevent the emergence in Near Eastern antiquity of recognisable markets for goods and factors of production. Their precise importance relative to subsistence production (and tax collection) is difficult to evaluate. The direct evidence for trade, occupational specialisation, supply-demand-determined prices, investment in material and human capital, and other 'modern' phenomena is uneven with respect to time and place but is, nevertheless, abundant. The availability of a large labour force for seasonal work in agriculture and irrigation canal repair testifies to significant economic differentiation and division of labour. Indirect evidence of the importance of trade is also provided by major transformations in the economies of Sumer, Pharaonic Egypt, and southern Babylonia to take advantage of new commercial opportunities.

If, however, as Polanyi (1981, p. 124) states, 'a full market system encompasses its society', then no such system has ever existed. Transaction costs alone would rule out complete markets. But the requisite functions demanded by Polanyi — the allocation of consumer goods, land, and labour (slave and free) through the supply-demand price mechanism; risk-bearing organised as a market function; and elaborate credit and investment markets — can be seen plainly at various points in the documents from the earliest times. Besides all these, the documents hint at an appreciation of opportunity costs and the free-rider problem. Indeed, the Old Babylonian period (first half of the second millennium) has been characterised by Hallo (1958, p. 98) as one in which 'there was a price on everything from the skin of a gored ox to the privilege of a temple office.' For good economic reasons, including tax exemptions, exclusive franchises, and, most importantly, a limited supply of individuals qualified to play the role of entrepreneur, many economic transactions took place within temple and palace where, no less than in today's large enterprises, they were mediated by authority. The evidence does not in the least suggest, however, that market-mediated transactions did not take place or were unimportant relative to hierarchy. As in the modern economy, we find, in the words of economist, D.H. Robertson, 'islands of conscious power in an ocean of unconscious cooperations'. (The importance of family firms and personal economics in the ancient economy was stressed earlier.) It is incorrect to magnify the economic flows of temple or palace to Amazonian proportions while shrinking the market to a mere brook. Polanyi (1981, p. 146) concedes that in Greece 'the part played by market elements . . . was of importance to the economy as a whole.' No less can be said for the ancient Near East, from the beginning of its spatially and temporally sporadic records to the end.

REFERENCES

Adams, Robert McC. (1974), 'Anthropological Perspectives on Ancient Trade', *Current Anthropology*, 15, 239-49
—— (1981), *Heartland of Cities*, Chicago: University of Chicago Press
—— and Hans J. Nissen (1972), *The Uruk Countryside: The Natural Setting of Urban Societies*, Chicago: University of Chicago Press
Aharoni, Yohanan (1968), 'Arad: Its Inscriptions and Temple', *Biblical Archaeologist*, 31, 2-32
—— (1974), 'The Horned Altar at Beer-Sheba', *Biblical Archaeologist*, 37, 2-6
—— (1982), *The Archaeology of the Land of Israel*, Philadelphia: Westminster
—— and Ruth Amiran (1964), 'Arad: A Biblical City in Southern Palestine', *Archaeology*, 11, 43-53
Ahmed, Sami Said (1968), *Southern Mesopotamia in the Time of Ashurbanipal*, The Hague: Mouton
Akerloff, George A. (1970), 'The Market for "Lemons": Qualitative Uncertainty and the Market Mechanism', *Quarterly Journal of Economics*, 84, 488-500
Albright, W.F. (1934), 'The North-Canaanite Poems of Alêyan Ba'al', *Journal of the Palestine Exploration Society*, 14, 101-40
—— (1968), *Yahweh and the Gods of Canaan*, Garden City, New York: Doubleday
Alchian, Armen A. (1969), 'Information Costs, Pricing, and Resource Unemployment', *Western Economic Journal*, 9, 109-27
—— (1977), 'Why Money?', *Journal of Money, Credit, and Banking*, 9, 133-40
Aldred, Cyril (1970), 'The Foreign Gifts Offered to Pharaoh', *Journal of Egyptian Archaeology*, 56, 105-16
—— (1978), *Jewels of the Pharaohs: Egyptian Jewelry of the Dynastic Period*, New York: Ballantine
Ali, Fadhil A. (1964), 'Blowing the Horn for Official Announcement', *Sumer*, 20, 66-8
Alster, Bendt (1974), *The Instructions of Suruppak: A Sumerian Proverb Collection*, Copenhagen: Akademisk Forlag
Angus, S. (1975), *The Mystery Religions*, New York: Dove
Arrow, Kenneth (1974), *The Limits of Organization*, New York: Norton
Artzi, P., and A. Malamat (1971), 'The Correspondence of Šibtu, Queen of Mari in ARM X'. *Orientalia*, 40, 75-89
Astour, Michael C. (1970), 'Ma'hadu, the Harbor of Ugarit', *Journal of the Economic and Social History of the Orient*, 13 April, 116-22
—— (1972), 'The Merchant Class of Ugarit', in Dietz Otto Edzard (ed.), *Gesellschaftsklassen im alten Zweistromland und in den angrenzenden gebieten*, Munich: Verlag der Bayerischen Akademie der Wissenschaften, 11-26
—— (1973), 'Ugarit and the Aegean: A Brief Summary of Archaeological and Epigraphic Evidence', *Alter Orient und altes Testament*, 22, 17-27
—— (1981a): 'Toponymic Parallels between the Nuzi Area and Northern Syria', in Morrison and Owen (eds), *Nuzi and the Hurrians*, 11-26
—— (1981b), 'Ugarit and the Great Powers', in Gordon D. Young (ed.), *Ugarit in Retrospect*, Winona Lake, Indiana: Eisenbrauns
Atkinson, Dorothy (1983), *The End of the Russian Land Commune, 1905-1930*, Stanford: Stanford University Press
Atkinson, K.T.M. (1972), 'A Hellenistic Land-Conveyance: the Estate of Mnesi-machus in the Plain of Sardis', *Historia*, 21, 45-74

Auster, R.D., and Morris Silver (1979), *The State as a Firm: Economic Forces in Political Development*, Boston, Martinus Nijhoff

Austin, M.M., and P. Vidal-Naquet (1977), *Economic and Social History of Ancient Greece: An Introduction*, Berkeley: University of California Press

Avigad, N. (1975), 'The Priest of Dor', *Israel Exploration Journal*, 25, 101-5

——— (1977), 'Hebrew Epigraphic Sources', in Abraham Malamat (ed.), *The Age of the Monarchies: Culture and Society, V. The World History of the Jewish People*, Jerusalem: Masada Press, 20-43

Avi-Yonah, Michael (1978), *Hellenism and the East*, Ann Arbor: University Microfilms for the Hebrew University, Jerusalem

Badawy, Alexander (1967), 'The Civic Sense of Pharaoh and Urban Development in Ancient Egypt'. *Journal of the American Research Center in Egypt*, 6, 103-9

——— (1983), 'Review of J. Vandier', *Journal of the American Oriental Society*, 103, 688-70

Baer, Klaus (1962), 'The Low Price of Land in Ancient Egypt', *Journal of the American Research Center in Egypt*, 1, 25-45

——— (1963), 'An Eleventh Dynasty Farmer's Letters to His Family', *Journal of the American Oriental Society*, 83, 1-19

Bakir, Abd El-Mohsen (1952), *Slavery in Pharaonic Egypt*, Cairo: Imprimerie de l'institut français d'archeologie orientale

Baldacci, M. (1981) 'The Ammonite Text from Tell Siran and North-West Semitic Philology', *Vetus Testamentum*, 31, 363-8

Balkan, Kemal (1967), 'Contributions to the Understanding of the Idiom of the Old Assyrian Merchants of Kanesh', *Orientalia*, 36, 393-415

——— (1974), 'Cancellation of Debts in Cappadocian Tablets From Kültepe', in K. Bittel *et al.* (eds), *Anatolian Studies*, 29-41

Balmuth, Miriam S. (1971), 'Remarks on the Appearance of the Earliest Coins', in David G. Mitten *et al.* (eds), *Studies Presented to George M.A. Hanfmann*, Cambridge, Massachusetts: Fogg Art Musuem, 1-7

——— (1975), 'The Critical Moment: The Transition from Currency to Coinage in the Eastern Mediterranean', *World Archaeology*, 6, 293-8

Barton, George A. (1929), *The Royal Inscriptions of Sumer and Akkad*, New Haven: Yale University Press

Barzel, Yoram (1977), 'An Economic Analysis of Slavery', *Journal of Law and Economics*, 20, 87-110

Batto, Bernard F. (1974), *Studies on Women at Mari*, Baltimore: Johns Hopkins University Press

——— (1980), 'Land Tenure and Women at Mari', *Journal of the Economic and Social History of the Orient*, 23, 209-39

Bauer, Josef (1975), 'Darlehensurkunden aus Gursu', *Journal of the Economic and Social History of the Orient*, 18, 189-218

Bayliss, Miranda (1973), 'The Cult of Dead Kin in Assyria and Babylonia', *Iraq*, 35, 115-25

Becker, Gary S. (1981), 'Altruism in the Family and Selfishness in the Marketplace', *Economica*, 48, 1-15

Beich, Ralph (1963), 'Nuzi Last Wills and Testaments', Unpublished PhD dissertation, Waltham, Massachusetts: Brandeis University

Bell, Lanny, Janet H. Johnson, and Donald Whitcomb (1984), 'The Eastern Desert of Upper Egypt: Routes and Inscriptions', *Journal of Near Eastern Studies*, 43, 27-46

Ben-Porath, Yoram (1980), 'The F-Connection: Families, Friends, and Firms and the Organization of Exchange', *Population and Development Review*, 6, 1-30

Ben-Tor, Amnon (1982), 'The Relations between Egypt and the Land of Canaan during the Third Millennium B.C.', *Journal of Jewish Studies*, 33, 3-17

Bietak, Manfred (1979), 'Urban Archaeology and the "Town Problem" in Ancient Egypt', in Kent R. Weeks (ed.), *Egyptology and the Social Sciences*, Cairo: American University in Cairo Press

Biran, Avraham (1980), 'Tell Dan Five Years Later', *Biblical Archaeologist*, 43, 168-82

Bittel, K., Ph. H.J. Houwink Ten Cate, and E. Reiner (eds) (1974), *Anatolian Studies Presented to Hans Gustav Güterbock on the Occasion of His 65th Birthday*. Istanbul: Nederlands Historisch-Archaeologisch Institut in het Nabije Oosten

Bivar, A.D. (1971), 'A Hoard of Ingot Currency of the Medians near Malayir', *Iran*, 9, 97-111

Blackman, Aylward M., and T. Eric Peet, (1925), 'Papyrus Lansing: A Translation with Notes', *Journal of Egyptian Archaeology*, 11, 284-98

Bleeker, C.J. (1966), 'Guilt and Purification in Ancient Egypt', *Numen*, 13, 81-7
——— (1967), *Egyptian Festivals*, Leiden: Brill
——— (1973), *Hathor and Thoth*, Leiden: Brill

Bloch, Herbert (1941), 'The Roman Brick Industry and Its Relationship to Roman Architecture', *Journal of the Society for Architectural Historians*, 1, 3-8

Blomquist, Thomas W. (1979), 'The Dawn of Banking in an Italian Commune: Thirteenth Century Lucca', in Center for Medieval and Renaissance Studies of the University of California, Los Angeles, *The Dawn of Modern Banking*, 53-72

Blum, Jerome (1971), 'The European Village as a Community: Origins and Functions', *Agricultural History*, 45, 157-78

Boardman, John (1980), *The Greeks Overseas: Their Early Colonies and Trade*, London: Thames & Hudson

Boese, Wayne Edward (1973), 'A Study of the Slave Trade and the Sources of Slaves in the Roman Republic and Early Empire', Unpublished PhD dissertation, Seattle: University of Washington

Bogaert, Raymond (1966), *Les origines antiques de la banque de depôt*, Leiden: Sijthoff
——— (1970), 'The Economic Functions of Greek Banks', in van der Wee (ed.), *Fifth International Congress*, V, 241-51

Bogoslowsky, Evgeni (1977), 'Die "Auf-den-Ruf-Hörenden" in den Privatwirtschaft unter der 18. Dynastie', in Erika Endesfelder *et al.* (eds), *Ägypten und Kusch*, Berlin: Akademie-Verlag, 81-95

Bohl, Franz M. Th. (1920), 'The Position of Women in Ancient Babylonia and Israel', *Bibliotheca Sacra*, 77, 4-13

Borowski, Oded (1982), 'A Note on the "Iron Age Cult Installation" at Tel Dan', *Israel Exploration Journal*, 32, 58

Bottéro, Jean (1967), 'The First Semitic Empire', in Bottéro *et al.* (eds), *The Near East*, 91-132

Bottéro, Jean, *et al.* (eds), (1967), *The Near East: The Early Civilizations*, New York: Delacorte

Boylan, Patrick (1922), *Thoth the Hermes of Egypt: A Study of Some Aspects of Theological Thought in Ancient Egypt*, London: Oxford University Press

Bradbur, Daniel A. (1980), 'Never Give a Shepherd an Even Break: Class and Labor among the Komachi', *American Ethnologist*, 7, 603-20

Breasted, James Henry (1906), *Ancient Records of Egypt, II*, Chicago: University of Chicago Press
——— (1909), *A History of Egypt*, New York: Scribner
——— (1912), *Development of Religion and Thought in Ancient Egypt*, New York: Harper & Row

Breneman, J. Mervin (1971), 'Nuzi Marriage Contracts', Unpublished PhD dissertation, Waltham, Massachusetts: Brandeis University

Breton, Albert and Ronald Wintrobe (1982), *The Logic of Bureaucratic Conduct*,

Cambridge: Cambridge University Press

Brinkman, J.A. (1968), *A Political History of Post-Kassite Babylonia, 1158-722 BC*, Rome: Pontificium Institutum Biblicum

—— (1981), 'Hurrians in Babylonia in the Late Second Millennium B.C.', in Morrison and Owen (eds), *Nuzi and the Hurrians*, 27–35

—— (1984), 'Settlement Surveys and Documentary Evidence: Regional Variations and Secular Trend in Mesopotamian Demography', *Journal of Near Eastern Studies*, 43, 169-80

Brothwell, Don, and Patricia Brothwell (1969), *Food in Antiquity*, New York: Praeger

Brown, Norman O. (1947), *Hermes the Thief: The Evolution of a Myth*, New York: Vintage

Brunner, Hellmut (1975), 'Osiris in Egypt', 27, 37-40

Brunner, Karl and Allan H. Meltzer (1971), 'The Use of Money: Money in the Theory of an Exchange Economy', *American Economic Review*, 61, 784-805

Bubenik, Vit (1974), 'Evidence for Alašija in Linear B Texts', *Phoenix*, 28, 245-50

Burford, Alison (1972), *Craftsmen in Greek and Roman Society*, Ithaca: Cornell University Press

Burke, Madeleine Lurton (1964), 'Lettres de Numushda-Nahrâri et de trois autres correspondants à Idiniatum', *Syria*, 41, 67-103

Burkert, Walter (1979), *Structure and History in Greek Mythology and Ritual*, Berkeley: University of California Press

Burns, A.R. (1927), *Money and Monetary Policy in Early Times*, New York: Knopf

Burrows, Millar (1938), *The Basis of Israelite Marriage*, New Haven: American Oriental Society

Butz, Kilian (1979), 'Ur in Altbabylonischer Zeit als Wirtschaftsfaktor', in Lipiński (ed.), *State and Temple Economy*, I, 257-409

Campbell, Edward F., Jr. (1970), 'The Amarna Letters and the Amarna Period', in Edward F. Campbell Jr. and David Noel Freedman (eds), *The Biblical Archaeologist Reader*, III, Garden City, New York: Doubleday, 54-74

Cardellini, Innocenzo (1981), *Die biblischen 'Sklaven'-Gesetze im Lichts des keilschriftlichen Sklavenrechts*, Königstein/Ts.-Bonn: Hanstein

Cassin, Elena (1952), 'Symboles de cession immobilière dans l'ancient droit mésopotamien', *L'Année sociologique*, 5, 107-61

Casson, L. (1980), 'The Role of the State in Rome's Grain Trade', in D'Arms and Kopff (eds), *Commerce of Ancient Rome*, 21-33

Center for Medieval and Renaissance Studies, University of California, Los Angeles (1979), *The Dawn of Modern Banking*, New Haven: Yale University Press

Černý, Jaroslav (1932), 'The Abnormal-Hieratic Tablet Leiden I 431', in Mond (ed.), *Studies Presented*, 46-56

—— (1933), 'Fluctuations in Grain Prices during the Twentieth Egyptian Dynasty', *Archiv Orientalni*, 6, 173-8

—— (1954), 'Prices and Wages in Egypt in the Ramesside Period', *Journal of World History*, 1, 903-21

—— and T. Eric Peet (1927), 'A Marriage Settlement of the Twentieth Dynasty: An Unpublished Document from Turin', *Journal of Egyptian Archaeology*, 13, 30-9

Champdor, Albert (1958), *Babylon*, London: Elek

Charvát, Petr (1979), 'Early Ur', *Archiv Orientalni*, 47, 15-20

Chittenden, Jacqueline (1947), 'The Master of Animals', *Hesperia*, 16, 89-114

Civil, Miguel (1983), 'The Sign LAK 384', *Orientalia*, 52, 233-40

Clark, L.R.T. Rundle (1960), *Myth and Symbol in Ancient Egypt*, New York: Grove

Clay, Rachel (1938), *The Tenure of Land in Babylonia and Assyria*, London: University of London Institute of Archaeology

Clower, R.D. (1969), 'Introduction', in R.D. Clower (ed.), *Monetary Theory*, Harmondsworth: Penguin, 7-21

Cohen, Mark E. (1981), *Sumerian Hymnology: The Eršemma*, Cincinnati: Hebrew Union College

Cohen, Rudolph (1981), 'Excavations at Kadesh-barnea', *Biblical Archaeologist*, 44, 93-107

Cohen, Sol (1973), 'Ernmerkar and the Lord of Aratta', Unpublished PhD dissertation, Philadelphia: University of Pennsylvania

Colini, A.M. (1980), 'Il Porto Fluviale del Foro Boario a Roma', in D'Arms and Kopff (eds), *Commerce of Ancient Rome*, 43-51

Contenau, Georges (1966), *Everyday Life in Babylon and Assyria*, New York: Norton

Crawford, Dorothy (1973), 'Garlic-Growing and Agricultural Specialization in Graeco-Roman Egypt', *Chronique d'Égypte*, 48, 350-63

Crawford, H.E.W. (1973), 'Mesopotamia's Invisible Exports in the Third Millennium', *World Archaeology*, 5, 232-41

Crook, J.A. (1967), *Law and Life of Rome*, Ithaca: Cornell University Press

Cross, Dorothy (1937), *Movable Property in the Nuzi Documents*, New Haven: American Oriental Society

Curtis, John B., and William W. Hallo, (1959), 'Money and Merchants in Ur III', *Hebrew Union College Annual*, 30, 103-39

Dahood, Mitchell (1981), 'Afterword: Ebla, Ugarit, and the Bible', in Pettinato, *The Archives of Ebla*, 271-321

Dalley, Stephanie (1977), 'Old Babylonian Trade in Textiles at Tell al Rimah', *Iraq*, 39, 155-9

—— (1980), 'Old Babylonian Dowries', *Iraq*, 42, 53-74

Dandamayev, Muhammad A. (1971), 'Die Rolle des *tamkārum*', in Klengel (ed.), *Beiträge zur Sozialen Struktur*, 69-78

—— (1975), 'Forced Labour in the Palace Economy in Achaemenid Iran', *Altorientalische Forchungen*, 2, 71-8

—— (1982) (ed.; preface), *Societies and Languages in the Ancient Near East*, Warminster: Aris & Phillips

Darby, William J., Paul Ghalioungui, and Louis Grivetti (1977), *Food: The Gift of Osiris*, II, London Academic Press

D'Arms, J.H., and E.C. Kopff, (eds) (1980), *The Seaborne Commerce of Ancient Rome: Studies in Archaeology and History*, Rome: American Academy of Rome

Davies, J.K. (1981), *Wealth and the Power of Wealth in Classical Athens*, Salem, New Hampshire: Ayer

Davies, Norman de Garis (1933), *The Tomb of Nefer-Hotep at Thebes*, New York: Metropolitan Museum of Art

—— and R.O. Faulkner (1947), 'A Syrian Trading Venture to Egypt', *Journal of Egyptian Archaeology*, 33, 40-6

Dayton, John (1974), 'Money in the Near East before Coinage', *Berytus Archaeological Studies*, 22, 41-52

Deimel, Anton (1931), *Sumerische Tempewirtschaft zur Zeit Urukaginas und seiner Vorgänger*, Rome: *Analecta Orientalia*, 71-113

Delougaz, Pinhas (1967), 'Remarks Concerning Dating and Function of the Northern Palace', in Delougaz *et al.* (eds), *Private Houses*, 196-8

Delougaz, Pinhas, Harold P. Hill and Seton Lloyd (eds) (1967), *Private Houses in the Diyala Region*, Chicago: University of Chicago Press

Denman, D.R. (1958), *Origins of Ownership*, London: Allen & Unwin

172   *References*

Dever, William G. (1983), 'Material Remains and the Cult in Ancient Israel: An Essay in Archaeological Systematics', in Carol L. Meyers and M. O'Connor (eds), *The Word of the Lord Shall Go Forth*, Winona Lake, Indiana: Eisenbrauns, 571-87

Diakonoff, I.M. (1969a), 'The Rise of the Despotic State in Ancient Mesopotamia', in Diakonoff (ed.), *Ancient Mesopotamia*, 173-202

—— (ed.) (1969b), *Ancient Mesopotamia: Social and Economic History*, Moscow: Central Department of Oriental Literature

—— (1974a), 'Slaves, Helots, and Serfs in Early Antiquity', *Acta Antiqua*, 22, 45-78

—— (1974b), 'The Commune in the Ancient Near East as Treated in the Works of Soviet Researchers', in Dunn and Dunn (eds), *Introduction*, 519-48

Dixon, D.M. (1969), 'A Note on Cereals in Ancient Egypt', in Peter J. Ucko and G.W. Dimbleby (eds), *The Domestication and Exploitation of Plants and Animals*, Chicago: University of Chicago Press, 131-42

Donkin, R.A. (1973), 'Changes in the Early Middle Ages', in H.C. Darby (ed.), *A New Historical Geography of England*, London: Cambridge University Press, 7-135

Dougherty, Raymond P. (1923), *The Shirkûtu of Babylonian Deities*, New Haven: Yale University Press

—— (1930), 'The Babylonian Principle of Suretyship as Administered by Temple Law', *American Journal of Semitic Languages*, 47, 73-103

Downey, Glanville (1951), 'The Economic Crisis at Antioch under Julian the Apostate', in P.R. Coleman-Norton (ed.), *Studies in Roman Economic and Social History*, Princeton: Princeton University Press, 312-21

—— (1955), 'Philanthropia', *Historia*, 2, 199-208

van Driel, G. (1970), 'Land and People of Assyria: Some Remarks', *Bibliotheca Orientalis*, 27, 168-75

Dubberstein, Waldo H. (1938), 'Comparative Prices in Later Babylonia (625-400 B.C.)', *American Journal of Semitic Languages*, 56, 20-43

Dumett, Raymond E. (1983), 'African Merchants of the Gold Coast, 1860-1905 — Dynamics of Indigenous Entrepreneurship', *Comparative Studies in Society and History*, 25, 661-93

Duncan-Jones, Richard (1974), *The Economy of the Roman Empire*, London: Cambridge University Press

Dunn, Stephen P., and Ethel Dunn (eds) (1974), *Introduction to Soviet Ethnography*, II, Berkeley, California: Highgate Road Social Science Station

During-Caspars, Elizabeth C.L. (1979), 'Sumer, Coastal Arabia, and the Indus Valley in Protoliterate and Early Dynastic Eras', *Journal of the Economic and Social History of the Orient*, 22, 121-35

Edelstein, Gershon and Shimon Gibson (1982), 'Ancient Jerusalem's Rural Food Basket', *Biblical Archaeology Review*, 8, 46-54

Edgerton, William F. (1947), 'The Nauri Decree of Seti I: A Translation and Analysis of the Legal Portion', *Journal of Near Eastern Studies*, 6, 219-30

Edwards, I.E.S., C.J. Gadd and N.G.L. Hammond (eds) (1971), *The Cambridge Ancient History*, 3rd ed., I, Pt 2: *Early History of the Middle East*, London: Cambridge University Press

—— and E. Sollberger (eds) (1973), *The Cambridge Ancient History*, 3rd ed., II, Pt 1: *History of the Middle East and Aegean Region c. 1800-1380*, London: Cambridge University Press

—— (eds) (1975), *The Cambridge and Ancient History*, 3rd ed., II, Pt 2: *History of the Middle East and Aegean Region c. 1380-1000*, London: Cambridge University Press

Edzard, Dietz Otto (1967a), 'The Early Dynastic Period', in Bottéro (ed.), *The Near East*, 52-90

—— (1967b), 'The Old Babylonian Period', in Bottéro (ed.), *The Near East*, 177-231

———— (1970), *Altbabylonische Rechts- und Wirtschaftsurkunden aus Tell ed-Der im Iraq Museum, Baghdad*, Munich: Verlag der Bayerischen Akademie der Wissenschaften

———— (1974), '"Soziale Reformen" im Zweistromland bis ca. 1600 v. Chr.: Realität oder literarischer Topos?' *Acta Antiqua*, 22, 145-56

Ehrlich, Isaac, and Gary Becker (1972), 'Market Insurance, Self-Insurance, and Self-Protection', *Journal of Political Economy*, 80, 623-48

Eichler, Barry L. (1973), *Indenture at Nuzi: the Personal Tidennūtu Contract and Its Mesopotamian Analogues*, New Haven: Yale University Press

Einzig, Paul (1949), *Primitive Money*, London: Eyre & Spottiswoode

———— (1962), *The History of Foreign Exchange*, New York: St Martin's Press

Ekelund, Robert B., Jr. and Robert D. Tollison (1981), *Mercantilism as a Rent-Seeking Society: Economic Regulation in Historical Perspective*, College Station: Texas A&M University Press

Elat, M. (1978), 'The Economic Relations of the Neo-Assyrian Empire with Egypt', *Journal of the American Oriental Society*, 98, 20-34

———— (1979), 'The Monarchy and the Development of Trade in Ancient Israel', in Lipiński (ed.), *State and Temple Economy*, II, 528-46

Elayi, Josette (1981), 'The Relations between Tyre and Carthage During the Persian Period', *Journal of the Ancient Near Eastern Society*, 13, 15-29

Ellis, Maria de J. (1976), *Agriculture and the State in Ancient Mesopotamia*, Philadelphia: Occasional Publications of the Babylonian Fund

Ellis, Richard S. (1968), *Foundation Deposits in Ancient Mesopotamia*, New Haven: Yale University Press

Emery, Walter B. (1961), *Archaic Egypt*, Baltimore: Penguin

———— (1967), *Lost Land Emerging*, New York: Scribner

Endesfelder, Erika (1980), 'Zur ökonomischen Entwicklung', *Altorientalishe Forschungen*, 7, 5-29

Engnell, Ivan (1967), *Studies in Divine Kingship in the Ancient Near East*, Oxford: Blackwell

Erman, Adolf (1971), *Life in Ancient Egypt*, New York: Dover

Evans, J.A.S. (1961), *A Social and Economic History of an Egyptian Temple in the Greco-Roman Period*, New Haven: Yale University Press

Eyre, C.J. in Marvin A. Powell (ed.), in press

Fabricus, Knud (1929), 'The Hittite System of Land Tenure in the Second Millennium B.C. (*saḫḫan* and *luzzi*)'. *Acta Orientalia*, 7, 275-92

Fadhil, Abdulillah (1981), 'Ein frühes *tuppi maruti* aus Tell al-Faḫḫār/Kurruḫanni', in Morrison and Owen (eds), *Nuzi and the Hurrians*, 363-76

Fakhry, Ahmed (1938), 'Stela of the Boat Captain Inikaf', *Annales du Service des Antiquités d'Égypte*, 38, 35-45

Fairservis, Walter A., Jr. (1962), *The Ancient Kingdoms of the Nile*, New York: Crowell

Falkenstein, Adam (1974), *The Sumerian Temple City*, Malibu, California: Undema

Farber, Howard (1974), 'An Examination of Long Term Fluctuations in Prices and Wages for North Babylonia during the Old Babylonian Period', Unpublished MA thesis, De Kalb: Northern Illinois University

———— (1978), 'A Price and Wage Study for Northern Babylonia during the Old Babylonian Period', *Journal of the Economic and Social History of the Orient*, 21, 1-51

Faulkner, R.O. (1953), 'Egyptian Military Organization', *Journal of Egyptian Archaeology*, 39, 32-47

Fenoaltea, Stefano (1976), 'Risk, Transaction Costs, and the Organization of Medieval Agriculture', *Explorations in Economic History*, 13, 129-5

Fensham, F.C. (1967), 'Shipwreck in Ugarit and Ancient Near Eastern Law Codes', *Oriens Antiquus*, 6, 221-4

Fine, Hillel, A. (1952-53), 'Studies in Middle Assyrian Chronology and Religion, Part I', *Hebrew Union College Annual*, 24, 187-272

Finkelstein, J.J. (1956), 'Assyrian Contracts from Sultantepe', *Anatolian Studies*, 6, 137-45

―――― (1961), 'Ammisaduqa's Edict and the Babylonian "Law Codes"', *Journal of Cuneiform Studies*, 15, 91-104

―――― (1962), 'Mesopotamia', *Journal of Near Eastern Studies*, 21, 73-92

―――― (1968a), 'The Edict of Ammisaduqa: A New Text', *Revue d'assyriologie et d'archéologie orientale*, 26, 45-64

―――― (1968b), 'An Old Babylonian Herding Contract and Genesis 31:38f', *Journal of the American Oriental Society*, 88, 30-6

―――― (1969a), 'The Laws of Ur-Nammu', *Journal of Cuneiform Studies*, 22, 66-82

―――― (1969b), 'The Edict of Ammisaduqa', in Pritchard (ed.), *Ancient Near Eastern Texts*, 526-8

―――― (1970), 'On Some Recent Studies in Cuneiform Law', *Journal of the American Oriental Society*, 90, 245-56

Finley, Moses (1965), *The World of Odysseus*, New York: Viking

―――― (1973), *The Ancient Economy*, Berkeley: University of California Press

―――― (1982), *Economy and Society in Ancient Greece*, Brent D. Shaw and Richard Sallee (eds), New York: Viking

Finn, R. Welldon (1973), *Domesday Book*, London: Phillimore

Fischer, Henry George (1961a), 'Land Records on Stelae of the Twelfth Dynasty', *Revue égyptologique*, 13, 107-9

―――― (1961b), 'Notes on the Moʿalla Inscriptions and Some Contemporaneous Texts', *Wiener Zeitschrift für die Kunde des Morgenlandes*, 57, 59-77

―――― (1964), *Inscriptions from the Coptite Nome: Dynasties VI-XI*, Rome: Pontificium Institutum Biblicum

Fish, T. (1938), 'The Sumerian City Nippur in the Period of the Third Dynasty of Ur', *Iraq*, 5, 157-79

―――― (1953), 'Gemé at Umma', *Manchester Cuneiform Studies*, 3, 47-55

Fisher, Loren, R. (1958), 'An Amarna Age Prodigal', *Journal of Semitic Studies*, 3, 113-20

Fitzmyer, Joseph A. (1971), 'A Re-Study of an Elephantine Aramaic Marriage Contract (*AP* 15)', in Hans Goedicke (ed.), *Near Eastern Studies in Honor of William Foxwell Albright*, Baltimore: Johns Hopkins University Press, 137-68

Fogel, Robert W. and Stanley L. Engerman (1970), 'A Comparison of the Relative Efficiency of Slave and Free Agriculture in the United States during the 1860s', in Van der Wee (ed.), *Fifth International Congress*, VI-VIII, 141-6

Forbes, R.J. (1964), *Studies in Ancient Technology*, II, V, VIII, IX, Leiden: Brill

Forquin, Guy (1976), *Lordship and Feudalism in the Middle Ages*, New York: Pica

Foster, Benjamin R. (1977), 'Commercial Activity in Sargonic Mesopotamia', *Iraq*, 39, 31-44

―――― (1981), 'A New Look at the Sumerian Temple State', *Journal of the Economic and Social History of the Orient*, 24, 225-41

―――― (1982), *Umma in the Sargonic Period*, Hamden: Connecticut Academy of Arts and Sciences

Francis, E.P., and Michael Vikers, (1984), 'Green Goddess: A Gift to Lindos from Amasis of Egypt', *American Journal of Archaeology*, 88, 68-9

Frankfort, Henri (1959), *The Birth of Civilization in the Near East*, Bloomington: Indiana University Press

Frayne, Douglas (1983), 'Šulgi, the Runner', *Journal of the American Oriental Society*, 103, 739-48

Friedman, Milton (1959), *A Program for Monetary Stability*, New York: Fordham University Press

Friedmann, Alec H. (1981), 'Economic Geography and the Administration at Nuzi', unpublished PhD dissertation, Cincinnati: Hebrew Union College — Jewish Institute of Religion

Frymer-Kensky, Tikva (1981), 'Supranational Legal Procedures in Elam and Nuzi', in Morrison and Owen (eds), *Nuzi and the Hurrians*, 115-31

Furley, William D. (1981), *Studies in the Use of Fire in Ancient Greek Religion*, Salem, New Hampshire: Ayer

Fussfeld, Daniel B. (1957), 'Economic Theory Misplaced: Livelihood in Primitive Society', in Karl Polanyi (ed.), *Trade and Market in Early Empires*, New York: Free Press, 342-55

Gadd, C.J. (1971), 'The Cities of Babylonia', in Edwards *et al.* (eds), *Early History*, 93-144

―――― (1973), 'Hammurabi and the End of His Dynasty', in Edwards *et al.* (eds), *Early History*, 176-227

―――― (1975), 'Assyria and Babylon, c. 1370-1300 B.C.' in Edwards *et al.* (eds), *History of the Middle East*, 21-48

al-Gailani, Lamia (1965), 'Tell edh-Dhibaʾi', *Sumer*, 21, 33-9

Ganshof, F.L. (1964), *Feudalism*, New York: Harper & Row

Gardiner, Alan H. (1930), 'Two Hieroglyphic Signs and the Egyptian Words for "Alabaster" and "Linen", etc.', *Bulletin de l'institut français d'archéologie orientale*, 30, 161-83

―――― (1935), 'A Lawsuit Arising from the Purchase of Two Slaves', *Journal of Egyptian Archaeology*, 21, 140-6

―――― (1941), 'Ramesside Texts Relating to the Taxation and Transport of Corn', *Journal of Egyptian Archaeology*, 27, 19-73

―――― (1947), *Ancient Egyptian Onomastica*, I, II, London: Oxford University Press

―――― (1948), *The Wilbour Papyrus*, II. London: Oxford University Press for the Brooklyn Museum

―――― (1951), 'A Protest against Unjustified Tax-Demands', *Revue d'Egyptologie*, 6, 115-27

Garelli, Paul (1963), *Les Assyriens en Cappadoce*, Paris: Librarie Adrien Maisonneuve

―――― (1979), 'Assur and its Temple in the Light of Old Texts', *Sumer*, 35, 411-08

Garnsey, Peter, Keith Hopkins, and C.R. Whittaker (1983), *Trade in the Ancient Economy*, London: Chatto & Windus

Gavin, Carney E.S. (1981), 'The Nuzi Collections in the Harvard Semitic Museum', in Morrison and Owen (eds), *Nuzi and the Hurrians*, 137-53

Gelb, I.J. (1965), 'The Ancient Mesopotamian Ration System', *Journal of Near Eastern Studies*, 24, 230-43

―――― (1968), 'The Word for Dragoman in the Ancient Near East', *Glossa*, 2, 93-104

―――― (1971), 'On the Alleged Temple and State Economies in Ancient Mesopotamia', *Studi in Onore di Edwardo Volterra*, 6, 137-54

―――― (1972), 'The Arua Institution', *Revue d'assyriologie et d'archéologie orientale*, 66, 1-32

―――― (1973), 'Prisoners of War in Early Mesopotamia', *Journal of Near Eastern Studies*, 32, 70-98

―――― (1979), 'Household and Family in Mesopotamia', in Lipiński (ed.), *State and Temple Economy*, II, 1-97

―――― (1980), 'Comparative Method in the Study of the Society and Economy of the

Ancient Near East', *Rocznik Orientalistyczny*, 2, 29-36

—————— (1982), 'Terms for Slaves in Ancient Mesopotamia', in Dandamayev (ed.), *Societies and Languages*, 81-98

—————— and E. Sollberger (1957), 'The First Legal Document from the Later Old Assyrian Period', *Journal of Near Eastern Studies*, 16, 163-75

Georgiou, Hara (1979), 'Relations between Cyprus and the Near East in the Middle and Late Bronze Age', *Levant*, 11, 84-100

Gerstenblith, Patty (1983), *The Levant at the Beginning of the Middle Bronze Age*, Winona Lake, Indiana: Eisenbrauns for American Schools of Oriental Research

Geva, Shulamit (1982), 'Archaeological Evidence for the Trade Between Israel and Tyre?' *Bulletin of the American Schools of Oriental Research*, 248, 69-72

Gibson, J.C.L. (1977), *Canaanite Myths and Legends*, Edinburgh: Clark

Gibson, McGuire, and Robert D. Biggs (eds) (1977), *Seals and Sealing in the Ancient Near East*, Malibu, California: Undema

Ginsberg, H.L. (1969), 'Ugaritic Myths, Epics, and Legends', in Pritchard (ed.), *Ancient Near Eastern Texts*, 129-55

Giorgadze, G. (1982), 'Einige Bemerkungen zum hethitischen Text KUB 48, 105', in Dandamayev *et al*, (eds), *Societies and Languages*, 110-16

Giveon, Raphael (1978), 'Ancient Egyptian Mining Centres in South-Sinai', in R. Giveon, *The Impact of Egypt on Canaan*, Göttingen: Universitätsverlag Freiburg Schweiz, 51-60

Glanville, S.R.K. (1935), 'Weights and Balances in Ancient Egypt', *Weekly Evening Meeting*, November 8, 10-40

Gledhill, John and Mogens Trolle Larsen, 'The Polanyi Paradigm and a Dynamic Analysis of Archaic States', unavailable

Glotz, Gustave (1925), *The Aegean Civilization*, London: Kegan Paul

—————— (1967), *Ancient Greece at Work*, New York: Norton

Goedicke, Hans (1969-70), 'An Egyptian Claim to Asia', *Journal of the American Research Center in Egypt*, 8, 11-27

—————— (1971-72), 'Tax Deduction for Religious Donations', *Journal of the American Research Center in Egypt*, 9, 73-5

—————— (1975a), *The Report of Wenamun*, Baltimore: Johns Hopkins University Press

—————— (1975b), 'Unity and Diversity in the Oldest Religion of Ancient Egypt', in Hans Goedicke and J.J.M. Roberts (eds), *Unity and Diversity: Essays in the History, Literature, and Religion of the Ancient Near East*, Baltimore: John Hopkins University Press, 201-17

—————— (1977), *The Protocol of Neferyt (The Prophecy of Neferti)*, Baltimore: Johns Hopkins University Press

Goetze, Albrecht (1962), 'Two Ur Dynasty Tablets Dealing with Labor', *Journal of Cuneiform Studies*, 16, 13-16

—————— (1965), 'Tavern Keepers and the Like in Ancient Babylonia', *Assyriological Studies*, 16, 211-15

—————— (1969a), 'The Laws of Eshnunna', in Pritchard (ed.), *Ancient Near Eastern Texts*, 161-3

—————— (1969b), 'The Hittite Laws', in Pritchard (ed.), *Ancient Near Eastern Texts*, 188-97

Goitein, S.D. (1967), *A Mediterranean Society, I, Economic Foundations*, Berkeley: University of California Press

Gomi, Tohru (1980), 'On Dairy Productivity at Ur in the Late Ur III Period', *Journal of the Economic and Social History of the Orient*, 23, 1-42

Goody, Jack (1983), *The Development of the Family and Marriage in Europe*, Cambridge: Cambridge University Press

Gophna, Ram (1976), 'Egyptian Immigration into Southern Canaan during the First

Dynasty?' *Tel Aviv*, 3, 31-7

Gordon, Cyrus H. (1936), 'The Status of Woman Reflected in the Nuzi Tablets', *Zeitschrift für Assyriologie*, 9, 146-69

Graesser, Carl F. (1972), 'Standing Stones in Ancient Palestine', *Biblical Archaeologist*, 35, 34-63

de Graeve, Marie-Christine (1981), *The Ships of the Ancient World*, Leuven: Department Oriëntalistiek

Graham, A.J. (1971), 'Patterns in Early Greek Colonisation', *Journal of Hellenic Studies*, 91, 35-47

Grant, Michael (1980), *The Etruscans*, New York: Scribner's

Graves, Philip E., Robert L. Sexton, and Richard K. Vedder (1983), 'Slavery, Amenities, and Factor Price Equalization: A Note on Migration and Freedom', *Explorations in Economic History*, 20, 156-62

Grayson, Albert K. (1972), *Assyrian Royal Inscriptions*, I, Wiesbaden: Harrassowitz

Green, Margaret Whitney (1975), 'Eridu in Sumerian Literature', unpublished PhD dissertation, Chicago: University of Chicago

Greenberg, Moshe (1951), 'Hebrew s^e*gulla* Akkadian *sikiltu*', *Journal of the American Oriental Society*, 71, 172-4

Greenfield, J.C. (1982a), 'Two Biblical Passages in the Light of Their Near Eastern Background—Ezekiel 16:30 and Malachi 3:17' (English summary), *Eretz-Israel*, 16, 253

—— (1982b), 'Babylonian-Aramaic Relationship', in Nissen and Renger (eds), *Mesopotamien und seine Nachbarn*, II, 471-82

Greengus, S. (1966), 'Old Babylonian Marriage Ceremonies and Rites', *Journal of Cuneiform Studies*, 20, 55-72

—— (1984), 'Review of Morrison and Owen', *Journal of the American Oriental Society*, 104, 364-6

Greenwald, Bruce, and Robert R. Glasspiegel (1983), 'Adverse Selection in the Market for Slaves: New Orleans, 1830-1860', *Quarterly Journal of Economics*, 98, 479-99

Grégoire, Jean-Pierre (1970), *Archives administratives sumériennes*, Paris: Geuthner

Grierson, Philip (1977), *The Origins of Money*, London: Athlone

Griffith, F. Ll. (1909), *Catalogue of the Demotic Papyri in the John Ryland Library*, III, Manchester: Manchester University Press

—— (1927), 'The Abydos Decree of Seti I at Nauri', *Journal of Egyptian Archaeology*, 13, 193-208

Griffiths, J. Gwyn (1970), *Plutarch's De Iside et Osiride*, Cambridge: Wales University Press

—— (1980), *The Origins of Osiris and His Cult*, Leiden: Brill

Grosz, Katarzna (1981), 'Dowry and Brideprice at Nuzi', in Morrison and Owen (eds), *Nuzi and the Hurrians*, 161-82

Gurney, O.R. (1966), *The Hittites*, Harmondsworth: Penguin

Gyles, Mary Francis (1959), *Pharaonic Policies and Administration, 663 to 323 B.C.*, Chapel Hill: University of North Carolina Press

Von Hagen, Victor W. (1967), *The Roads That Led to Rome*, Cleveland: World

Hallo, William W. (1958), 'Contributions to Neo-Sumerian', *Hebrew Union College Annual*, 29, 69-107

—— (1963), 'Lexical Notes on the Neo-Sumerian Metal Industry', *Bibliotheca Orientalis*, 20, 136-42

—— (1964), 'The Road to Emar', *Journal of Cuneiform Studies*, 18, 57-88

—— (1965), 'A "Persian Gulf" Seal on an Old Babylonian Mercantile Agreement', *Assyriological Studies*, 16, 199-203

—— (1970), 'Antediluvian Cities', *Journal of Cuneiform Studies*, 23, 57-67

—— (1973), 'The Date of the Fara Period: A Case Study of the Historiography of

Early Mesopotamia', in Giorgio Buccellati (ed.), *Approaches to the Study of the Ancient Near East*, Rome: Biblical Institute Press, 228-38

────── (1981), 'A Letter Fragment from Tel Aphek'. *Tel Aviv*, 8, 18-24

Hammershaimb, E. (1957), 'Some Observations on the Aramaic Elephantine Papyri', *Vetus Testamentum*, 7, 17-34

Hammond, Mason (1972), *The City in the Ancient World*, Cambridge: Harvard University Press

Har-El, Menashe (1977), 'The Valley of the Craftsmen', *Palestine Exloration Quarterly*, 109, 75-86

Harmatta, J., and G. Komoróczy (eds) (1976), *Wirtschaft und Gesellschaft im alten Vorderasien*, Budapest: Akademiai Kiado

Harris, Rivkah (1955), 'The Archive of the Sin Temple in Khafajah (Tutub)', *Journal of Cuneiform Studies*, 9, 31-58, 59-69, 91-105

────── (1960), 'Old Babylonian Temple Loans', *Journal of Cuneiform Studies*, 14, 126-37

────── (1963), 'The Organization and Administration of the Cloister in Ancient Babylonia', *Journal of the Economic and Social History of the Orient*, 6, 121-57

────── (1964), 'The *Nadītu* Woman', in Robert M. Adams (ed.) (forward), *Studies Presented to A. Leo Oppenheim*, Chicago: Oriental Institute of the University of Chicago, 106-35

────── (1965), 'The Journey of the Divine Weapon', *Assyriological Studies*, 16, 217-24

────── (1968), 'Some Aspects of the Centralization of the Realm under Hammurabi and His Successors', *Journal of the American Oriental Society*, 88, 727-37

────── (1972), 'Notes on the Nomenclature of Old Babylonian Sippar', *Journal of Cuneiform Studies*, 24, 102-4

────── (1975), *Ancient Sippar: A Demographic Study of an Old Babylonian City*, Istanbul: Nederlands Historisch-Archåologisch Institut Te Istanbul in het Nabije Oosten

Harrison, A.R.W. (1968), *The Law of Athens, The Family and Property*, London: Oxford University Press

Hawkins, J.D. (1979), 'Some Historical Problems of the Hieroglyphic Luwian Inscriptions', *Anatolian Studies*, 29, 153-67

Hayden, Roy Edmund (1962), 'Court Procedure at Nuzi', unpublished PhD dissertation, Waltham, Massachusetts: Brandeis University

Hayes, William C. (1946), 'Royal Decrees from the Temple of Min at Coptos', *Journal of Egyptian Archaeology*, 32, 3-23

────── (1955), *A Papyrus of the Late Middle Kingdom in the Brooklyn Museum*, New York: Brooklyn Museum

Heichelheim, Fritz M. (1958), *An Ancient Economic History*, I, II, III, Leiden: Sijthoff

Heimpel, Wolfgang (1981), 'The Nanshe Hymn', *Journal of Cuneiform Studies*, 33, 65-139

Helck, W. (1970), 'Ein Indiz früher Handelfahrten syrischer Kaufleute', *Ugarit Forschungen*, 2, 35-7

────── (1975), *Wirtschaftsgeschichte des alten Ägypten im 3. und 2. Jahrtausend vor Chr*, Leiden: Brill

────── (1979), 'Einige Betrachtungen zu den frühesten Beziehungen zwischen Ägypten und Vorderasien', *Ugarit Forschungen*, 11, 357-63

Hellie, Richard (1971), *Enserfment and Military Change in Muscovy*, Chicago: University of Chicago Press

Heltzer, Michael (1969), 'Problems of the Social History of Syria in the Late Bronze Age', in M. Liverani (ed.), *La Siria nel Tardo Bronzo*, Rome: Centro per le Antichita e la Storia dell'Arte del Vicion Oriente, 31-46

——— (1976a), 'Mortgage of Land Property and Freeing It in Ugarit', *Journal of the Economic and Social History of the Orient*, 19, 89-95

——— (1976b), *The Rural Community in Ancient Ugarit*, Wiesbaden: Reichert

——— (1978a), *Goods, Prices, and the Organization of Trade in Ugarit*, Wiesbaden: Reichert

——— (1978b), 'The *Rabbaᵗum* in Mari and the *Rpi(m)* in Ugarit', *Orientalis Lovaniensia Periodica*, 9, 5-20

——— (1982), *The Internal Organization of the Kingdom of Ugarit: Royal Service-System, Taxes, Royal Economy, Army, and Administration*, Wiesbaden: Reichert

Hemming, W.B. (1956), 'The "Coin" with Cuneiform Inscription', *Numismatic Chronicle*, 16, 327-8

Hill, Harold P. (1967), 'Tell Asmar: The Private Home Area', in Delougaz *et al.* (eds), *Private Houses*, 143-81

Hillers, Delbert R. (1971), 'Hebrew Cognate of *Unuššu/ᵗUnt* in Is. 33:8'. *Harvard Theological Review*, 64, 257-9

Hinz, Walther (1973a), 'Persia c. 1800-1550 B.C.', in Edwards *et al.* (eds), *History of Middle East*, 256-88

——— (1973b), *The Lost World of Elam*, New York: New York University Press

Hirschmeier, Johannes, and Tsunehiku Yui (1975), *The Development of the Japanese Economy, 1600-1973*, Cambridge: Harvard University Press

Hirshleifer, Jack (1980), *Price Theory and Applications*, Englewood Cliffs: Prentice Hall

Hodges, Henry (1977), *Technology in the Ancient World*, New York: Knopf

Hodjash, Svetlana, and Oleg D. Berlev, 'A Market Scene in the Mastaba of *D3d3-m-ᶜnh*', *Altorientalische Forschungen*, 7, 31-49

Hoffman, Richard D. (1975), 'Medieval Origins of the Common Fields', in William W. Parker and Eric L. Jones (eds), *European Peasants and Their Markets*, Princeton: Princeton University Press, 23-71

Hoffner, Harry A., Jr. (1968), 'A Hittite Text in Epic-Style about Merchants', *Journal of Cuneiform Studies*, 22, 34-45

——— (1973), 'The Hittites and Hurrians', in D.J. Wiseman (ed.), *Peoples of Old Testament Times*, London: Oxford University Press, 197-228

——— (1974), 'The Arzana House', in K. Bittel *et al.* (eds), *Anatolian Studies*, 113-21

Holmes, Y. Lynn (1975), 'The Foreign Trade of Cyprus during the Late Bronze Age', in Noel Robertson (ed.), *The Archaeology of Cyprus: Recent Developments*, Park Ridge, New Jersey: Noyes, 90-110

Hopkins, Keith (1978), *Conquerors and Slaves: Sociological Studies in Roman History*, I, Cambridge: Cambridge University Press

——— (1983), 'Models, Ships, and Staples', in Peter Garnsey and C.R. Whittaker (eds), *Trade and Famine in Classical Antiquity*, Cambridge: Cambridge Philological Society, 84-109

Hopper, R.J. (1979), *Trade and Industry in Classical Greece*, London: Thames & Hudson

Horn, Siegfried H. (1963), 'Byblos in Ancient Records', *Andrews University Seminary Studies*, 1, 52-61

Hornung, Erik (1982), *Conceptions of God in Ancient Egypt*, Ithaca: Cornell University Press

Howard-Carter, Theresa (1981), 'The Tangible Evidence for the Earliest Dilmun', *Journal of Cuneiform Studies*, 33, 210-23

Hruška, B. (1974), 'Die Reformtexte Urukaginas: Der verspätete Versuch einer Konsolidierung des Stadtstaates von Lagaš', in Paul Garelli (ed.), *XIXᵉ rencontre assyriologique international: le palais et la royauté*, Paris: Geuthner, 151-61

———— (1976), 'Das Drehem-Archiv und die Probleme der neusumerischen Viehwirtschaft ', in Harmatta and Komoróczy (eds), *Wirtschaft und Gesellschaft*, 91-101

———— and Komoróczy, G. (eds) (1978), *Festschrift Lubor Matouš*, Budapest: no publisher

Hughes, Diane (1975), 'Domestic Ideals and Social Behavior: Evidence from Medieval Genoa', in Charles E. Rosenberg (ed.), *The Family in History*, Philadelphia: University of Pennsylvania Press, 115-43

Hughes, George Robert (1952), *Saite Demotic Land Leases*, Chicago: University of Chicago Press

Humphreys, S.C. (1978), *History, Economics and Anthropology: The Work of Karl Polanyi*, London: Routledge & Kegan Paul

———— (1983), *The Family, Women, and Death: Comparative Studies*, London: Routledge & Kegan Paul

Isager, Signe, and Mogens Herman Hansen (1975), *Aspects of Athenian Society in the Fourth Century*, Odense: Odense University Press

Israelit-Groll, Sarah (1982), 'Diachronic Grammar as a Means of Dating Undated Texts', in S. Israelit-Groll (ed.), *Egyptological Studies*, Jerusalem: Magnes, 11-104

Jacobsen, Thorkild (1960), 'The Waters of Ur', *Iraq*, 22, 174-85

———— (1970), 'On the Textile Industry at Ur under Ibbi Sin', in William L. Moran (ed.), *Towards the Image of Tammuz and Other Essays on Mesopotamian History and Culture by Thorkild Jacobsen*, Cambridge: Harvard University Press, 216-29, 422-7

———— (1976), *Treasures of Darkness: A History of Mesopotamian Religion*, New Haven: Yale University Press

———— (1979), 'Iphur-Kishi and His Times', *Archiv für Orientforschung*, 36, 1-14

———— (1982), *Salinity and Irrigation Agriculture in Antiquity*, Malibu: California: Undema

James, T.G.H. (1984), Pharaoh's People, Chicago: University of Chicago Press

Jankowska, Ninel B. (1970), 'Private Contracts in the Commerce of Ancient Western Asia (2nd Millennium B.C.)', in Van Der Wee (ed.), *Fifth International Congress*, V, 150-68

———— (1982), 'The Mittanian Šattiwasa in Arraphe', in Dandamayev (ed.), *Societies and Languages*, 138-49

Janssen, Jacob J. (1961), *Two Ancient Egyptian Ship's Logs*, Leiden: Brill

———— (1975a), 'Prolegomena to the Study of Egypt's Economic History during the New Kingdom', *Studien zur altägyptischen Kultur*, 3, 127-85

———— (1975b), *Commodity Prices from the Ramessid Period: An Economic Study of the Village of the Necropolis Workers*, Leiden: Brill

———— (1982), 'Gift-Giving in Ancient Egypt as an Economic Feature', *Journal of Egyptian Archaeology*, 68, 253-8

Janssen, Jozef M.A. (1955-56), 'Egyptological Remarks on the Story of Joseph', *Ex Oriente Lux*, 14, 63-72

Jelinkova, E.A.E. (1957), 'Sale of Inherited Property in the First Century B.C.', *Journal of Egyptian Archaeology*, 43, 45-55, 61-74

Jensen, William C., and William H. Meckling (1976), 'Theory of the Firm: Managerial Behavior, Agency Costs and Ownership Structure', *Journal of Financial Economics*, 3, 305-60

Jones, Robert H. (1976), 'The Origin and Development of Media of Exchange', *Journal of Political Economy*, 84, 757-75

Jones, Tom B. (1962), *The Silver-Plated Age*, Sandoval, New Mexico: Coronado

———— and John W. Snyder (1961), *Sumerian Economic Texts from the Third Ur Dynasty*, Minneapolis: Minnesota University Press

Kadish, Gerald E. (1966), 'Old Kingdom Egyptian Activity in Nubia: Some Reconsiderations', *Journal of Egyptian Archaeology*, 52, 23-33

Kalluveettil, Paul (1982), *Declaration and Covenant*, Rome: Biblical Institute

Kanawati, Naguib (1977), *The Egyptian Administration in the Old Kingdom*, Warminster: Aris & Phillips

Kaplony, P. (1962), 'Miszellen', *Zeitschrift für ägyptische Sprache und Altertumskunde*, 88, 73-4

Kaster, Joseph (1968), *Wings of the Falcon: Life and thought in Ancient Egypt*, New York: Holt, Rinehart, and Winston

Katzenstein, H. Jacob (1979), 'Tyre in the Early Persian Period (539-486 B.C.E.)', *Biblical Archaeologist*, 42, 23-34

Kemp, Barry J. (1983), 'Old Kingdom, Middle Kingdom and Second Intermediate Period c. 2686-1552 B.C.', in B.G. Tirgger *et al.* (eds), *Ancient Egypt*, 71-182

Kenyon, Kathleen M. (1960), *Archaeology in the Holy Land*, New York: Praeger

Kienast, Burkhart (1960), *Die altassyrischen Texte des orientalischen Seminars der Universität Heidelberg und der Sammlung Erlenmeyer-Basel*, Berlin: de Gruyter

Killen, J.T. (1979), 'The Linear B Tablets and Economic History: Some Problems', *Bulletin of the Institute of Classical Studies*, 26, 133-4

Kilmer, Anne Draffkorn (1974), 'Symbolic Gestures in Akkadian Contracts from Alalakh and Ugarit', *Journal of the American Oriental Society*, 94, 177-83

Kitchen, K.A. (1971), 'Punt and How to Get There', *Orientalia*, 40, 190-207

Klein, Jeffrey (1972), 'A Greek Metalworking Quarter: Eighth Century Excavations on Ischia', *Expedition*, 14, 34-9

Klengel, Horst (ed.) (1971a), *Beiträge zur sozialen Strucktur des alten Vorderasien*, Berlin: Akademie-Verlag

——— (1971b), 'Soziale Aspeckte der altbabylonischen Dienstmiete', in Klengel (ed.), *Beiträge zur sozialen Strucktur*, 39-52

——— (1975), 'Zur ökonomischen Funktion der hethitischen Tempel', *Studi Micenei ed Egeo-Anatolici*, 10, 181-200

——— (1980), 'Zum Bewässerungsbodenbau am mittleren Euphrat nach den Texten von Mari', *Altorientalische Forschungen*, 7, 77-87

——— (ed.) (1982), *Gesellschaft und Kultur im alten Vorderasien*, Berlin: Akademie-Verlag

Knapp, A. Bernard (1983), 'An Alashiyan Merchant at Ugarit', *Tel Aviv*, 10, 38-45

Kochavi, Moshe (1974), 'Khirbet Rabûd = Debir', *Tel Aviv*, 1, 2-33

Kocka, Jürgen (1971), 'Family and Bureaucracy in German Industrial Management', *Business History Review*, 45, 133-56

Kohl, Philip L. (1978), 'The Balance of Trade in Southwestern Asia in the Mid-Third Millennium B.C.', *Current Anthropology*, 19, 463-75

Komoróczy, Géza (1973), 'Berosos and the Mesopotamian Literature', *Acta Antiqua*, 21, 119-52

——— (1976), 'Work and Strike of Gods: New Light on the Divine Society in the Sumero-Akkadian Mythology', *Oikumene*, 1, 9-37

——— (1978), 'Landed Property in Ancient Mesopotamia and the Theory of the So-called Asiatic Mode of Production', *Oikumene*, 2, 1-18

Kovalevsky, Maxime (1891), *Modern Customs and Ancient Laws of Russia*, London: Nutt

Kraay, Colin M. (1976), *Archaic and Classical Greek Coins*, Berkeley, California: University of California Press

Kraemer, Ross S. (1979), 'Ecstasy and Possession: The Attraction of Women to the Cult of Dionysus', *Harvard Theological Review*, 72, 55-80

Kramer, Samuel Noah (1952), *Enmerkar and the Lord of Aratta*, Philadelphia: University Museum of the University of Pennsylvania

—— (1963), *The Sumerians*, Chicago: University of Chicago Press

—— (1969a), 'The Curse of Agade', in Pritchard (ed.), *Ancient Near Eastern Texts*, 646-51

—— (1969b), 'Lipit-Ištar Lawcode', in Pritchard (ed.), *Ancient Near Eastern Texts*, 159-61

—— (1969c), 'Sumerian Hymns', in Pritchard (ed.), *Ancient Near Eastern Texts*, 573-86

—— (1981), *History Begins at Sumer*, Philadelphia: University of Pennsylvania

Krecher, J. (1976), 'Die Aufgliederung des Kaupfreises nach sumerischen Kaufverträgen der Fara- und der Akkade-Zeit', in Harmatta and Komoröczy (eds), *Wirtschaft und Gesellschaft*, 29-32

Kruchten, J.M. (1979), 'L'Évolution de la Gestion Domaniale Sous le Nouvel Empire Egyptien', in Lipiński (ed.), *State and Temple Economy*, II, 517-25

Labuschagne, L.L. (1974), 'The *Našû-Nadanu* Formula and Its Biblical Equivalent', in Van Voss et al., *Travels in the World of the Old Testament*, 176-80

Laessoe, Jorgen (1951), 'The Irrigation System at Ulḫu, 8th Century B.C.', *Journal of Cuneiform Studies*, 5, 21-32

Lambert, Maurice (1953), 'Textes commerciaux de Lagash', *Revue d'assyriologie et d'archéologie orientale*, 47, 57-69

—— (1963), 'L'Usage de l'argent-metal à Lagash au temps de la IIIe dynastie d'Ur', *Revue d'assyriologie et d'archéologie orientale*, 57, 79-92, 193-200

Lambert, W.G. (1960), *Babylonian Wisdom Literature*, Oxford: Oxford University Press

Lane, Frederic C. (1944), 'Family Partnerships and Joint Ventures in the Venetian Republic', *Journal of Economic History*, 4, 78-96

Langdon, Stephen (1907), 'An Early Babylonian Tablet of Warnings for the King', *Journal of the American Oriental Society*, 28, 145-54

Larsen, Mogens Trolle (1974), 'The Old Assyrian Colonies in Anatolia', *Journal of the American Oriental Society*, 94, 468-75

—— (1976), *The Old Assyrian City-State and Its Colonies*, Copenhagen: Akademisk Forlag

—— (1977a), 'Partnerships in Old Assyrian Trade', *Iraq*, 39, 119-45

—— (1977b), 'Seal Use in the Old Assyrian Period', in Gibson and Biggs (eds), *Seals and Sealing*, 92-105

—— (1982), 'Your Money or Your Life: A Portrait of an Assyrian Businessment', in Dandamayev (ed.), *Societies and Languages*, 214-45

Lattimore, Owen (1962), *Studies in Frontier History: Collected Papers, 1929-1958*, London: Oxford University Press

Lattimore, Richmond (trans. and introd.) (1951), *The Iliad of Homer*, Chicago: University of Chicago Press

Leemans, W.F. (1950a), *The Old Babylonian Merchant*, Leiden: Brill

—— (1950b), 'The Rate of Interest in Old Babylonian Times', *Revue internationale des droits de l'antiquité*, 5, 7-34

—— (1954), *Legal and Economic Records from the Kingdom of Larsa*, Leiden: Brill

—— (1960a), *Foreign Trade in the Old Babylonian Period*, Leiden: Brill

—— (1960b), *Legal and Administrative Documents of the Time of Hammurabi and Samsuiluna*, Leiden: Brill

—— (1960c), 'Some Marginal Remarks on Ancient Technology', *Journal of the Economic and Social History of the Orient*, 3, 217-37

—— (1961), 'The Asiru.' *Revue d'assyriologie et d'archéologie orientale*, 55, 57-76

—— (1968), 'Old Babylonian Letters and Economic History', *Journal of the Economic and Social History of the Orient*, 11, 171-226

—— (1975), 'The Role of Land Lease in Mesopotamia in the Early Second

Millennium', *Journal of the Economic and Social History of the Orient*, 18, 134-48

—— (1977), 'The Importance of Trade: Some Introductory Remarks', *Iraq*, 39, 2-10

—— (1983), '*Trouve-t-on des "communautés rurales" dans l'ancienne Mésopotamie?*' Recueils de la société Jean Bodin pour l'histoire comparative des institutions, XLI, Paris: Dessain et Tolra

Leighton, Albert C. (1972), *Transport and Communication in Early Medieval Europe, A.D. 500-1100*, New York: Barnes & Noble

Lemche, Niels Peter (1979), '*Andurārum* and *Mīšarum*: Comments on the Problem of Social Edicts and Their Application in the Ancient Near East', *Journal of Near Eastern Studies*, 38, 11-22

Levey, M. (1959), *Chemistry and Chemical Technology in Ancient Mesopotamia*, Amsterdam: Elsevier

Levine, Baruch A. (1968), '*Mulūgu/Melûg*: The Origins of a Talmudic Institution', *Journal of the American Oriental Society*, 88, 271-85

—— (1974), *In the Presence of the Lord: A Study of Cult and Some Cultic Terms in Ancient Israel*, Leiden: Brill

Levmore, Saul (1982), 'Monitors and Freeriders in Commercial and Corporate Settings', *Yale Law Journal*, 92, 49-83

Lévy, Jean-Phillippe (1967), *The Economic Life of the Ancient World*, Chicago: University of Chicago Press

Lewis, Naghtali (1960), 'On Timber and Nile Shipping', *Transactions of the American Philological Society*, 91, 137-41

Lewy, Hildegard (1956), 'On Some Old Assyrian Cereal Names', *Journal of the American Oriental Society*, 76, 201-4

—— (1964a), 'The Assload, the Sack, and Other Measures of Capacity', *Rivista degli Studi Orientali*, 39, 181-97

—— (1964b), 'Notes on the Political Organization of Asia Minor at the Time of the Old Assyrian Texts', *Orientalia*, 33, 181-98

Lewy, Julius (1950-51), 'Tabor, Tibar, Atabyros', *Hebrew Union College Annual*, 23, 357-86

—— (1955), 'Old Assyrian *ḫusârum* and Sanchunyâtôn's Story about Chusor', *Israel Exploration Journal*, 5, 154-62

—— (1958a), 'Some Aspects of Commercial Life in Assyria and Asia Minor in the Nineteenth Pre-Christian Century', *Journal of the American Oriental Society*, 78, 89-101

—— (1958b), 'The Biblical Institution of $D^e r\hat{o}r$ in the Light of Akkadian Documents', *Eretz-Israel*, 5, 21-31

—— (1961), 'Amurritica', *Hebrew Union College Annual*, 32, 31-74

—— and Hildegard Lewy (1942-43), 'The Origin of the Week and the Oldest West Asiatic Calendar', *Hebrew Union College Annual*, 17, 1-152

Lichtheim, Miriam (1973, 1976, 1980), *Ancient Egyptian Literature: A Book of Readings*, I, II, III, Berkeley: University of California Press

Lieberman, Stephen J. (1969), 'An Ur III Text from Drēhem Recording "Booty from the Land of Mardu"', *Journal of Cuneiform Studies*, 22, 53-62

Liebermann, Yehoshua (1983), 'The Economics of *kethubah* Valuation', *History of Political Economy*, 15, 519-28

Limet, Henri (1960), *Le Travail Du Metal Au Pays De Sumer Au Temps De La IIIe Dynastie D'Ur*, Paris: Faculté de Philosophie et Lettres l'Université de Liege

—— (1979), 'Le Rôle du palais dans l'économie néo-sumérienne', in Lipiński (ed.), *State and Temple Economy*, I, 235-48

Lipiński, Edward (1979a), 'Les temples néo-assyriens et les origines du monnayage', in Lipiński (ed.), *State and Temple Economy*, II, 565-88

—— (ed.) (1979b), *State and Temple Economy in Ancient Mesopotamia*, I, II,

Leiden: Brill

——— (1982), 'Sale, Transfer and Delivery in Ancient Semitic Terminology', in Klengel (ed.), *Gesellschaft und Kultur*, 173-85

Liverani, M. (1979a), *Three Amarna Essays* (Matthew L. Jaffe, introd. and trans.), Malibu, California: Undema

——— (1979b), 'Dono, Tributo, Commercio, Ideologia dello Scambia nella Tarda Età del Bronzo', *Annali dell'Istituto Italiano di Numismatica*, 26, 9-28

Lloyd, Seton (1978), *The Archaeology of Mesopotamia*, London: Thames & Hudson

Loane, Helen Jefferson (1938), *Industry and Commerce in the City of Rome (50B.C.-200 A.D.)*, Baltimore: John Hopkins University Press

Loding, Darlene Marilyn (1974), 'A Craft Archive from Ur', unpublished PhD dissertation, Philadelphia University of Pennsylvania

Loewe, Raphael (1955), 'The Earliest Biblical Allusion to Coined Money?' *Palestine Exploration Quarterly*, 141-50

Lopez, Robert S. (1964), 'Market Expansion: The Case of Genoa', *Journal of Economic History*, 24, 415-64

——— (1971), *The Commercial Revolution of the Middle Ages, 950-1350*, Englewood Cliffs: Prentice-Hall

Lorton, David (1974), *The Juridical Terminology of International Relations in Egyptian Texts through Dynasty XVIII*, Baltimore: Johns Hopkins University Press

Lucas, A., and J.R. Harris (1962), *Ancient Egyptian Materials and Industries*, New York: Praeger

Lutz, Henry Frederick (1931), *Legal and Economic Documents from Ashjâly*, Berkeley: University of California Press

——— (1932), 'Babylonian Partnership', *Journal of Economic and Business History*, 4, 552-70

McCloskey, Donald N., and John Nash (1984), 'Corn at Interest: The Extent and Cost of Grain Storage in Medieval England', *American Economic Review*, 74, 174-87

McCown, Chester C. (1943), *The Ladder of Progress in Palestine*, New York: Harper

MacDonald, John (1972), 'Egyptian Interests in Western Asia to the End of the Middle Kingdom: An Evaluation', *Australian Journal of Biblical Archaeology*, 2, 72-98

——— (1980), 'The Supreme Warrior Caste in the Ancient Near East', in R.Y. Ebied and M.J.L. Young (eds), *Oriental Studies*, Leiden: Brill, 39-71

McDonald, William A. (1964), 'Overland Communications in Greece During LH III', in Emmett L. Bennett, Jr. (ed.), *Mycenaean Studies*, Madison: University of Wisconsin Press, 217-40

Machinist, Peter (1983), 'Assyria and Its Image in the First Isaiah', *Journal of the American Oriental Society*, 103, 719-37

Mackaay, Ejan (1982), *Economics of Information and Law*, Boston: Kluwer-Nijhoff

MacMullen, Ramsey (1970), 'Market-Days in the Roman Empire', *Phoenix*, 34, 333-41

——— (1980), 'Woman in Public in the Roman Empire', *Historia*, 29, 208-19

McNeil, Robert Clayton (1970), 'The "Messenger Texts" of the Third Ur Dynasty', unpublished PhD dissertion, Philadelphia: University of Pennsylvania

Macqueen, James (1964), *Babylon*, London: Hale

——— (1975), *The Hittites and Their Contemporaries in Asia Minor*, Boulder: Westview

Macnamara, Ellen (1973), *Everyday Life of the Etruscans*, New York: Putnam

Maekawa, Kazuya (1973-74), 'The Development of the *É-Mí* in Lagash during Early Dynastic III', *Mesopotamia*, 8-9, 77-144

—— (1974), 'Agricultural Production in Ancient Sumer', *Zinbun*, 13, 1-60

—— (1977), 'The Rent of the Tenant Field (*gán-APIN.LAL*) in Lagash', *Zinbun*, 14, 1-54

Maidman, Maynard P. (1976), 'A Socio-Economic Analysis of a Nuzi Family Archive', unpublished PhD dissertation. Philadelphia: University of Pennsylvania

—— (1981), 'The Office of *halsuhlu* in the Nuzi Texts', in Morrison and Owen (eds), *Nuzi and the Hurrians*, 233-46

Maisler, B. (1946), 'Canaan and the Canaanites', *Bulletin of the American Schools of Oriental Research*, 102, 7-12

Makkay, J. (1983), 'The Origins of the "Temple Economy" as Seen in the Light of Prehistoric Evidence', *Iraq*, 45, 1-6

Malamat, A. (1962), 'Mari and the Bible: Some Patterns of Tribal Organization and Institutions', *Journal of the American Oriental Society*, 82, 142-50

—— (1966), 'The Ban in Mari and the Bible', in *Biblical Essays*, Proceedings of the 9th Meeting of 'Die Ou-Testam Werkgemeenskop in Suid-Afrika', 40-9

—— (1971), 'Syro-Palestinian Destinations in a Mari Tin Inventory', *Israel Exploration Journal*, 21, 31-8

Mallowan, M.E.L. (1965a), *Early Mesopotamia and Iran*, New York: McGraw-Hill

—— (1965b), 'The Mechanics of Ancient Trade in Western Asia', *Journal of Persian Studies*, 3, 1-7

Marcus, Abraham (1983), 'Men, Women, and Property', *Journal of the Economic and Social History of the Orient*, 26, 137-63

Martirossian, A. (1983), 'Notes Concerning the Economic Activities of the Babylonian Temple in the First Millennium B.C.', *Iraq*, 45, 128-30

Marzal, A. (1971), 'The Provincial Governor at Mari: His Title and Appointment', *Journal of Near Eastern Studies*, 30, 186-217

Matouš, L. (1974), 'Der Aššur-Tempel nach altassyrischen Urkunden aus Kültepe, in Van Voss *et al.* (eds), *Travels in the World of the Old Testament*, 181-9

Matthews, Victor Harold (1978), *Pastoral Nomadism in the Mari Kingdom (ca. 1830-1760 B.C.)*, Cambridge, Massachusetts: American Schools of Oriental Research

Mauss, Marcel (1967), *The Gift*, New York: Norton

Mazar, A. (1973), 'Excavations at Tell Qasile, 1971-72', *Israel Exploration Journal*, 23, 65-71

Meek, Theophile (1969a), 'Mesopotamian Legal Documents', in Pritchard (ed.), *Ancient Near Eastern Texts*, 217-22

—— (1969b), 'The Code of Hammurabi', in Pritchard (ed.), *Ancient Near Eastern Texts*, 163-80

—— (1969c), 'The Middle Assyrian Laws', in Pritchard (ed.), *Ancient Near Eastern Texts*, 180-88

Megally, Mounir (1977), *Recherches sur l'économie, l'administration et la comptabilité égyptiennes à la XVIIIe dynastie: d'après le Papyrus E. 3226 du Louvre*, Cairo: Institut Français d'archéologie Orientale du Caire

Melitz, Jacques (1970), 'The Polanyi School of Anthropology: An Economist's View', *American Anthropologist*, 72, 1020-40

—— (1974), *Primitive and Modern Money: An Interdisciplinary Approach*, Reading, Massachusetts: Addison Wesley

Mellink, Machteld J. (1969), 'Archaeology in Asia Mïnor', *American Journal of Archaeology*, 73, 204-27

Mendelsohn, Isaac (1949), *Slavery in the Ancient Near East*, New York: Oxford University Press

—— (1955), 'On Slavery in Alalakh', *Israel Exploration Journal*, 5, 65-72

—— (1959), 'A Ugaritic Parallel to the Adoption of Ephraim and Manasseh, *Israel*

Exploration Journal, 9, 180-3

Mercer, Samuel Alfred B. (1912), *The Oath in Babylonian and Assyrian Literature*, Paris: Geuthner

—— (1914), 'The Oath in Cuneiform Inscriptions, Part III, *American Journal of Semitic Languages*, 30, 196-211

Merrillees, R.S. (1972), 'Aegean Bronze Age Relations with Egypt', *American Journal of Archaeology*, 76, 281-94

Mettinger, Tryggve (1971), *Solomonic State Officials*, Lund: Gleerup

—— (1976), *King and Messiah*, Lund: Gleerup

Michell, H. (1957), *The Economics of Ancient Greece*, New York: Barnes & Noble

Milgrom, Jacob (1976), 'The Legal Terms *šlm* and *Brʾšw* in the Bible, *Journal of Near Eastern Studies*, 35, 271-3

Millard, A.R. (1973), 'Cypriot Copper in Babylonia, c. 1745 B.C.', *Journal of Cuneiform Studies*, 25, 211-13

Miller, Patrick D., Jr., and J.J.M. Roberts (1977), *The Hand of the Lord: A Reassessment of the 'Ark Narrative' of 1 Samuel*, Baltimore: Johns Hopkins University Press

Millett, Paul (1983), 'Maritime Loans and the Structure of Credit in Fourth Century Athens', in Garnsey *et al.* (eds), *Trade in the Ancient Economy*, 36-52

Mireaux, Emile (1959), *Daily Life in the Time of Homer*, New York: Macmillan

Moeller, Walter O. (1976), *The Wool Trade of Ancient Pompeii*, Leiden: Brill

Mond, Robert (introd.) (1932), *Studies Presented to F. Ll. Griffith*, London: Egypt Exploration Society

Montet, Pierre (1968), *Lives of the Pharaohs*, Cleveland: World

—— (1981), *Everyday Life in Egypt in the Days of Rameses the Great*, Philadelphia: University of Pennsylvania Press

Moorey, P.R.S. (1982), 'The Archaeological Evidence for Metallurgy and Related Technologies in Mesopotamia, c. 5500-2100 B.C.', *Iraq*, 44, 13-38

Morenz, Siegfried (1973), *Egyptian Religion*, Ithaca: Cornell University Press

Morgan, Willis D. (1927), 'The History and Economics of Suretyship', *Cornell Law Quarterly*, 90, 153-71

Morrison, Martha A. (1974), 'Šilwa-Tešup: Portrait of a Hurrian Prince', unpublished PhD dissertation, Waltham, Massachusetts: Brandeis University

—— (1983), 'The Jacob and Laban Narrative in Light of Near Eastern Sources', *Biblical Archaeologist*, 46, 155-64

—— and D.I. Owen (eds) (1981), *Studies on the Civilization and Culture of Nuzi and the Hurrians*, Winona Lake, Indiana: Eisenbrauns

Mueller, Dieter (1975), 'Some Remarks on Wage Rates in the Middle Kingdom', *Journal of Near Eastern Studies*, 34, 249-63

Muffs, Yohanan (1969), *Studies in the Aramaic Legal Papyri from Elephantine*, Leiden: Brill

Muhly, James D. (1973), *Copper and Tin: The Distribution of Mineral Resources and the Nature of the Metals Trade in the Bronze Age*, Hamden, Connecticut: Connecticut Academy of Arts and Sciences

—— (1980), 'The Bronze Age Setting', in Theodore A. Wertime and James D. Muhly (eds), *The Coming of the Age of Iron*, New Haven: Yale University Press, 25-67

Müller, Manfred (1971), 'Sozial- und wirtschaftspolitische Rechterlässe im Lande Arrapha', in Klengel (ed.), *Beiträge zur sozialen Struktur*, 53-60

—— (1981), 'Ein Prozess um einen Kreditkauf in Nuzi', in Morrison and Owen (eds), *Nuzi and the Hurrians*, 443-54

Müller, W. Max (1906, 1910, 1920), *Egyptological Researches*, I, II, III, Washington, D.C.: Carnegie Institution

Mullen, E. Theodore, Jr. (1980), *The Divine Council in Canaanite and Early Hebrew Literature*, Chico, California: Scholars Press

Munn-Rankin, J.M. (1956), 'Diplomacy in Western Asia in the Early Second Millennium B.C.', *Iraq*, 18, 68-110

Muntingh, L.M. (1967), 'The Social and Legal Status of a Free Ugaritic Female', *Journal of Near Eastern Studies*, 26, 102-12

Mylonas, George E. (1966), *Mycenae and the Mycenaean Age*, Princeton: Princeton University Press

Na'aman, Nadav (1981), 'Economic Aspects of the Egyptian Occupation of Canaan', *Israel Exploration Journal*, 31, 172-85

Nakata, Ichiro (1971), 'Mesopotamian Merchants and Their Ethics', *Journal of the Ancient Near Eastern Society*, 32, 90-101

Naveh, Joseph, and Shaul Shaked (1973), 'Ritual Texts or Treasury Documents?', *Orientalia*, 42, 445-57

Nel, Philip (1977), 'The Concept "Father" in the Wisdom Literature of the Ancient Near East', *Journal of Northwest Semitic Languages*, 5, 53-66

Nelson, Philip (1970), 'Information and Consumer Behavior', *Journal of Political Economy*, 78, 311-29

Newberry, Percy E. (1938), 'Three Old-Kingdom Travellers to Byblos and Pwenet', *Journal of Egyptian Archaeology*, 24, 182-4

Nilsson, Martin P. (1949), *A History of Greek Religion*, London: Oxford University Press

Nissen, Hans-Jorg and Johannes Renger (eds) (1982), *Mesopotamien und seine Nachbarn: politische und kulturelle Wechselbeziehungen im alten Vorderasien vom 4. bis 1. Jahrtausend v. Chr.*, I, II, Berlin: Reimer

North, Douglass C. (1977), 'Markets and Other Allocation Systems in History: The Challenge of Karl Polanyi', *Journal of European Economic History*, 6, 703-16

────── (1981), *Structure and Change in Economic History*, New York: Norton

────── (1984), 'Government and the Cost of Exchange in History', *Journal of Economic History*, 44, 255-64

────── and Robert Paul Thomas (1973), *The Rise of the Western World*, London: Cambridge University Press

Oates, Joan (1978), 'Mesopotamian Social Organization', in J. Friedman and M.J. Rowlands (eds), *The Evolution of Social Systems*, Pittsburgh: University of Pittsburgh Press, 457-85

────── (1979), *Babylon*, London: Thames & Hudson

Oelsner, J. (1976), 'Neue Daten zur sozialen und wirtschaftlichen Situation Nippurs in altbabylonischen Zeit', in Harmatta and Komoróczy (eds), *Wirtschaft und Gesellschaft*, 259-65

Ogilvie, R.M. (1969), *The Romans and Their Gods in the Age of Augustus*, New York: Norton

Özgüç, Nimet (1969), 'Assyrian Trade Colonies in Anatolia', *Archaeology*, 22, 250-5

Oliver, Henry Edmund (1907), *Roman Economic Conditions to the Close of the Republic*, Toronto: University of Toronto Press

Olmstead, A.T. (1923), *The History of Assyria*, Chicago: University of Chicago Press

────── (1930), 'Materials for an Economic History of the Ancient Near East', *Journal of Economic and Business History*, 2, 219-40

────── (1948), *History of the Persian Empire*, Chicago: University of Chicago Press

Oppenheim, A. Leo (1947), 'A Fiscal Practice of the Ancient Near East', *Journal of Near Eastern Studies*, 6, 116-20

────── (1948), *Catalogue of the Cuneiform Tablets of the Wilberforce Eames*

Babylonian Collection, New Haven: American Oriental Society
—— (1954), 'The Seafaring Merchants of Ur', *Journal of the American Oriental Society*, 74, 6-17
—— (1955), 'A Note on ṣòn barzel', *Israel Exploration Journal*, 5, 89-92
—— (1967a), *Letters from Mesopotamia*, Chicago: University of Chicago Press
—— (1967b), 'Essay on Overland Trade in the First Millennium B.C.' *Journal of Cuneiform Studies*, 21, 236-54
—— (1969a), 'Review of R. Bogaert', *Journal of the Economic and Social History of the Orient*, 12, 198-9
—— (1969b), 'Mesopotamia: Land of Cities', in Ira M. Lapidus (ed.), *Middle Eastern Cities*, Berkeley: University of California Press, 13-18
—— (1970), 'Trade in the Ancient Near East', in Van der Wee (ed.), *Fifth International Congress*, V, 125-49
—— (1973), 'Towards a History of Glass in the Ancient Near East', *Journal of the American Oriental Society*, 93, 259-66
—— (1974), 'Old Assyrian *Magāru* or *Makāru*', in Bittel (ed.), *Anatolian Studies*, 229-37
—— and Erica Reiner (1977), *Ancient Mesopotamia*, Chicago: University of Chicago Press
Orlin, Louis Lawrence (1970), *Assyrian Colonies in Cappadocia*. The Hague: Mouton
Ortiz, S. (ed.) (1983), *Economic Anthropology: Topics and Theories*, Lanham, Maryland: University Press of America
Owen, David I. (1969), 'The Loan Documents from Nuzu', unpublished PhD dissertation, Waltham, Massachusetts: Brandeis University
—— (1981a), 'Widow's Rights in Ur III Sumer', *Zeitschrift für Assyriologie*, 70, 170-84
—— (1981b), 'An Akkadian Letter from Ugarit at Tel Aphek', *Tel Aviv*, 8, 1-17
Paradise, Jonathan (1980), 'A Daughter and Her Father's Property at Nuzi', *Journal of Cuneiform Studies*, 32, 189-210
Pardee, Dennis (1975), 'The Ugaritic Text 2106: 10-18. A Bottomry Loan?', *Journal of the American Oriental Society*, 95, 612-19
Parker, B. (1954), 'The Nimrud Tablets, 1952: Business Documents', *Iraq*, 16, 29-58
Parpola, Simo, Asko Parpola, and Robert H. Brunswig Jr. (1977), 'The Meluḫḫa Village: Evidence of Acculturation of Harappan Traders in Late Third Millennium Mesopotamia.' *Journal of the Economic and Social History of the Orient*, 20, 129-63
Peet, Thomas Eric (1930), *The Great Tomb-Robberies of the Twentieth Egyptian Dynasty*, I. Oxford: Oxford University Press
—— (1932), 'The Egyptian Words for "Money", "Buy", and "Sell"', in Mond (ed.), *Studies Presented*, 122-7
Pestman, P.W. (1961), *Marriage and Matrimonial Property in Ancient Egypt*. Leiden: Brill
—— (1969), 'The Laws of Succession in Egypt', in J. Brugman *et al.* (eds), *Essays on Oriental Laws of Succession*, Leiden: Brill, 58-77
Petrie, W.F. Flinders (1923), *Social Life in Ancient Egypt*, New York: Cooper Square
Pettinato, Giovanni (1981), *The Archives of Ebla: An Empire Inscribed in Clay*, Garden City, New York: Doubleday
—— and Hartmut Waetzoldt (1975), 'Saatgut und Furchenabstand beim Getreidenbau', *Studia Orientalia*, 46, 259-90
Pflüger, Kurt (1946), 'The Edict of King Haremhab', *Journal of Near Eastern*

Studies, 5, 260-8
—— (1947), 'The Private Funerary Stelae of the Middle Kingdom and Their Importance for Ancient Economic History', *Journal of the American Oriental Society*, 5, 127-35
Pirenne, Jacques (1961), *Histoire de la Civilisation de l'Égypte Ancienne*, Paris: Michel
Plescia, Joseph (1970), *The Oath and Perjury in Ancient Greece*, Tallahassee, Florida: State University Press
Poebel, Arno (1909), *Babylonian Legal and Business Documents From the Time of the First Dynasty of Babylon*, Philadelphia: Department of Archaeology, University of Pennsylvania
Polanyi, Karl (1981), *The Livelihood of Man*, edited by Harry W. Pearson, New York: Academic Press
Pollard, Sidney (1965), 'The Genesis of the Managerial Profession in Britain', *Studies in Romanticism*, 4, 57-80
Pomeroy, Sarah B. (1975), *Goddesses, Whores, Wives, and Slaves*, New York: Schocken
—— (1984), *Women in Hellenistic Egypt*, New York: Shocken
Posner, Richard A. (1981), *Economics of Justice*, Cambridge: Harvard University Press
Postgate, J.N. (1971), 'Land Tenure in the Middle Assyrian Period: A Reconsideration', *British School of Oriental and African Studies*, 34, 496-520
—— (1975), 'Some Old Babylonian Shepherds and Their Flocks', *Journal of Semitic Studies*, 20, 1-18
—— (1976), *Fifty Neo-Assyrian Legal Documents*, Warminster: Aris & Phillips
—— (1979), 'The Economic Structure of the Assyrian Empire', in Mogens Trolle Larsen (ed.), *Power and Propaganda: A Symposium on Ancient Empires*, Copenhagen: Academisk Forlag, 193-221
Potts, Daniel T. (1982), The Zagros Frontier and the Problem of Relations between the Iranian Plateau and Southern Mesopotamia in the Third Millennium B.C.', in Nissen and Renger (eds), *Mesopotamien und seine Nachbarn*, I, 33-55
—— (1983), 'Barber Miscellanies', in Daniel T. Potts (ed.) *Dilmun, New Studies in the Archaeology and Early History of Bahrain*, Berlin: Reimer, 127-39
Powell, Marvin A. (1977), 'Sumerian Merchants and the Problem of Profit', *Ircq*, 39, 23-9
—— (1978a), 'A Contribution to the History of Money in Mesopotamia Prior to the Invention of Coinage', in Hruška and Komoróczy (eds), *Festshrift*, II, 211-43
—— (1978b), 'Non-Slave Labor in Sumer', in Michael Flinn (ed.), *Proceedings of the Seventh International Economic History Congress*, Edinburgh: Edinburgh University Press, 169-77
Price, Ira M. (1915-16), 'Some Observations on the Financial Importance of the Temple in the First Dynasty of Babylon', *American Journal of Semitic Languages*, 32, 250-60
—— (1923), 'Transportation by Water in Early Babylonia', *American Journal of Semitic Languages*, 40, 111-16
Pritchard, James B. (1962), *Gibeon Where the Sun Stood Still*, Princeton: Princeton University Press
—— (ed.) (1969), *Ancient Near Eastern Texts Relating to the Old Testament*, 3rd edition, Princeton: Princeton University Press
Pruessner, A.H. (1927), 'The Earliest Traces of Negotiable Instruments', *American Journal of Semitic Languages*, 44, 88-107
—— (1930), 'Date Culture in Ancient Babylonia', *American Journal of Semitic Languages*, 47, 213-32
Pryor, J.H. (1984), 'Commenda: The Operation of the Contract in Long Distance

Commerce at Marseilles During the Thirteenth Century', *Journal of European Economic History*, 13, 397-440

Rabinowitz, Jacob J. (1961), 'The Susa Tablets, The Bible, and the Aramaic Papyri', *Vetus Testamentum*, 11, 55-76

Rainey, A.F. (1964), 'Business Contracts at Ugarit', *Israel Exploration Journal*, 13, 313-21

—— (1965), 'Family Relationships in Ugarit', *Orientalia*, 34, 10-22

—— (1967), '*Aširu* and *Asiru* in Ugarit and the Land of Canaan', *Journal of Near Eastern Studies*, 26, 296-301

Reece, David W. (1969), 'The Technological Weakness of the Ancient World', *Greece and Rome*, 16, 32-47

Rees, Albert (1966), 'Information Networks in Labor Markets', *American Economic Review*, 56, 559-66

Reineke, Walter F. (1979), 'Wären die *swtjw* wirklich Kaufleute?' *Altorientalische Forschungen*, 6, 5-14

Reiner, Erica (1961), 'The Etiological Myth of the "Seven Sages"', *Orientalia*, 30, 1-11

—— (1969), 'Akkadian Treaties from Syria and Assyria', in Pritchard (ed.), *Ancient Near Eastern Texts*, 531-41

Renger, Johannes (1967), 'Untersuchungen zum Priestertum in der altbabylonischen Zeit', *Zeitschrift für Assyriologie*, 58, 110-188

—— (1971), 'Notes on Goldsmiths, Jewelers, and Carpenters of Neobabylonian Eanna', *Journal of the American Oriental Society*, 91, 499-503

—— (1979), 'Interaction of Temple, Palace, and Private Enterprise in the Old Babylonian Economy', in Lipiński (ed.), *State and Temple Economy*, I, 249-56

Ringgren, Helmer (1973), *Religion of the Ancient Near East*, Philadelphia: Westminster

Roaf, Michael (1982), 'Weights on the Dilmun Standard', *Iraq*, 44, 137-41

Robertson, Noel (1982), 'The Ritual Background of the Dying God in Cyprus and Syro-Palestine', *Harvard Theological Review*, 75, 313-59

Röllig, Wolfgang (1976), 'Der altmesopotamische Markt', *Die Welt des Orients*, 8, 286-95

Rosenberg, Nathan (1982), *Inside the Black Box: Technology and Economics*, Cambridge: Cambridge University Press

Rosengarten, Yvonne (1960), *Le Concept Sumérien De Consommation Dans La Vie Économique et Religieuse*, Paris: De Boccard

Rostovtzeff, M. (1941), *The Social and Economic History of the Hellenistic World*, II, London: Oxford University Press

Roth, Martha T. (1980), 'The Scholastic Exercise "Laws about Rented Oxen",' *Journal of Cuneiform Studies*, 32/3, 127-46

Rougé, Jean (1981), *Ships and Fleets of the Ancient Mediterranean*, Middletown, Connecticut: Wesleyan University Press

Rupp, Kalman (1983), *Entrepreneurs in Red: Structure and Organizational Innovation in the Centrally Planned Economy*, Albany: State University of New York Press

Saggs, H.W.F. (1960), 'Review of G. Boyer', *Journal of Semitic Studies*, 5, 411-17

—— (1962), *The Greatness That Was Babylon*, New York: Hawthorn

—— (1984), *The Might That Was Assyria*, London: Sidgwick & Jackson

Saleh, Abdel-Aziz (1973), 'An Open Question on Intermediaries in the Incense Trade during Pharaonic Times', *Orientalia*, 42, 370-82

Samuel, Alan E. (1965), 'The Role of Paramone Clauses in Ancient Documents', *Journal of Juristic Papyrology*, 15, 221-311

—— (1966), *The Mycenaeans in History*, Englewood Cliffs: Prentice-Hall

Sandman-Holmberg, Maj (1946), *The God Ptah*, Lund: Gleerup

Sasson, Jack M. (1966a), 'Canaanite Maritime Involvment in the Second Millennium

B.C.', *Journal of the American Oriental Society*, 86, 126-38

—— (1966b), 'A Sketch of North Syrian Economic Relations in the Middle Bronze Age', *Journal of the Economic and Social History of the Orient*, 9, 161-81

—— (1968), 'Instances of Mobility among Mari Artisans', *Bulletin of the American Schools of Oriental Research*, 190, 46-54

—— (1977), 'Treatment of Criminals at Mari: A Survey', *Journal of the Economic and Social History of the Orient*, 20, 90-113

—— (1979), *Ruth*, Baltimore: Johns Hopkins University Press

—— (1980), 'The Old Babylonian Tablets from Al-Rimah', *Journal of the American Oriental Society*, 100, 453-60

Säve-Söderbergh, Torgny (1946), *The Navy of the Eighteenth Egyptian Dynasty*, Uppsala: Lundequistka

Sayed, Abdel Monem A.H. (1978), 'The Recently Discovered Port on the Red Sea Shore', *Journal of Egyptian Archaeology*, 64, 69-71

Schaeffer, Claude F.A. (1939), *The Cuneiform Texts of Ras-Shamra-Ugarit*, London: Oxford University Press

Schaps, David M. (1979), *Economic Rights of Women in Ancient Greece*, Edinburgh: University of Edinburgh Press

Schwabe, Calvin W. (1984), 'A Unique Surgical Operation on the Horns of African Bulls in Ancient and Modern Times', *Agricultural History*, 58, 138-56

Scott, James C. (1976), *The Moral Economy of the Peasant*, New Haven: Yale University Press

de Selincourt, Aubrey (1972), *Herodotus: The Histories*, Harmondsworth: Penguin

van Selms, A. (1958), 'The Canaanites in the Book of Genesis', in B. Gemser *et al.* (eds), *Studies on the Book of Genesis*, Leiden: Brill, 182-213

Semenov, Ia. I. (1974), 'The Problem of the Socioeconomic Order of the Ancient Near East', in Dunn and Dunn (eds), *Introduction to Soviet Ethnography*, 575-604

van Seters, John (1966), *The Hyksos: A New Interpretation*, New Haven: Yale University Press

—— (1975), *Abraham in History and Tradition*, New Haven: Yale University Press

Shapiro, Carl (1983), 'Premiums for High Quality Products as Returns to Reputation', *Quarterly Journal of Economics*, 98, 659-79

Shea, William H. (1983), 'Two Palestinian Segments from the Eblaite Geographical Atlas', in Carol L. Meyers and M. O'Connor (eds), *The Word of the Lord Shall Go Forth*, Winona Lake, Indiana: Eisenbrauns for the American Schools of Oriental Research, 589-612

Sheffer, Avigail (1981), 'The Use of Perforated Clay Balls on the Warp-Weighted Loom', *Tel Aviv*, 8, 81-3

Shelmerdine, Cynthia W. (1973), 'The Pylos Ma Tablets Reconsidered', *American Journal of Archaeology*, 77, 261-75

Shendge, J. (1983), 'The Use of Seals and the Invention of Writing', *Journal of the Economic and Social History of the Orient*, 26, 113-36

Shlomowitz, Ralph (1979), 'The Origins of Southern Sharecropping', *Agricultural History*, 53, 557-75

Siegel, Bernard J. (1947), *Slavery during the Third Dynasty of Ur*, Washington, D.C.: American Anthropological Association

Silver, Morris (1980), *Affluence, Altruism, and Atrophy: The Decline of Welfare States*, New York: New York University Press

—— (1981), 'Adaptations to Information Impactedness: A Survey', in Malcolm Galatin and Robert D. Leiter (eds), *Economics of Information*, Boston: Martinus Nijhoff, 104-18

—— (1983a), *Prophets and Markets: The Political Economy of Ancient Israel*, Boston: Kluwer-Nijhoff

———— (1983b), 'A Non-Neo Malthusian Model of English Land Values, Wages, and Grain Yields Prior to the Black Death', *Journal of European Economic History*, 12, 631-50

———— (1983c), 'Karl Polanyi and Markets in the Ancient Near East: The Challenge of the Evidence', *Journal of Economic History*, 53, 795-829

———— (1984), *Enterprise and the Scope of the Firm: The Role of Vertical Integration*, Oxford: Martin Robertson

Singer, Itamar (1975), 'Hittite *ḫilam mar* and Hieroglyphic Luwian **ḫilana*', *Zeitschrift für Assyriologie*, 65, 69-103

———— (1983), 'Takuḫlinu and Ḫaya: Two Governors in the Ugarit Letters from Tel Aphek', *Tel Aviv*, 10, 3-25

Skaist, Aaron (1975), 'Inheritance Laws and Their Social Background', *Journal of the American Oriental Society*, 95, 242-7

Smith, C.S. (1970), 'Art, Technology, and Science: Notes on their Historical Imperatives', *Technology and Culture*, 11, 493-549

Smith, H.S. (1976), *The Fortress of Buhen: The Inscriptions*, London: Egypt Exploration Society

———— and Alexandrina Smith (1976), 'A Reconsideration of the Kamose Texts', *Zeitschrift für ägyptische Sprache und altertumskunde*, 103, 48-76

Smith, Sidney (1922), 'A Pre-Greek Coinage in the Near East', *Numismatic Chronicle*, 2, 176-85

Smith, William Robertson (1889), *The Religion of the Semites: The Fundamental Institutions*, New York: Meridan

Smith, William Stevenson (1935), 'The Old Kingdom Linen List', *Zeitschrift für ägyptische Sprache und Altertumskunde*, 71, 134-49

———— (1965), *Interconnections in the Ancient Near East*, New Haven: Yale University Press

———— (1969), 'Influence of the Middle Kingdom on Western Asia Especially in Byblos', *American Journal of Archaeology*, 73, 277-81

Snaith, N.H. (1966), 'The Daughters of Zelophedad', *Vetus Testamentum*, 16, 124-7

Snell, Daniel C. (1982), *Ledgers and Prices: Early Mesopotamian Merchant Accounts*, New Haven: Yale University Press

Snodgrass, Anthony (1981), *Archaic Greece: The Age of Experiment*, Berkeley: University of California Press

Spar, Ira (1972), 'Studies in Neo-Babylonian Economic and Legal Texts', unpublished PhD dissertation, Minneapolis: University of Minnesota

Speiser, E.A. (1955), 'Akkadian Documents from Ras Shamra', *Journal of the American Oriental Society*, 75, 154-65

———— (1963), 'A Significant New Will from Nuzi', *Journal of Cuneiform Studies*, 17, 65-71

———— (1964), *Genesis: Introduction, Translation, and Notes*, Garden City, New York: Doubleday

———— (1967), *Oriental and Biblical Studies*, Philadelphia: University of Pennsylvania Press

Spencer, Patricia (1984), *The Egyptian Temple: A Lexicographical Study*, Kegan Paul International

Stager, E. (1982), 'The Archaeology of the East Slope of Jerusalem and the Terraces of the Kidron', *Journal of Near Eastern Studies*, 41, 111-21

———— and Samuel R. Wolff (1981), 'Production and Commerce in Temple Courtyards: An Olive Press in the Sacred Precinct at Tel Dan', *Bulletin of the American Schools of Oriental Research*, 243, 95-102

Starr, Chester G. (1977), *The Economic and Social Growth of Early Greece, 800-500 B.C.*, New York: Oxford University Press

Steinkeller, Piotr (1981a), 'The Renting of Fields in Early Mesopotamia and the Development of the Concept of "Interest" in Sumerian', *Journal of the Economic and Social History of the Orient*, 24, 113-45

—— (1981b), 'Early History of the Hamrin Basin in the Light of Textual Evidence', in McGuire Gibson (ed.), *Uch Tepe I*, Chicago: The Oriental Institute, University of Chicago, 163-81

—— (1982a), 'Two Sargonic Sale Documents Concerning Women', *Orientalia*, 51, 355-68

—— (1982b), 'On Editing Ur III Economic Texts', *Journal of the American Oriental Society*, 102, 639-44

Stephens, Ferris J. (1955), 'Notes on Some Economic Texts of the Time of Urukagina', *Revue d'assyriologie et d'archéologie orientale*, 49, 129-36

Stieglitz, Robert R. (1979), 'Commodity Prices at Ugarit', *Journal of the American Oriental Society*, 99, 14-23

Stol, M. (1982), 'State and Private Business in the Land of Larsa', *Journal of Cuneiform Studies*, 34, 127-230

Stolper, Matthew Wolfgang (1974), 'Management and Politics in Late Achaemenid Babylonia: New Texts from the Murašû Archive', unpublished PhD dissertation, Ann Arbor: University of Michigan

Stone, Elizabeth C. (1977), 'Economic Crisis and Social Upheaval in Old Babylonian Nippur', in Louis D. Levine and T. Cuyler Young (eds), *Mountains and Lowlands*, Malibu, California: Undema, 267-89

—— (1982), 'The Social Role of the *Nadītu* Women in Old Babylonian Nippur', *Journal of the Economic and Social History of the Orient*, 25, 50-70

Strange, John (1980), *Caphtor/Keftiu: A New Investigation*, Leiden: Brill

Stroud, Ronald S. (1975), 'An Athenian Law on Silver Coinage', *Hesperia*, 44, 157-88

Struve, V.V. (1969), 'The Problem of the Genesis, Development, and Disintegration of the Slave Societies of the Ancient Orient', in Diakonoff (ed.), *Ancient Mesopotamia*, 17-67

Sumner, B.H. (1943), *A Short History of Russia*, New York: Reynal and Hitchcock

Sventsitskaya, I.S. (1976), 'The Interpretation of Data on Landholding in the *Iliad* and *Odyssey*', *Vestniki Drevnei Istarii*, 1, 63

Sweet, Ronald F.G. (1958), 'Prices, Moneys, and Money Uses in the Old Babylonian Period', unpublished PhD dissertation, Chicago: University of Chicago.

Swidler, Leonard (1976), 'Greco-Roman Feminism and the Reception of the Gospel', in Bernd Jaspert and Rudolf Mohr (eds), *Traditio Krisis- Renovation aus theologischer Sicht*, Marburg: Elwert, 41-55

Thédoridès, Aristide (1958), 'A propos de Pap. Lansing, 4, 8-5, 2 et 6, 8-7, 5', *Revue international des droits de l'antiquité*, 5, 65-119

Thirsk, Joan (1964), 'The Common Fields', *Past and Present*, 29, 3-25

Thomas, D. Winton (1958), *Documents From Old Testament Times*, London: Nelson

Thompson, Herbert (1934), *A Family Archive From Siut: Text*, Oxford: University University Press

—— (1941), 'Two Demotic Self-Dedications', *Journal of Egyptian Archaeology*, 26, 68-78

Thompson, Thomas L. (1974), *The Historicity of the Patriarchal Narratives*, Berlin: de Gruyter

—— (1978), 'The Background of the Patriarchs: A Reply to William Dever and Malcolm Clarke', *Journal for the Study of the Old Testament*, 9, 2-43

Thompson, Wesley E. (1979), 'A View of Athenian Banking', *Museum Helveticum*, 36, 224-41

Thrupp, Sylvia L. (1977), *Society and History*, Ann Arbor: University of

Michigan

Toumanoff, Peter (1981), 'The Development of the Peasant Commune in Russia', *Journal of Economic History*, 41, 179-84

Trigger, Bruce G. (1976), *Nubia under the Pharaohs*, Boulder: Westview

—— (1983), 'The Rise of Egyptian Civilization', in B.G. Trigger *et al.* (eds), *Ancient Egypt*, 1-70

—— B.J. Kemp, D. O'Connor and A.B. Lloyd (eds) (1983), *Ancient Egypt: A Social History*, Cambridge: Cambridge University Press

Tsevat, Matitiahu (1958), 'Alalakhiana', *Hebrew Union College Annual*, 29, 109-34

—— (1978), 'A Window for Baal's House', in Yitschak Avischur and Joshua Blau (eds), *Bible and Ancient Near East*, Jerusalem: Rubenstein, 151-61

Tucker, Gene M. (1963), 'Contracts in the Old Testament: A Form Critical Investigation', unpublished PhD dissertation, New Haven: Yale University

—— (1966), 'The Legal Background of Genesis 23', *Journal of Biblical Literature*, 65, 77-84

Tyumenev, K.I. (1969), 'The State Economy of Ancient Sumer', in Diakonoff (ed.), *Ancient Mesopotamia*, 7-87

Uchitel, Alexander (1981), 'Women at Work: Pylos and Knossos, Lagash and Ur', *Historia*, 33, 257-82

Udovitch, Abraham L. (1977), 'Formalism and Informalism in the Social and Economic Institutions of the Medieval Islamic World', in Amin Banani and Speros Vyronis, Jr. (eds), *Individualism and Conformity in Classical Islam*, Wiesbaden: Harrassowitz, 61-81

—— (1979), 'Bankers without Banks: Commerce, Banking, and Society in the Islamic World of the Middle Ages', in Center for Medieval and Renaissance Studies, *The Dawn of Modern Banking*, 255-74

Vanstiphout, Herman (1970), 'Political Ideology in Early Sumer', *Orientalia Lovaniensia Periodica*, 1, 7-38

de Vaux, Roland (1978), *The Early History of Israel*, Philadelphia: Westminster

Veenhof, K.R. (1966), 'Review of Ernest Kutsch', *Bibliotheca Orientalis*, 23, 308-13

—— (1972), *Aspects of Old Assyrian Trade and Its Terminology*, Leiden: Brill

—— (1977), 'Some Social Effects of Old Assyrian Trade', *Iraq*, 39, 109-18

—— (1978), 'An Ancient Anatolian Moneylender', in Hruška and Komoróczy (eds), *Festschrift*, 279-311

—— (1982), 'The Old Assyrian Merchants and Their Relations with the Native Population of Anatolia', in Nissen and Renger (eds), *Mesopotamien und seine Nachbarn*, I, 147-60

Velde, H. Te (1977), *Seth, God of Confusion: A Study of His Role in Egyptian Mythology and Religion*, Leiden: Brill

Vercoutter, Jean (1967a), 'Egypt under the Old Kingdom', in Bottéro *et al.* (eds), *The Near East*, 276-319

Vercoutter, Jean (1967b), 'Egypt in the Middle Kingdom', in Bottéro *et al.* (eds), *The Near East*, 347-82

Vermeule, Emily (1964), *Greece in the Bronze Age*, Chicago: University of Chicago

Vernant, Jean-Pierre (1982), *The Origins of Greek Religious Thought*, Ithaca: Cornell University Press

Vinogradoff, Paul (1904), *The Growth of the Manor*, London: Allen & Unwin

Van Voss, M.S., H.G. Heerma, Ph.H.J. Hovwink, Ten Cate and N.A. Van Uchelen (eds) (1974), *Travels in the World of the Old Testament*, Assen: Van Gorcum

De Vries, Jan (1976), *Economy of Europe in an Age of Crisis*, London: Cambridge University Press

Waetzoldt, Hartmut (1972), *Untersuchungen zur neusumerischen Textilindustrie*,

Rome: Centro per le Antchità e la Storia dell'Arte del Vicino Oriente
—————— (1978), 'Zu den Feldpachtverträgen aus Nippur', *Die Welt des Orients*, 9, 201-5
Wainwright, G.A. (1938), *The Sky-Religion in Egypt*, London: Cambridge University Press
Walters, Stanley D. (1970), *Water for Larsa*, New Haven: Yale University Press
Ward, Richard David (1973), 'The Family History of Silli-Ištar', unpublished PhD dissertation, Minneapolis: University of Minnesota
Ward, William A. (1963), 'Egypt and the East Mediterranean from Predynastic Times to the End of the Old Kingdom', *Journal of the Economic and Social History of the Orient*, 6, 1-57
—————— (1965), *The Spirit of Ancient Egypt*, Beirut: Khayats
—————— (1971), *Egypt and the East Mediterranean World, 2200-1900 B.C.,*, Beirut: American University of Beirut
Watson, Alan (1970), *The Law of the Ancient Romans*, Dallas: Southern Methodist University Press
Watts, Ross L., and Jerold L. Zimmerman (1983), 'Agency Problems, Auditing, and the Theory of the Firm: Some Evidence', *Journal of Law and Economics*, 26, 613-33
Van der Wee, Hermann (ed.) (1970), *Fifth International Congress of Economic History, Leningrad, 1970*. The Hague: Mouton
Weeks, Noel Kenneth (1971), 'The Real Estate Interests of a Nuzi Family', unpublished PhD dissertation, Waltham, Massachusetts: Brandeis University
Weill, Raymond (1940), *Phoenicia and Western Asia*, London: Harrap
Weinberg, J.P. (1976), 'Die Agrarverhältnisse in der Bürger-Tempel-Gemeinde der achämeniden Zeit', in Harmatta and Komoróczy (eds), *Wirtschaft und Gesellschaft*, 473-85
Weinfeld, Moshe (1982a), 'The Council of the "Elders" to Rehoboam and Its Implications', *MAARAV*, 3, 27-53
—————— (1982b), '"Justice and Righteousness" in Ancient Israel against the Background of "Social Reform" in the Ancient Near East', in Nissen and Renger (eds), *Mesopotamien und seine Nachbarn*, 491-519
Weisberg, David B. (1967), *Guild Structure and Political Allegiance in Early Achaemenid Mesopotamia*, New Haven: Yale University Press
Wellard, James (1972), *Babylon*, New York: Schocken
Wenig, Steffen (1962), 'Ein Siegelzylinder mit dem Namen Pepi's I', *Zeitschrift für ägyptische Sprache und Altertumskunde*, 88, 66-9
Wensky, Margaret (1982), 'Women's Guilds in Cologne in the Later Middle Ages', *Journal of European Economic History*, 11, 631-50
Wente, E. F. Jr. (1972), 'The Report of Wenamon', in William Kelly Simpson (ed.), *The Literature of Ancient Egypt*, New Haven: Yale University Press, 142-55
Westbrook, Raymond (1971), 'Redemption of Land', *Israel Law Review*, 6, 367-75
Westenholz, Joan Gronick (1983), 'Review of B. Kienast', *Journal of Near Eastern Studies*, 92, 219-28
Westermann, William L. (1955), *The Slave Systems of Greek and Roman Antiquity*, Philadelphia: American Philosophical Society
Wheeler, Tamara Stech, James D. Muhly and Robert Maddin (1979), 'Mediterranean Trade in Copper and Tin in the Late Bronze Age', *Istituto Italiano di Numismatica Annali*, 26, 139-52
Wiedemann, Thomas (1981), *Greek and Roman Slavery*, London: Croom Helm
Willetts, Ronald F. (1967), *The Law Code of Gortyn*, Berlin: de Gruyter
Williams, R.J. (1981), 'The Sages of Ancient Egypt in the Light of Recent Scholarship', *Journal of the American Oriental Society*, 101, 1-19
Wilson John A. (1948), 'The Oath in Ancient Egypt', *Journal of Near Eastern Studies*, 7, 129-56
—————— (1951), *The Culture of Ancient Egypt*, Chicago: University of Chicago

Press
———— (1969a), 'Egyptian Oracles and Prophecies', in Pritchard (ed.), *Ancient Near Eastern Texts*, 441-44
———— (1969b), 'Egyptian Historical Texts', in Pritchard (ed.), *Ancient Near Eastern Texts*, 227-64
———— (1969c), 'Observations on Life and the World', in Pritchard (ed.), *Ancient Near Eastern Texts*, 431-34
———— (1969d), 'Egyptian Rituals and Incantations', in Pritchard (ed.), *Ancient Near Eastern Texts*, 325-30
Wilson, Rodney (1983), *Banking and Finance in the Arab Middle East*, New York: St Martin's Press
Wiseman, D.J. (1953), *The Alalakh Tablets*, London: British School of Archaeology at Ankara
———— (1964), 'Rahab of Jericho', *Tyndale House Bulletin*, 14, 8-11
———— (1982), '"Is it Peace?" — Covenant and Diplomacy', *Vetus Testamentum*, 32, 311-26
Witt, R.E. (1971), *Isis in the Graeco-Roman World*, London: Thames & Hudson
Wood, Merry Wiesner (1981), 'Paltry Peddlars or Essential Merchants? Women in the Distributive Trades in Early Modern Nuremberg', *Sixteenth Century Journal*, 12, 3-13
Wooley, C. Leonard (1982), *Ur of the Chaldees* (rev. ed. P.R.S. Moorey), Ithaca: Cornell University Press
Wycherly, R.E. (1978), *The Stones of Athens*, Princeton: Princeton University Press
Yadin, Yigael (1975), *Hazor: The Rediscovery of a Great Citadel of the Bible*, New York: Random House
Yaron, Reuven (1958), 'On Defension Clauses of Some Oriental Deeds of Sale from Mesopotamia and Egypt', *Bibliotheca Orientalis*, 15, 15-22
———— (1959), 'Redemption of Persons in the Ancient Near East', *Revue internationale des droits de l'antiquité*, 6, 155-76
———— (1960a), 'Aramaic Deeds of Conveyance, II', *Biblica*, 41, 379-94
———— (1960b), 'A Document of Redemption from Ugarit', *Vetus Testamentum*, 10, 83-90
———— (1969a), 'Foreign Merchants at Ugarit', *Israel Law Review*, 4, 70-9
———— (1969b), *The Laws of Eshnunna*, Jerusalem: Magnes
Yeo, Cedric (1946), 'Transportation in Imperial Italy', *Transactions of the American Philological Society*, 77, 221-44
Yoffee, Norman (1977), *The Economic Role of the Crown in the Old Babylonian Period*, Malibu, California: Undema
———— (1979), 'The Decline and Rise of Mesopotamian Civilization: An Ethno-archaeological Perspective on the Evolution of Social Complexity', *American Antiquity*, 44, 5-35
———— (1981), *Explaining Trade in Ancient Western Asia*, Malibu, California: Undema
Zaccagnini, Carlo (1975), 'The Yield of the Fields at Nuzi', *Oriens Antiquus*, 14, 181-225
———— (1976), 'Review of R.S. Merrillees', *Oriens Antiquus*, 15, 159-63 (Italian)
———— (1977), 'The Merchants at Nuzi', *Iraq*, 39, 171-89
———— (1978), 'Review of H. Lanz', *Oriens Antiquus*, 17, 233-7 (in Italian)
———— (1979), 'The Price of Fields at Nuzi', *Journal of the Economic and Social History of the Orient*, 22 (January), 1-31
———— (1983a), 'Patterns of Mobility among Ancient Near Eastern Craftsmen', *Journal of Near Eastern Studies*, 42, 245-64
———— (1983b), 'On Gift Exchange in the Old Babylonian Period', *Studi Orientalistici*

in Ricordo di Franco Pintore, Pavia: 189-253

van Zijl, Peter J. (1972), *Baal: A Study of Texts in Connexion with Baal in the Ugaritic Epics*, Vluyn: Verlag Butzon

⸺ Zimmern, Alfred (1928), *Solon and Croesus and Other Greek Essays*, London: Oxford University Press (The quote in the preface comes from page 172.)

APPENDIX

Chronological Table

Mesopotamia

Period	Dates		
Early Dynastic I	c. 2900	–	c. 2700
Early Dynastic II	c. 2700	–	c. 2500
(Fara	26th or 25 century)		
Early Dynastic III	c. 2500	–	c. 2300
(Lagash	2570	–	2342)
Akkadian (Sargonid)	2334	–	2154
Post-Akkadian (Gutian)	2154	–	2112
Neo-Sumerian (Ur III)	2112	–	2004
Old Babylonian	c. 2000	–	c. 1600
(Isin-Larsa	2000	–	1800)
(First Dynasty of Babylon —			
the Dynasty of Hammurabi	1894	–	1595)
(Assyrian kings	1813	–	1741)
Middle Babylonian and Middle Assyrian	c. 1600	–	c. 1000
Kassite Dynasty	1570	–	1157)
(Second Dynasty of Isin	1158	–	1027)
Neo-Assyrian	c. 1000	–	626
Neo-Babylonian	626	–	539
Persian (Achaemenid)	539	–	351

Western Iran

Elam

Kings of Awan	c. 2600	–	c. 2220(?)
Kings of Simashki	2038	–	1850(?)
House of the Eparti	1850	–	1505
House of the Igehalkids	1350	–	1210
House of the Shutrukids	1205	–	1110(?)
Later Elamite Kings	760(?) –		644(?)
Achaemenid Kings	560		330

Asiatic Turkey (Anatolia)

Assyrian trade with Cappadocia	c. 1940	–	c. 1800

Hittites

Old Kingdom	1740	– 1460
Empire	1460	– c. 1215

Syria

Ebla	mid-third millennium	
Mari	c. 1825	– c. 1759
Alalakh	18th and 15th centuries	
Ugarit	c. 1400	– c. 1200

Israel

Early Canaanite (Early Bronze Age)	c. 3150	– c. 2200
Middle Canaanite (Middle Bronze Age)	c. 2200	– c. 1550
Late Canaanite (Late Bronze Age)	c. 1550	– c. 1200
Israelite (Iron Age)	c. 1200	– 586
(United Monarchy	c. 1000	– 925)
(Divided Kingdoms – Israel and Judah	925	– 721)
(Judah alone	721	– 586)

Egypt

Archaic Period (1st and 2nd Dynasties)	c. 3000	– c. 2780
Old Kingdom (3rd to 6th Dynasties)	c. 2780	– 2260
	(alternative:	
	2686	– 2181)
First Intermediate Period (7th to 10th Dynasties)	2260	– 2040
Middle Kingdom (11th to 12th Dynasties)	2160	– 1785
Second Intermediate Period (13th to 14th Dynasties and 17th Dynasty)	1785	– 1580
(Hyksos 15th to 16th Dynasties	1730	– 1580)
New Kingdom (18th to 20th Dynasties)	1580	– 1085
(Ramessids	1314	– 1085)
Divided Kingdom and Libyan Epoch (21st to 24th Dynasties)	1085	– 715
Late Period	730	– 656
Assyrian domination	671	– 669
	666	– 660(?)
26th Dynasty (Saite)	663	– 525
Persian	525	– 333
Alexander and Ptolemies	332	– 30

Greece

Mycenaean civilisation	c. 1700	– c.	1200
Archaic	800	–	500
Classical	500	–	300
Hellenistic	300	–	0

INDEX

á 91, 105
Abraham n. 8:27, 33, 48, 49, 95,
  96–7, 124, 127
Adad 101
Adams, Robert M. 148, 154, 155,
  n. 4:157
Adapa 24
Addu-dūri 43, 45
Admission Torah 22
Admonitions of Ipuwer 83–4, 151,
  n. 2, 156
Adonis 13, n. 10:27
adoption 49–50, 140–1, n. 22:144,
  159, 160
advertising 120
'Advice to a Prince' n. 29:30
Aegyptus 14
affluence 21–2, 149, 158
agents 19, 34, 39, 48, 49, 74, 75,
  135, 137, 158
Agora 7, 11, 119
agricultural manual 155
Ahab 74
Aharoni, Yohannan 10
Ahaziah 74
Akhenaten 37, 76
Akkad n. 10:27, 39
Alalakh 39, 42, 45, 63, 86, 95, 124,
  129, 160
Alashiya 37, 108
Albright, W.F. 7
Alchian, Armen A. 122, 123
Aldred, Cyril 36, n. 35, 117
Alexandria 41, 65
Ali, Fadhil A. 120
Alster, Bendt 89
Amarna 35, 36, 37, 112
Amasis 14, 76
Amiran, Ruth 10
Ammisaduqa 86, n. 7:113
Amon (Amun) 24, 102, 136
Amos 22, 26, 82
amphictyonies 11, n. 6:26
Amunemhet III 111
ancestral gods 40, 49
andurārum 159
animal fat 153

Ankhmahor 151
Ankhtyfy 62, 127
annuity 49, 97
Any 88
Aphek 65, 96, 121
Aphrodite 8
Apollo 15, 23, n. 14:28
apprenticeship 49, 102
Arad 10, n. 6:26
Aratta 13, 62
archaism 47, 98
Arinna 20
ark n. 18:29
aroura n. 2:156
artificial pollination 109, 164
arua n. 24:30, n. 7:52
Ashdod n. 6:27, n. 10:27
Assur 15, 16, 17, 38, 40, 43, 45, 47,
  59, 63, 64, 88, 107, 108, 118,
  121, 129, 159, 164
Assurbanipal 78
Assur-Uballit I 37
Assyria 15
Astarte 13, 153
Astour, Michael C. 9, 50, 90, 137,
  n. 20:144
Aswan 111, 150
Atarshua 16
Athena 7, 14
Athens 7, 11, 47, 48, 49, 50, 87,
  n. 13:114, 118, 119, 158, 163
audits 87, 134
Auster, Richard D. ix
awīlum 34

Baal 7, 8, 13, n. 10:27, 152, 153
Babylon 159, 160, 163
Badawy, Alexander 106, 154
Baer, Klaus 95, 149, n. 3:156
Bakir, Abdel-Mohsen 103
balanced silver accounts 78, 81, 131,
  133
Baldacci, M. 110
Balkan, Kemal 90, 91, 134, 159
Balmunamhe 154
Balmuth, Miriam S. 125, 127, 128,
  129

202 *Index*